*For Caron – for making every day seem like the first day that I saw you*

# Welfare Theory

Also by Tony Fitzpatrick:

*Freedom and Security: An Introduction to the Basic Income Debate*

Also published by Palgrave

# Welfare Theory: An Introduction

**Tony Fitzpatrick**

**Consultant Editor: Jo Campling**

palgrave

First published 2001 by
PALGRAVE
Houndmills, Basingstoke, Hampshire RG21 6XS and
175 Fifth Avenue, New York, N. Y. 10010
Companies and representatives throughout the world

PALGRAVE is the new global academic imprint of
St. Martin's Press LLC Scholarly and Reference Division and
Palgrave Publishers Ltd (formerly Macmillan Press Ltd).

ISBN 978-0-333-77843-2
Transferred to Digital Printing 2012

This book is printed on paper suitable for recycling and
made from fully managed and sustained forest sources.

A catalogue record for this book is available
from the British Library.

Library of Congress Cataloging-in-Publication Data

Fitzpatrick, Tony, 1966–
    Welfare theory : an introduction / Tony Fitzpatrick.
        p. cm.
    Includes bibliographical references and index.
    ISBN 0–333–77842–1 (cloth) — ISBN 0–333–77843–X (paper)
        1. Social policy—Philosophy. 2. Public welfare—Philosophy. I. Title.

HN28 .F57 2001
361.6′5′01—dc21                                                                    2001024724

10   9   8   7   6   5   4   3   2   1
10   09   08   07   06   05   04   03   02   01

# Contents

# Preface and Acknowledgements

Commissioning editors and academics should never drink wine at conferences, or certainly not while they are in the same room together. I can only assume this is what happened when Catherine Gray of Palgrave mentioned to Chris Pierson that she was looking for someone to write a textbook on welfare theory. Do you remember that moment in every party when you deflect attention away from yourself by pointing at that hapless bloke alone in the corner? So it was that my name was mentioned. I may have inadvertently come close to wrecking Chris's life and career on many occasions but there was really no need for this! Anyway, once the fog had lifted Catherine contacted me and – ah, how naive I was in those far-off days of 1998 – I agreed to give it a shot. And so the fog descended again. Had I known how painful a delivery this project was going to be I would either have kept my virginity, or else demanded a much bigger fee. And so, more than two years later, here we are.

Apart from Catherine Gray of Palgrave there are several people who assisted with the birth. Hartley Dean read an early chapter before fainting at the first sight of blood. Jo Campling has been an effective midwife, having seen it all so many times before! Nick Manning and Bill Silburn paced up and down in the waiting room, by which time I was on the laughing gas, and offered valuable support. An anonymous reviewer patted my forehead just as I lost consciousness for the final time. And Dr Pierson himself read tirelessly through the manuscript in the minutest detail before delivering a verdict that only an academic of his brilliance and experience can get away with: 'Yeah, looks fine.' In short, you are holding my baby in your hands. An ugly little sprog, perhaps, but he is mine.

Dear Caron, this is what I managed to write when I wasn't writing about you.

Tony Fitzpatrick
University of Nottingham

# Abbreviations

| | |
|---|---|
| BWS | Bretton Woods System |
| CCTV | closed circuit television |
| EU | European Union |
| FDI | foreign direct investment |
| GDP | gross domestic product |
| GM | genetically modified |
| ICTs | information and communication technologies |
| IGOs | intergovernmental organisations |
| IMF | International Monetary Fund |
| INGOs | international non-governmental organisations |
| ISA | ideological state apparatus |
| KWNS | Keynesian Welfare National State |
| MNCs | multinational corporations |
| NHS | National Health Service |
| NSMT | new social movement theory |
| OECD | Organisation for Economic Co-operation and Development |
| RCT | rational choice theory |
| RMT | resource mobilisation theory |
| RSA | repressive state apparatus |
| SWPR | Schumpetarian Workfare Postnational Regime |
| TNCs | transnational corporations |
| UN | United Nations |
| WTO | World Trade Organization |

# Introduction

Although I lived only a few minutes away, the evening air was so cold and piercing that the walk to the university library through the granite canyons of Buccleuch Place seemed to take a long time. This was in Edinburgh in the early winter of 1992. After the first few months of my doctoral research it was clear that I would have to familiarise myself with a whole new subject. Armed with an academic background in literature, philosophy and politics it was my initial intention to get a feel for this subject by browsing the relevant shelves of the short-loan collection. Once inside, warmed up, and able to look out over the rain-scoured street, I perused some of the most prominent Social Policy books. They had titles such as *Blood Donation in Britain and America*, *A History of German Social Insurance* and *Social Services in Albania* (Vol. 3). 'Oh wow,' I remember thinking to myself, 'can any subject really be this dull?'

And yet, I persevered. I learned that Social Policy demonstrates a degree of commitment and humanity that so many governments have perversely forgotten how to demonstrate. At its best, Social Policy squeezes itself through the cracks of social surfaces, the minutiae of everyday life, and reveals the historical and political realities that background even the most apparently mundane activities. This is why *The Gift Relationship* by Richard Titmuss (1970) is so fondly remembered. The blood donation systems of Britain and America are not simply administratively distinct but symbolise divergent ways of thinking about individuality and society. Since Titmuss, our societies have consumed and then discarded any number of self-images. But through the apocalyptic crises of the 1970s, the authoritarian populism of the 1980s, the self-congratulatory triumphalism of the early 1990s and the introspective anxieties of the pre-millennium years, Social Policy has always been prodding and poking society in the side of its conscience. Sometimes like an enthusiastic child who won't sit still and sometimes like an exasperated elderly relative who has seen it all before, Social Policy keeps reminding us today of what we will try to forget again tomorrow: that a just and decent society costs time, effort and compassion. Oh, and money.

I also discovered that my academic background had been the best possible training for Social Policy. To some extent, the subject is an offshoot of other disciplines within the social sciences – sociology, politics, economics (with history, philosophy and some criminology and cultural studies thrown in, just to be on the safe side). Yet Social Policy also underpins these other subjects. Social policies often predated these disciplines, or at least accompanied their emergence; if social science was forged in the fires of industrial capitalism then welfare systems have been there from the beginning, stoking the flames. So when we study welfare theory we are not stealing from other subjects but retracing a lineage that leads back to a common ancestry. Nor are we dabbling in theory for the sake of it. For the Greeks, the modern tendency to distinguish between thinking and doing would have been meaningless. Philosophy was not a secluded, cloistered activity but a social interaction, a training in the mental and physical virtues that enabled people (well, privileged men) to engage more effectively with public affairs. At its best, welfare theory amplifies the echoes of this earlier tradition.

That brings me to the first aim of this textbook: to map the historical genesis of welfare theory and reclaim for it ideas and thinkers that are too often confined to social or political thought. This is not to argue that there is an entirely distinct school of thought called welfare theory; no, 'welfare', 'social' and 'political' are clearly intertwined. Yet it *is* to insist that welfare and welfare systems can no longer be relegated to footnotes and parentheses without omitting what is crucial about the modern world of the last 500 years: the pursuit of social progress has been a collective effort which has taken improvements in well-being as one of its main criteria of success. The welfare state may still be a relatively recent innovation but it is as dependent on ideas that are centuries, and even millennia, old as a cruise liner is on primitive efforts to mould iron and bronze.

I was far less conscious of the book's second aim and only fully identified it once I had drafted the 10 chapters that lie ahead of us. Recent books dealing with theories of Social Policy have adopted a heavy ideological structure – although there has also been a recent trend towards using the distinction between the premodern, modern and postmodern as an organising structure. This is an entirely worthwhile approach, but one that can be too restrictive and limiting. I wanted to stretch my legs a bit and exercise in a wider, more comprehensive playground. Nevertheless, it emerged that an ideological spectrum is central to my way of thinking about welfare theory and this spectrum underscores much, but certainly not all, of what follows. Yet isn't this to take the spectrum too seriously, critics might ask? In truth, I have little time for those who argue that the spectrum is redundant. First, because it has formed the background to the last two centuries of social interaction and organisation, and the weight of the past cannot dissolve very quickly, no matter how impatient the fashions of the present might be. Second, because the spectrum has only ever been a partial and imperfect means for explaining the social world, there is little reason to believe that it has become any *more* imperfect. A Left–Right spectrum is a tool for understanding which is useful in some ways and less so in others. It is certainly *not* intended to be a perfect reflection of the world. In fact, it is the people who would ditch the spectrum altogether who might be accused of taking it too seriously. So, the ground within which this book plays is broad, but the compass we use to orient ourselves has ideological markings. There are many different ways of telling the story of welfare theory, obviously, but this is mine.

Of course, some people fear theory because it makes them feel as if they are trapped on a particularly sadistic snakes and ladders board, where they are always sliding helplessly back towards the first square. Others love theory for the same reason, although they regard the endless journey to and from first principles as precisely what is enjoyable. Writing a textbook on theory has been a testing experience in this respect. I still enjoy the exhilarating fall and the long trek back to the top of the slide, yet I also now appreciate more fully how tiring it can be. What this gives me is both a God's eye and a worm's eye view of welfare theory. As I set out to read about welfare theory again I am not necessarily in any better position than the reader. I have some idea of the terrain that lies ahead, yet it feels new every time I venture out.

What I do not claim is that everything that *could* be covered *has* been covered. You will not find anything about religion or law in the pages that follow because I know very little about each and am inclined to know even less. Nor can I claim to have achieved a perfect introduction to the subjects which are included. Just as some scientists posit the existence of parallel universes, so there exist in these other quantum realities a multitude of Fitzpatricks who have written different versions of the book you are currently holding. Some of them are better luckily; some are a damn sight worse. In fact, even this Fitzpatrick could no doubt stitch together another three or four books from the fat that had to be trimmed and the spare parts that had to be thrown away. Some of these virtual monsters may haunt the pages that follow, but I think I have managed to exorcise most of them.

In fact, while I'm in a contrite mood I may as well apologise for making the bibliography too long. This may seem like a strange apology when the purpose of a textbook is offer an example of good practice when it comes to referencing. Yet the other side of the coin is that students can use books such as these to claim a familiarity with ideas that they do not possess. To students: please don't; to lecturers: sorry, some of them will anyway. The bibliography could have been shorter but I got carried away. You see, I never did escape from that library.

Chapter 1 deals with issues that arise out of the basic question: what is welfare? However, in any book dealing with theory it is often the most basic questions which gives rise to the most intricate and complex arguments. To be honest, the debates covered in Chapter 1 are those that I became familiar with most recently. To my own frustration as a student, many authors would mention the relevant issues without going into the depth that I felt to be appropriate. In short, Chapter 1 is a large and particularly jagged pill to swallow but the rest of the book will digest that much easier if you hold your nose and take the medicine all in one go.

Chapters 2–4 really need to be regarded as a unit. Chapter 2 discusses equality and egalitarianism. What is it that egalitarians wish to see equalised? What do we mean by distributive justice and how is equality to be reconciled with liberty? To what extent has the welfare state been an egalitarian institution? The chapter underlines the point that neither equality nor liberty can be discussed in isolation from the other. Indeed, many of the controversies with which welfare theory is concerned stem from the attempt to work out when equality and liberty are compatible with one another and when they are not!

Chapter 3 looks at the other side of the coin: liberty. It examines so-called 'classic' liberalism where the market was expected to take on the role of social unifier that, in premodern times, had been accorded to the feudal hierarchy. It shows how classic liberalism gradually came under challenge from those who felt that only a state concerned with the welfare of all could properly defend individual freedom. However, classic liberalism has made a comeback over the last few decades and the chapter analyses the work of Robert Nozick and Friedrich Hayek in this context. It concludes that, although the Left–Right spectrum is of considerable relevance, we should not fall into the trap of simplifying the equality–liberty distinction along those lines.

Chapter 4 brings the arguments of the previous two chapters together through an extended discussion of citizenship. It looks at the complex arguments concerning rights and obligations, introducing us to communitarianism along the way. To what extent must citizenship imply exclusion? Can people be coerced into being social participants and, if so, how? How do we retain the universalism of a citizenship ethic while making allowances for differences, for example of gender?

We then take a look at some key political and sociological concepts in Chapters 5 and 6, respectively. Chapter 5 deals with the political concepts of the state, power, poverty and social exclusion, and human nature. It defines the main theories of the state and then reviews the main theories of power, from those that treat power as a 'surface feature' of society to those who believe that power swarms through the hidden depths of the social body. We then move onto poverty and social exclusion, revisiting in a theoretical context some of the arguments with which many Social Policy students will already be familiar. To what extent are poor individuals responsible for their deprivation? Are poverty and social exclusion the same or different? Finally, the chapter looks at human nature and why it might be regarded as a political rather than, say, a biological concept. In particular, we examine needs and the importance of needs to the notion of human flourishing and well-being.

Chapter 6 concentrates on class, explaining the Marxist and Weberian interpretations of class and class society. It details some of the changes to the class system that have occurred in recent years and the effects which the welfare state has had upon that system, both in the past and the present. The chapter ends by reviewing some of the debates concerning social movements and ponders whether social movements have taken over from classes as the main collective actors of contemporary society.

Chapters 7 and 8 then analyse the old and new ideologies of welfare. Chapter 7 covers the traditional ideologies: the radical Right, conservatism, social democracy and Marxism. The main ideas of each are reviewed in turn, their critiques of social policy are examined and an account is offered of each ideology's principal strengths and weaknesses.

Chapter 8 performs a similar function. However, its focus is not so much on ideologies (although many ideological characteristics are undoubtedly present) as on those ideas which have developed along with the 'new' social divisions – the quotation marks highlight the point that it is our theories which are relatively new rather than the divisions themselves. Therefore, we look, in turn, at ideas and critiques associated with feminism and the women's movement, the anti-racist movement, the disability rights movement, age and the construction of dependency and, finally, sexuality and the gay/lesbian movement.

Chapters 9 and 10 round off this introduction to welfare theory by bringing the story as up to date as possible. Chapter 9 deals with certain economic developments that allegedly define the age in which we live. Some attention is paid to the thesis of post-industrialism before we review post-Fordism and the implications of post-Fordism for the welfare state. Most of Chapter 9, though, is dedicated to an outline of globalisation and the economic, political, cultural and welfare-related aspects of the relevant debates. Do we live in a globalised environment or has the death of the nation-state been greatly exaggerated? What are the possible implications of globalisation for universal and high-spending welfare systems? Are they incompatible or can welfare systems be re-adapted to cope with globalising processes?

Finally, Chapter 10 sketches the main theoretical developments of recent years. Inevitably, this chapter reflects my own view of what is and is not important, but this view is hopefully not too idiosyncratic. The chapter deals with postmodernism and post-structuralism, communitarianism, environmentalism, theories of risk, information and communication technologies, social control and surveillance, the body and the new genetics. Despite the weight of history that the book tries to convey, Chapter 10 should make the point that welfare theory is a thriving and dynamic area of study.

# 1

# Welfare

This chapter provides an overview of many of the debates that are often neglected in Social Policy textbooks. Consequently, many students of the subject – myself included! – only start asking some of the most important questions towards the end of their studies rather than at the beginning. The single most important question being: 'what is welfare or well-being?' The principal answers that have been given to this question are reviewed in sections 1.3 and 1.4, having been preceded by a discussion of why an understanding of welfare theories is essential. We then go on to address some of the key issues about how welfare can be measured and applied. Is there such a property as *social* welfare (section 1.5)? What are public goods (section 1.6)? Can individual well-being be translated or aggregated into a collective form of well-being (sections 1.7–1.9)?

## 1.1 The Two Utopias of Social Policy

As an academic subject Social Policy is still relatively young. As an ever-widening tributary of sociology, it only established its own identity in the 1950s and 60s under the title of Social Administration. Yet the concepts and ideas with which Social Policy deals have roots that stretch back to the beginning of the modern period and, in some cases, far earlier. Any introduction to those concepts and ideas therefore has to encompass the subject's academic novelty *and* its intellectual maturity.

For instance, at some point during 1515 and 1516 Thomas More (1478–1535) composed the following comments about poverty and inequality:

If you don't try to cure these evils, it is futile to boast of your severity in punishing theft. Your policy may look superficially like justice, but in reality it is neither just nor practical. If you allow young folk to be abominably brought up and their characters corrupted, little by little, from childhood; and if you then punish them as grownups for committing the crimes to which their training has inclined them, what else is this, I ask, but first making them thieves and then punishing them for it? (More, 1989: 21)

In other words, if crime is a product of unjust social conditions, then the only moral and effective way of tackling it is by eliminating those conditions. More gives a hypothetical description of such a perfect society in his book *Utopia*, a word that he invented and which literally means 'no-place'. Regardless of whether he himself thought such a society to be desirable (Ackroyd, 1999: 167–75), More's observation captures an idea about social injustice which has endured throughout the centuries that separate him from us. Zygmunt Bauman has recently made a metaphorical distinction between 'tourists' (the affluent and economically secure) and 'vagabonds' (the poor and socially excluded):

> *A world without vagabonds is the utopia of the society of tourists.* Much of the politics in the society of tourists – like the obsession with 'law and order', the criminalisation of poverty, recurrent spongers-bashing, etc. – can be explained as an ongoing, stubborn effort to lift social reality, against all odds, to the level of that utopia. (Bauman, 1998: 97)

Like More, Bauman is accusing contemporary politics of seeking the elimination of the *poor* rather than the elimination of the *conditions that create poverty* and, in so doing, both men have managed to express the parameters within which the subject of Social Policy resides.

What are those parameters? It could be claimed that modern society exists somewhere between two extremes, two dreams of perfection. On the one hand, there is an 'environmental' utopia where social problems are explained in terms of social conditions; on the other, there is a 'pathological' utopia where social problems are attributed to the supposed failings and immorality of individuals. At their most general level, social policies are a means by which society moves itself in one direction or the other: some policies address the social injustice of underlying conditions, some are concerned with improving the behaviour and habits of individuals. Of course, it might be claimed that we must always fall short of either extreme (utopias are, by their very definition, unattainable), meaning that we should always factor both the 'social' and the 'individual' into our decision-making. To ignore this point is to risk creating one of two *dystopias*: either a collectivist society that stifles individuality (and More's utopia is a fairly unpleasant place) or an individualistic society that fractures the interdependent ties that hold us together. This implies that social policies are essentially paradoxical. They aim at utopia but must always fall short of their target if they are not to create utopia's opposite.

In simpler terms, we can state that it is this focus on deliberate social change which is the essential theme of Social Policy. In this book, a 'welfare system' is defined as a socioeconomic system that employs the principle of welfare in effecting social change; a 'welfare state' is defined here as a welfare system within which the state plays a central role in driving such change forward (cf. Goodin, 1988: 11). All welfare states are welfare *systems* but not all welfare systems are welfare *states* – due to the predominance of the market sector in some nations. As such, the term 'social policy' is sometimes used here to refer to the particular services contained within welfare systems (income mainten- ance, health care, and so on) and sometimes to the more general processes of deliberate social change. (Whenever Social Policy appears in this book with capitals, the reference is to the academic discipline.)

In the twentieth century there were two attempts to drive society in the direction of the environmental utopia. The first of these was the communist experiment which was based upon a belief that since social injustice derives from the private ownership of property then the abolition of the latter will effect the abolition of the former. The failure of that experiment does not necessarily invalidate the basic idea, but it does suggest that this approach to social reform is not available to us for the foreseeable future. An important question mark also hangs over the second attempt and we will see why throughout this book. The endeavour to create and maintain state welfare systems in liberal democratic societies continues, but without the momentum and certainty that once prevailed. As we venture into the twenty-first century we need to ask whether this experiment is worth continuing and, if so, in what form. This book will not address such issues systematically but it will arm students with the basic theoretical tools that will enable them to pursue such questions themselves.

## 1.2 What is Welfare Theory?

Analysing theories about the meaning of 'theory' can be a tedious business, so I propose to make a straightforward distinction between two types of theoret- ical inquiry.

First, theory can be interpreted as a form of transcendence. Throughout our lives we inhabit certain locations, know certain people, trust and believe in certain things, and accumulate a certain familiarity with the world and our societies. In one sense, theorising is the attempt to transcend our immediate contexts, to look beyond what is apparent, visible, common and easily know- able: we understand the social world by trying to look at it from the outside. For instance, the very first philosophical inquiry was supposed to have been made by Thales (625–545 BC) when he asked the question: 'What is the world made of?' Since it is not obvious, just by looking around us, what the world is made of, we need philosophical theories that will enable us to look beyond the apparent, the visible and the common. In short, 'transcendent theory' is the means by which we transcend the contexts of our immediate experience. In our time one of the most brilliant exponents of such theorising is the German philosopher and sociologist Jürgen Habermas.

Second, theory can also be interpreted as a form of immanence. This means that rather than transcending our contexts, theorising enables us to delve into those contexts still further: we understand the social world by looking at it from the inside. Let me try to illustrate the difference at work here. What should we be doing when we formulate theories about history? According to 'transcendence theorists' we should be identifying the underlying causes of historical progression: a Marxist, for instance, says that the fundamental dynamic of history is class struggle. But according to 'immanence theorists' that kind of approach risks being too abstract and ignoring the way in which the messiness and disorderliness of past events cannot be forced into neat categorical boxes without distorting the very object of our studies. The French intellectual Michel Foucault (1926–84) believed that knowing something requires us to immerse ourselves in the contingencies of the intended object of knowledge (Foucault, 1984). For Habermas (1984), by contrast, knowledge requires us to achieve a critical distance from the object of knowledge and the immediate contexts within which knowing takes place.

My own view is that, rather than engaging in endless debates as to which type of theorising is superior, we need recourse to both types.

So what of *welfare* theory then? What does this imply? Without too much simplification, we can distinguish between two Social Policy traditions. The first of these is the tradition of social administration which is basically concerned with the 'how' and the 'what' of Social Policy, for example how do welfare services operate and what effects do they have on individuals and society? The second is the theoretical tradition which is concerned with the 'why', for example why do we need a welfare state? It is difficult and probably meaningless to ask one type of question without also asking the other, so that few people lock themselves into one tradition exclusively. This means that welfare theory could be defined as follows:

> Welfare theory is a means of gaining both a transcendent and an immanent knowledge of the concepts and principles that underpin the design and delivery of social policies in order to understand the ways in which those policies affect the well-being of individuals and society as a whole.

If you can see that this raises still more questions you have learned the first important lesson that this book has to teach: the point of theory is not to ask questions that will receive correct answers (although that has been known to happen!) but to ask questions more intelligent than those we would ask otherwise and to detect which answers are likely to be *incorrect*. Theoretical debate resembles an ear-splitting conversation that goes on among countless numbers of people and between numerous generations. It is a debate which never ends and this book invites you to join the conversation. In order to make a start, the rest of this chapter analyses the possible meaning and basic implications of welfare or well-being.

## 1.3 What is Welfare?

Carl Schmitt (1888–1985) made a famous definition of politics as the process by which friends recognise each other in opposition to a set of enemies (Schmitt, 1976). Politics, he thought, is about an *identification* with those who are similar to oneself and a *differentiation* from those who are dissimilar. If this friend/enemy dichotomy is a useful way of defining politics, can we perform a similar exercise for Social Policy? The most obvious approach would be to define Social Policy as a process whereby welfare, or well-being, is maximised and diswelfare is minimised: so, a welfare/diswelfare distinction performs for Social Policy the same role as a friend/enemy distinction performs for politics. As shorthand definitions go this can probably suffice as well as any other, but it obviously begs the question as to what we mean by welfare.

This question is not an easy one to address and theorists have been struggling with it for centuries. Consequently, the scope of the debate is vast and we can do no more here than review six of the main perspectives on welfare: happiness, security, preferences, needs, desert, relative comparisons.

### 1.3.1 Happiness

There are basically two ways of defining happiness. First, the 'shallow' definition regards happiness as a particular and identifiable mental and physical experience, such as that we might feel when we win a competition or steal a kiss. Although happiness obviously does include such immediate experiences, there is also a second, 'deeper' definition. This is to regard happiness more as a general state of experience, one that is not necessarily reducible to a particular feeling of euphoria or joy but which is most often referred to as satisfaction or contentment. The ancient Greeks termed this *eudaimonia* which translates roughly as 'being well and doing well'. It means that I may be happy in general, perhaps because my ambitions are being realised, even when I suffer setbacks and misfortunes that leave me sad and frustrated from time to time.

The shallow definition of happiness captures very little of what welfare can be about. Although being in a state of welfare may render me happy in this sense, if welfare is nothing more than shallow happiness then this is a green light for all sorts of social and psychological conditioning. What if people were given the opportunity to plug themselves into some form of happiness machine after which they could experience, although only inside their heads, lives of immense joy? Would those who chose to do so be in a state of welfare? Or would this be too superficial a form of welfare, akin to spending one's life in a drug-induced haze such as Tennyson's lotus eaters? The deeper definition of happiness as *eudaimonia* is far more profound but this, too, requires the existence of autonomy and authenticity if such happiness is to be real rather than artificial. Therefore, on either definition we have to move beyond simple considerations of happiness per se.

### 1.3.2 Security

Security is another obvious candidate. Someone who enjoys security of income, employment and housing would seem to be in a greater condition of welfare than someone who experiences insecurity and uncertainty. Security implies a foreknowledge that one's circumstances are not going to decline for the foreseeable future and this anticipation may be valuable in itself even for a person whose circumstances may not be enviable otherwise. For instance, somebody who lives in a cheap bedsit but has a stable job may be said to experience more security, and therefore welfare, than somebody who can no longer pay an expensive mortgage and may soon lose their home through repossession.

However, defining welfare in terms of security also has its problems. It might be that the price of security is too high. In previous generations, many women believed (often incorrectly) that they could gain a financial security through marriage that they were unlikely to receive on their own in the job market, but only at the price of surrendering their independence and freedom. In short, if security implies dependency, then the level of welfare being experienced might be less than appears at first glance.

### 1.3.3 Preferences

It also seems reasonable to describe someone whose preferences have been satisfied as enjoying more welfare than someone whose desires have been left unfulfilled. If I want to buy a new car and can afford to do so, my 'want-satisfaction', and therefore my level of welfare, is higher than the person who also wants that vehicle but cannot afford to buy it. The attraction of defining welfare in this way is that it potentially renders the concept quantifiable. According to some welfare economists, the value of something depends on how much an individual would be willing to pay for it in the market (see the discussion of Pigou in section 1.5). If you and I are equally wealthy and I am willing to spend ten per cent of my wealth on a Van Gogh painting whereas you would only spend five per cent, the ownership of that painting enhances my welfare by twice the level it would enhance yours.

There are, however, several difficulties with defining welfare in this way. For instance, it might be that my preferences are superficial or artificially induced, in which case being in a state of want-satisfaction does not increase my level of welfare after all. If I am addicted to smoking, I may experience more moments of sheer want-satisfaction than someone who is not, yet my welfare may still be considerably lower due to the long-term health risks. It is also easy to think of welfare-enhancing experiences that do not derive from want-satisfaction, still less from the kinds of want-satisfactions associated with the market. Finally, we also have to remember that the satisfaction of my desires may reduce the ability of others to satisfy theirs, for example I want a cigarette whereas you want clean air to breathe. Preferences may, then, be too narrow and individualistic a concept to fully capture what is meant by well-being.

### 1.3.4 Needs

Treating needs and need-fulfillment as a proxy for welfare is popular among social policy commentators because of their egalitarian implications (cf. Goodin, 1988: 27–50, 278–305). This is because a need seems to describe something about human nature that is more essential than preferences and therefore less individualistic (needs seem to be far more general and commonly shared than wants). Needs also lend themselves to forms of objective measurement and definition, but not ones that are dependent on market behaviour. Since needs are so highly regarded within the Social Policy literature we will deal with them in section 2.2. when discussing equality and at greater length in Chapter 5 in our review of key political concepts.

However, it is worth pointing out that not all types of need-fulfillment can be regarded as important vis-à-vis welfare. My need for food is more important than your need for a cigarette. In other words, we have to distinguish between (a) *basic* needs, (b) *non-basic* needs and (c) preferences: basic needs might be regarded as relevant to welfare but not necessarily the other two categories. The trouble lies in defining basic needs (Doyal and Gough, 1991). If our definition is too modest, that is, it covers only the biological essentials of food, water and so on, we are left with a limited and unoriginal definition of welfare; but if our definition is too generous, that is, it refers to non-basic needs, welfare becomes too vague a guide for the design and assessment of social policies.

## 1.3.5 Desert

There is another school of thought which suggests that desert makes a better principle for the distribution of social goods than need. Desert implies an equivalence between contribution and reward. For instance, if I contribute twice as much as you to the design of a money-making invention, my share of the profits should be twice as high as yours. If I receive more than this amount, you have suffered an injustice; if I receive less, I have suffered the injustice. Yet desert is also a moral principle. Conservatives often appeal to desert as a concept that stresses the organic interdependency of society, while allowing us to morally sanction those who take more from society than they contribute. Yet others on the Right point out that desert is a remarkably difficult value to quantify: the prices which are set in a market are related to consumer demand and not to any notion of desert on the part of workers and companies. If consumers prefer to buy my substandard sketches to your expert oil paintings, the fact that you might deserve more than I do in an artistic sense means absolutely nothing. Markets are about entitlements rather than desert (Nozick, 1974). This might suggest that if the principle is to be preserved, we need to look beyond the market. Indeed, many on the Left think that social justice should be based upon desert rather than need. Marx appealed to both: in a socialist society people would be rewarded according to their labour, while in a communist society wealth would be distributed according to need.

It might well be that welfare is closely related to desert, so that someone who receives less than they deserve experiences less well-being than someone whose rewards are proportionate to their contributions. The problem with desert lies in deciding who is deserving. For the Right, the poor are undeserving because they are held to take from society more than they give; yet the Left use exactly the same argument against the wealthiest. So, although desert is a principle to which we constantly appeal, the value of such appeals is heavily dependent on the ideological context within which they are made. The conclusion is that, although desert may be related to well-being, we should not regard the two terms as synonymous.

## 1.3.6 Relative comparisons

So far we have largely been treating an individual's welfare as if it is something unrelated to the welfare of others. In reality, the level of well-being that I experience is dependent on the levels of well-being experienced by those with whom I make comparisons. Throughout our lives we compare ourselves constantly to two categories of people: those we know and those we do not. The people that we know can be divided into relatives, partners, friends, rivals, enemies and acquaintances. My level of welfare is likely to increase if the people that I like are in a state of well-being and/or if the people that I dislike are experiencing diswelfare. The people that we do not know bear much less of an immediate impact on a person's well-being, although I may experience the latter if, for example, my favourite team is playing well or my favourite actress wins an Oscar.

It seems inevitable that welfare is somehow related to the human characteristic of making constant comparisons with others. If I own two goats and everybody else owns four, my level of well-being is lower than it would be in a society where everyone owns just two goats, even though the quantity of my possessions is the same in both cases. We must be on our guard, however, as it may be that people compare the wrong things or have a distorted image of themselves and of others.

For instance, the extent to which our self-images and sense of self-worth is tied to ideal representations of attractiveness that are presented to us in films, TV, magazines, and so on has long been documented. There is a gender issue here, as women in particular are subjected to images of beauty and desirability, and so may be more vulnerable than men to the emotional and physical problems that attend a 'failure' to measure up to those images. Therefore, somebody who successfully aspires to such ideals may experience more welfare in a comparative sense than those who do not, yet this may well be an inferior and artificial form of well-being, one induced by companies trying to sell the products that supposedly bring those ideals within reach. We could therefore claim that there are both *authentic* and *inauthentic* types of welfare comparison, although deciding which is which is not an easy exercise to perform.

Each of the above six headings captures something of what we mean by welfare, but none is sufficient on its own. Rather than get lost in the details of that debate, therefore, we shall now review some of the theoretical parameters within which the debate actually takes place.

## 1.4 Three Important Distinctions

There are at least three distinctions that usefully enable us to elaborate on the possible definitions of welfare that have just been proposed.

### 1.4.1 Subjective or objective?

Is welfare a subjective or an objective condition? If welfare is subjective, this means it relates to the feelings, perceptions, understandings and experiences of the person to whom the term is being applied. Subjective welfare is dependent on the subject or self. If welfare is objective, by contrast, it can be described as such in two senses. By 'strong objective welfare' we mean that welfare *in no way relates* to the feelings, perceptions, understandings and experience of the person to whom the term is being applied, that is, welfare is not dependent on subjectivity *at all*. By 'weak objective welfare' we mean that welfare *is* subject related but also corresponds to some form of objective standard, allowing us to compare the welfare experienced by Jack with that experienced by Jill. What can we say about these three categories?

It seems nonsensical to describe welfare as strongly objective since this is equivalent to claiming that Jack can be in a state of welfare even though he does not actually know it or feel it himself. While there may be fictional scenarios where this could be true, for example if Jack is a prisoner who does not realise he is imprisoned because he is plugged into a virtual reality machine, the category seems unhelpful in relation to our everyday under-standing of well-being. However, we should hesitate before defining welfare purely in subjective terms since this might reduce welfare to a hedonistic and internal state of mind (cf. Sumner, 1996). For instance, somebody high on drugs and alcohol may be enjoying the time of their life yet be putting their long-term health in danger. Perhaps we need recourse to both the subjective and the weak objective categories of welfare, meaning that welfare has got something to do with feeling, perception and experience but not with just *any* sort of feeling, perception and experience. Perhaps objective standards are necessary if we are to be capable of (1) judging *when* one form of subjective welfare conflicts with another, and (2) deciding *which* form is better for the overall good of the person in question.

Amartya Sen's ideas offer one such compromise. Sen (1984, 1985) distin-guishes between functionings (the achievement of things such as health and literacy) and capabilities (the opportunity to realise a functioning). His distinc-tion avoids the pitfalls of strong objectivism and acknowledges the extent to which well-being is related to the contingencies and accidental circumstances of life, but it also avoids the vague and capricious implications of a purely sub-jective account of welfare. Defining welfare in terms of functionings and cap-abilities therefore seems to effect a neat compromise between the two extremes.

## 1.4.2 *Universal or relative?*

Is welfare the same for all people, regardless of their location in space and time, or is it context dependent, that is, relative to the era and places in which we live? If we defined welfare only in universal terms, we might miss the extent to which our perceptions, feelings and experiences are conditioned by the particular environments in which we live. However, if welfare is purely context dependent, we may lose the ability to speak meaningfully about welfare altogether. For instance, if everything is relative, there can be no such thing as basic needs, since by *basic* we mean 'that which is common to everyone'.

So it may be that, as with the previous distinction, we are being tricked by a misleading dichotomy. For example, we could think of welfare as referring to a universal core of needs, a core from which our 'weak objective' standards can be derived, but also to a context-dependent series of desires that are relative to time and place. As before, Sen (1983) has made some important contributions in this respect. He argues against a straightforward relativist account of poverty, claiming that 'the poor' and the 'less well-off' are not necessarily the same (poverty is another of the political concepts that we will review in Chapter 5). Relativist definitions and explanations must therefore be underpinned by an absolute and universalist foundation which allows us to avoid the problems with the concept of relative deprivation. So, someone may be described as poor if they have been deprived of dignity and esteem, but the nature of the commodities, the lack of which will create this absence of dignity and self-worth, will vary from society to society and generation to generation.

## 1.4.3 Individual or collective?

Is welfare a property of individuals or can collectives (groups, societies) be described as being in a state of well-being? Here, it is more difficult to sit on the fence and suggest that we should refer to *both* individualism *and* collectivism, as a great deal of the social and political thought of the last two centuries has concerned itself with this problem. Nevertheless, there is a fundamental point that needs to be made. Welfare *must* be an individual characteristic or property to some extent, for, even if it is also a property of a society, such social well-being cannot be disassociated from the welfare of the individuals who live in that society. Dictatorships are adept at pretending that social welfare is high even when most of that society's members are obviously miserable, but we recognise this as a pretence precisely because it offends our common-sense understanding of what welfare is and is not. Therefore, although collectives *may* be describable in such terms, they cannot be so described without a considerable amount of reference to the welfare of the individuals who comprise them.

The problem can be restated as follows: is welfare a property of individuals only or of individuals *and* collectives? For theorists the essential question is: can individual welfare be aggregated together, so that the sum of individual welfares adds up to a collective welfare? It is this question that we shall spend the rest of the chapter addressing, as the answer that is given to it can alter profoundly our approach to social policy.

# 1.5 Social Welfare

Is there such a thing as social welfare and, if so, what might this imply? There are four key theorists who have argued that the concept of social welfare is meaningful and applicable.

The philosopher Jeremy Bentham (1748–1832) was among the first to analyse this question (Bentham, 1984). Although he agreed with Adam Smith (1723–90) that society was no more than the sum of its parts, he further believed that we are not limited to discussions of individual welfare alone. For Bentham, welfare was equivalent to utility, by which he meant happiness, and therefore measurable: indeed, he actually formulated an 'hedonic calculus', enabling my pleasure at eating chocolate to be measured against your pleasure at dieting. It is the measurability of utility which allows us to add individual welfares together and so quantify the aggregate level of social welfare.[1] For Bentham, this method has three advantages.

First, we arm ourselves with a yardstick which enables us to evaluate different social states of affairs and supplement market outcomes with a system of statutory social and public policies. Second, we can, on this basis, make rational and deliberate decisions as to which are the most efficacious policies. Finally, we can compare different societies in order to decide which corresponds most closely to the principle of the greatest happiness of the greatest number. For Bentham, social welfare = social utility = the greatest happiness of the greatest number, and his influence extended well into the nineteenth century and to a series of reforms dealing with income maintenance, workplace conditions and public works.

The basic problem with his philosophy is that it reduces well-being to utility and reduces utility to a shallow notion of happiness. If your pleasure at watching soap operas is greater than my pleasure at reading *Ulysses*, Bentham would define your well-being as greater than mine, even if I benefit more in the long term by successfully completing Joyce's book. But if this is too facile a notion of well-being, there is a question mark as to whether social welfare can be regarded as the simple, mechanical aggregation of individual welfares.

Similarly, one of the most contentious aspects of this 'utilitarian' account of welfare concerns the claim that we can make interpersonal comparisons of welfare, for example between the pleasure of watching soap operas and finishing *Ulysses*. If welfare has a strong subjectivist element, how is this possible? How can my experiences be reliably compared to yours? The welfare economist A. C. Pigou (1877–1959) argued that interpersonal comparisons *are* possible because well-being is a matter of desire and *desire can be measured in monetary terms*: the more I am willing to pay for something then the more I desire it and the higher will be my level of welfare should I achieve/acquire it (Pigou, 1965). Therefore, individual welfare is closely related to market choice and social welfare can be said to rise and fall when national wealth rises and falls, as measured by certain economic indicators such as Gross Domestic Product.

There are, however, several criticisms that can be made of this argument. We have already questioned the link between well-being and desire (in section 1.3.3) on the grounds that desire is too subjective and vulnerable a concept to bear such a weight; and we might also question the link between desire and monetary payment, for example we all need and desire to breathe unpolluted air but there is a limited extent to which we determine the value of the latter by asking how much we might be willing to pay for it in a market!

The economist Vilfredo Pareto (1848–1923) was one of those who argued that interpersonal comparisons are not possible to make, but that we can nevertheless talk meaningfully about social and collective states of welfare. According to Pareto (Aron, 1970), a society that is making at least one person better off can be described as improving its level of welfare so long as nobody is becoming worse off as a result. However, there will come a time when it can only make some better off by making others worse off.[2] At this time the society in question has reached the point of 'optimum efficiency', making any further change unwarranted. Therefore, we can have a meaningful discussion of 'social welfare' without having to make Benthamite comparisons between my utility and yours. But the problem with defining social welfare in terms of Pareto-efficiency is that it is biased in favour of the status quo: if a change makes just one person worse off, the change is unjustified *no matter how unequal the society in question and how rich the 'worse-off' person remains.*

A more recent attempt to define social welfare without reducing it to Pareto-efficiency has been made by the political philosopher John Rawls (1972). We shall examine Rawls in more depth in the next chapter but it is worth observing here that Rawls directs welfare away from the criterion of efficiency and back towards matters of justice and morality, although he rejects utilitarian accounts of justice and morality. For Rawls, a society with a just distribution of resources is in a higher state of welfare than one with an unjust distribution, and a just distribution is that which is of benefit to the least advantaged. Social welfare therefore requires the elimination of *unjust* inequalities, rather than inequality per se, and Rawls's arguments offer an important justification for redistributive social policies, as we shall see in more depth in Chapter 2.

Figure 1.1 illustrates how these theories of social welfare relate to one another: one axis defines social welfare in terms of either ethics/justice or efficiency/economics; the other axis relates to whether it is or is not possible to make interpersonal comparisons of well-being.

## 1.6 Public Goods

A debate that relates to questions of social welfare is that concerning public goods and here we begin to understand why some theorists reject the concept of social welfare altogether.

Public goods are distinguishable from private goods. A private good is excludable: my consumption of the good prevents you from consuming it as well; public goods are non-excludable: my consumption of the good does not and cannot prevent you from consuming it also. Food is an obvious private

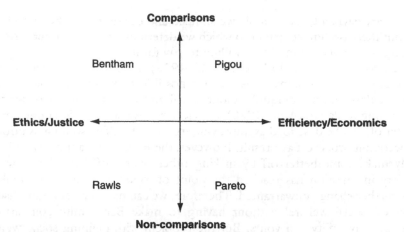

**Figure 1.1** Four perspectives on social welfare

good but food *safety* is a public good because ensuring hygiene is too costly and complicated a business for each individual alone and my enjoyment of safe food does not contravene your enjoyment of the same. It is also the case that the value of food safety to me does not decrease just because you experience it also (whereas I may not fancy a doughnut into which you have bitten).[3] *Social (and public) policies are therefore concerned with the production and distribution of public goods.*

The question is this: what counts as a public good? There are obvious candidates such as clean air, street lighting, national defence, law and order, but should we also include health care, education and minimum income maintenance? At the risk of putting it too simplistically, we can say the following. Those on the Right believe that these latter items are not public goods because they are privately consumable, and consequently the market should play a large and perhaps exclusive role in their provision. Those on the Left believe that the private consumability of education and so on does not contradict their status as semi-public (or *lumpy*) goods, that is, goods too expensive for individual purchase and from which public benefits can be derived (known as *merit* goods). Consequently, collective action is necessary because in a market economy public/lumpy/merit goods are underproduced: a political authority is needed to compel payment for such goods and this means giving a large role to the state. *The welfare state is a system of collective action that facilitates the production and distribution of public, lumpy and merit goods designed to increase the sum of social welfare.*

Part of the problem with public goods is that they are invitations to free-riders. Let us imagine that all the inhabitants of a port agree to build a lighthouse for reasons of public safety but that ten per cent of the town then refuse to take part in building and/or financing its construction (White,

1997). Unless we resort to coercive measures that may be inconsistent with a free society, those ten per cent cannot be excluded from enjoying the benefits of the lighthouse: they are free-riders. *Free-riders enjoy the benefits of social cooperation without shouldering the burdens of cooperative activity.* Although free-riders probably cannot be abolished altogether, one of the arguments of the Right is that a welfare state is an invitation to free-riders, for example benefit fraudsters, and leads to a society where people in general are more prepared to take rather than to give and where the hard working are exploited by the lazy (de Jasay, 1989). The Left reply either that such free-riding is a necessary price to be paid for the greater good, or that the Right have too narrow a definition of free-riding, for example Fraser (1997) argues that an extensive welfare system is needed to correct the free-riding of men on the unpaid, undervalued work of women.

## 1.7 The Prisoners' Dilemma

These issues all lead us towards a discussion of the nature of social cooperation and this means appreciating the prisoners' dilemma. The prisoners' dilemma is a branch of game theory, a mathematical attempt to understand social interaction. Any game includes a number of components – players, rules, strategies and outcomes – that are heavily interlinked: my strategy will develop and alter depending on my perceptions of your strategy and vice versa. Therefore a game is a constant feedback process of mutual readjustments and game theorists believe that social interaction can be understood as a complex game in which each participant (or social member) tries to secure the best outcome for him or herself based upon their interpretations of, and responses to, the 'moves' of others.

There are basically two types of game: conflictual and cooperative. Conflictual games are those in which there is a fixed stock of resources to be won (a zero-sum game or 'negative game'), meaning that players are more likely to fight it out than to collaborate: this might suggest a politics of market-based individualism or class-based group conflict (depending on whether the players are defined as individuals or classes). Cooperative games are those in which the stock of resources is not fixed (a non-zero-sum game or 'positive game') so that there may be a benefit for all if all agree to work together (indeed, resources may increase as a result of this cooperation). This cooperation may be associative and spontaneous, originating from the 'bottom' of society, or it may be enforced and centralised, originating from the 'top'. *A welfare state may be defined as a liberal democratic form of enforced 'top-down' cooperation.* The prisoners' dilemma is a theoretical means of debating whether social interaction conforms to the conflictual model or the cooperative model.

Two criminals have been arrested and separated from each other. The police are already in a position to convict both of robbery but they need a confession if either is to be convicted of the murder that was committed during the robbery. Both prisoners are informed that they have two alternatives: each man can either stay silent or confess that they both committed the murder. Prisoner 1 is then offered a deal and told that prisoner 2 is being offered the same deal. If both he and his partner confess to murder, they will each receive 15 years in jail; if he stays silent but his partner confesses, he will serve 20 years whereas his partner will go free; if both men stay silent, they will only be convicted for robbery and serve two years. Prisoner 1 reasons that the best alternative is to stay silent and hope that his partner does the same. But can his partner be trusted to do so? If not, it would be best to confess and at least serve five years less than he would serve if he stayed silent while his partner betrayed him. Prisoner 2 follows the same reasoning. Although it is in the best interests of both men to stay silent, self-interest, lack of communication and the knowledge that others act in similar circumstances leads each prisoner to confess, condemning them both to 15 years in jail. The prisoners' dilemma illustrates how self-interest can lead to a worse situation for everyone but also why self-interest can be a more rational strategy than selfless altruism (Axelrod, 1984).

In this version of the prisoners' dilemma, the conflictual model of social interaction predominates and suggests that the market is the best way of coordinating the self-interested actions of rational individuals. However, it is possible to revise the above thought-experiment so that cooperation and a reciprocal altruism is more rational after all; in other hypothetical scenarios, the prisoners are allowed to communicate, or the rules of the game are altered, or the players are naturally more altruistic, or the game is played several times (allowing the players to learn from past mistakes). In short, game theory is a means of theoretical illustration and does not tell us which social model is superior. Society is neither inherently conflictual nor cooperative: it is not inherently anything. Therefore, *social policies are not responses to social facts, they are means by which social facts are constructed in the first place. Normative and prescriptive positions in the subject of Social Policy are based not so much on the society we live in as the society we want to create.*

The conflictual model and the cooperative model correspond broadly to the two theories outlined in sections 1.8 and 1.9.

## 1.8 Rational Choice Theory

Rational choice theory (RCT) is the theory that society can be understood in terms of the self-interested actions of rational individuals (Elster, 1986a; Coleman and Fararo, 1993). Individuals act rationally when they try to maximise the benefits and minimise the costs that they experience according to whatever hierarchy of values and preferences they hold. RCT therefore regards all forms of social, group and organisational behaviour as reducible to the individual actions of voters and consumers, so that cooperative and collective forms of action are only explicable according to this basic unit of analysis. That such a theory has prospered in recent years is no great surprise: a rational choice interpretation reflects the shift in our societies towards greater individualism, and, because it places the emphasis on choice, with markets assumed to offer people more choice than public bureaucracies, there is a presumption within the theory in favour of markets and the greater efficiency that markets are often assumed to generate. In short, RCT is individualistic and subjective, and traces ultimately back to neoclassical economics, although some Marxists have adopted a rational choice perspective in recent years (Elster, 1986b).

RCT suggests that social policies must be explained in terms of rational, individual self-interest. At best, this could imply a pro-welfare state stance that is quite limited, since the welfare state would be interpreted in individualistic rather than collectivist terms. At worst, it could encourage an anti-welfare state stance with state services being read as serving the interests of producers (teachers, doctors and so on) rather than the welfare of service consumers. As such, RCT easily lends itself to the privatisation and marketisation of state welfare systems.

However, there are a number of reasons why this theory can be rejected as an inadequate explanation of society and social activity (cf. Zey, 1998: 87–113). First, it works with too restrictive a definition of the subject. By treating the individual as the basic unit of analysis, as the atom of society, RCT merely reproduces the Robinson Crusoe figure beloved of classical economics and ignores the many theories that, over the last century and a half, have demonstrated the extent to which subjects are interdependent and socially determined beings. By treating preferences and values as given, RCT is biased in favour of the existing order of things. Second, the theory is not very good at accounting for power. By treating inequalities in power as the product of rational, self-interested decisions, it overlooks the role that coercion, violence, exploitation and oppression play in human affairs, for example the fact that people often remain in situations where the costs outweigh the benefits either because of a real or perceived lack of choice. Again, therefore, RCT presumes in favour of the status quo. Third, the theory is not very good at explaining the existence of altruism and collective behaviour. Geras (1998) draws our attention to the remarkable sacrifices that many made during the Second World War, sacrifices that cannot be reduced to selfish calculations of profit and loss, benefit and cost. Finally, RCT underestimates the extent to which market exchange and activity is dependent on non-quantifiable qualities such as trust, friendship and cooperation: markets are not simply about the kind of economic calculations that RCT wants to focus upon. In conclusion, RCT is probably inadequate as an explanation of social behaviour in general and social policy in particular.

## 1.9 Collective Action

Yet if rational self-interest is unlikely to constitute the basis of social activity and cooperation, explanations that appeal to collective action seem to be flawed also.

One of the earliest critiques of collective action was offered by Hardin (1977) who imagines what would happen to an open pasture, a commons, when it is used for grazing. Although there is only so much grazing that the commons can absorb, this limit is certain to be breached because the cost for each individual herder of allowing his animals to overgraze is outweighed by the returns: the costs are borne by everybody but the benefits accrue to the individual alone. In short, where people receive most of the benefits but few of the costs for their actions, environmental degradation is likely to result. According to Hardin, there are two basic solutions to this 'tragedy of the commons'. On the one hand, we could make people act responsibly through a system of 'mutual coercion, mutually agreed upon' (Ophuls, 1977; cf. Ostrom, 1990). This seems to suggest that collective action can only be effective if it is coerced. On the other, we could raise the costs and lower the benefits of acting irresponsibly by abandoning any notion of collective action and privatising the commons, that is, parcelling out bits of land to everyone on the Aristotelian grounds that people care most about what they personally own. Such arguments resemble those of Olson (1965), who observed that people are unlikely to act according to the common welfare, because if each individual knows that they cannot be excluded from enjoyment of a public good, nobody has much of an incentive to contribute to the creation of such public goods in the first place.

These arguments therefore relate back to the issues of social welfare, free-riding and the prisoners' dilemma, the basic message being that (1) collective action is irrational from an individual point of view, and (2) public goods are either the unintended consequence of uncoordinated exchange between private owners within the market, or the result of a coercive authority. Its critics can therefore acknowledge that the welfare state has created and/or enabled the formation of public goods but still argue that the price has been too high in terms of personal freedom and efficiency (cf. Goodin, 1988: 229–56). The solution therefore might be to fall back on some version of RCT and privatise the ownership and control of social resources.

Is this the conclusion to which we are inevitably drawn? Perhaps not. First, because we have recourse to the objections already mentioned. The advocates of rational self-interest are too simplistic in their view of the subject, too naive in their interpretation of power, too reductionist when it comes to altruism and selflessness, and too facile in their interpretation of markets (it might be possible to privatise the land, but how can we privatise the sea and the air?). Second, we might treat the proposed alternatives as too polarised. What if

Hardin's original commons is *collectively* owned rather than *unowned*, what if people can engage in egalitarian, democratic debate with their neighbours about the best way of using the commons and what if the free-rider problem can be dealt with by a central, regulatory authority that is less coercive than an authoritarian state? If, in short, we alter the terms of the hypothesis, Hardin's pessimistic conclusions about the efficacy of collective action *can* be avoided.

The contrast between RCT and collective action lies at the heart of a political contrast that will be drawn throughout the book. Those on the Right insist that welfare is an individualistic concept through and through (Barry, 1999) because collective aggregation is not possible, because most goods are private in nature, because of the danger of free-riders and because individual self-interest is the most rational strategy for people to adopt. Social policies should therefore be based upon free-market principles. Those on the Left insist that welfare is individualistic *and* collectivist because there *is* such a thing as social welfare, because there are numerous public, lumpy and merit goods, because we are all free-riders to some extent and because cooperation is the most rational strategy if and when the circumstances are right. Social policies must therefore be geared towards the collective interest of all, implying the involvement of the state.

According to the Right, there is a limited extent to which I can care for the welfare of others, unless these others are actually known to me. Apart from occasional acts of philanthropy and charity, it is best that each person rationally pursues their self-interest and leaves the free market to coordinate these individual actions so that the social consequences are at least better than those that deliberate design can create. According to the Left, we do and should care for the generality of humankind, most of whom we do not know: self-interest is and should be tempered by some measure of cooperation, mutuality and altruism because my welfare is interdependent with the welfare of others.

In this chapter we have wound our way through some of the more intricate and complex aspects of Social Policy. We saw that welfare theory is a crucially important aspect of the discipline but that it resembles an open-ended discussion and does not provide a set of easily digestible solutions to the key questions that we have to ask. Sections 1.3 and 1.4 illustrated this observation by suggesting that welfare or well-being has no single, simple meaning or defining quality. Instead, we must allow a number of perspectives to illuminate our understanding of the concept. We then sketched the key issues surrounding the measurement of welfare and whether or not it is a characteristic of individuals alone. Throughout sections 1.6–1.9 we found a contrast between those who interpret well-being in terms of private goods, individual self-interest and market provision, and those who interpret it in terms of public goods, altruism, cooperation and collective provision.

So, having reviewed some of its more abstract heights, our journey across the terrain of welfare theory becomes a bit easier as we are now in a position to familiarise ourselves with ideas that relate more directly and more obviously to the kind of debates that must occupy anyone who takes an interest in social policies. We begin by introducing ourselves to the debates about equality.

# Equality

The first chapter has reviewed some of the main debates regarding the concept of welfare and we saw that those debates are characterised by certain political cleavages, particularly between Left and Right. During the next three chapters we shall witness how these cleavages extend across an even wider range of concepts and debates. As such, Chapters 2 to 4 should really be read as a whole since the meaning of equality is dependent on that of liberty, and vice versa, and both come together in complex ways under the heading of citizenship.

In this chapter we begin to sketch some of the issues at stake, looking at why equality is such an attractive yet controversial concept (sections 2.1–2.3), examining what it is that should be equalised (section 2.4), outlining the main theories of social justice (section 2.5) and the relevance of equality to social policy (section 2.6), and concluding with a look at some recent and significant theoretical developments (section 2.7).

## 2.1 Introducing Equality

Equality is both a philosophical concept and a political principle (Callinicos, 2000). As a concept, equality has been an object of reflection for many centuries. For instance, Aristotle (384–322 BC) distinguished between numerical equality (sameness in number or size) and proportionate equality (an equivalence in terms of ratio) (Aristotle, 1988: 111). As an illustration of this difference, imagine that we have a pie which we have to divide between a group of four hungry people. If everyone is equally hungry, it seems fair to divide the pie into numerically equal parts, that is, quarters. However, if two members of the group are twice as hungry as the other two, the division of the pie should not be strictly numerical but should be proportionate to this ratio between the hungry and the not-so-hungry. In short, the pie should be divided into *unequal* slices in order to reflect fairly the different levels of hunger and so ensure that all appetites are *equally* satisfied. Aristotle's distinction seems to suggest that equality be defined as *the fair distribution of shares in respect of x* (hunger, in the above example). The nature of equality therefore depends upon the nature of *x*.

However, such philosophical definitions do not actually require us to support equality as a moral and political principle. For instance, we might prefer to let the group fight for the pie, irrespective of any considerations of equality. To treat it as a principle, then, is to regard the concept as an ethical and political virtue. Both Plato (427–347 BC) and Aristotle made a philosophical association between equality and democracy, but the idea that society should be organised on this basis was not widely adopted until the democratic revolutions 2000 years after they lived. One of the first people to recognise that equality had been adopted as an organising principle of modern society was Alexis de Tocqueville (1805–59) who, in his travels around America in the 1820s, recognised that the French and American revolutions had made equality an irreversible, institutional feature of modern societies. In this sense, most of us are egalitarians because most of us are democrats. However, de Tocqueville (1990) also recognised the tensions that can arise between equality and other important principles and he correctly anticipated that modern societies would spend much of their time, energy and resources attempting to cope with these tensions.

Before we can go any further several points have to be made. First, we will be concerned mainly with *social* equality rather than, say, legal or political equality. Second, we should remember that social equality is not necessarily an absolute. It is common to hear people object to equality on the grounds that it would be unrealistic and undesirable for everyone to have the *same* income or the *same* level of wealth. Yet by social equality we might mean not a crude, absolute equality but a degree of equalisation. For instance, social equality could imply defining a minimum level of wealth, below which nobody should be allowed to fall, and a maximum level of wealth, beyond which nobody should be allowed to rise. Finally, some claim that we cannot all be equal because we are all different. Yet one of the mistakes that this objection makes is to confuse equality with uniformity. An egalitarian can easily acknowledge that there are some qualities in respect of which humans are different from each other, in addition to some qualities in respect of which we are the same.

## 2.2 Why Support Social Equality?

What is it that justifies social equality (Goodin, 1988: 51–69)? Why should social goods be distributed according to some notion of fairness? Perhaps the most common answer to these questions has centred around the relationship between the natural and the social: if there is such a thing as natural equality then we have a substantial reason to support and create a corresponding social equality.

In the above examples, what justified a fair distribution of the pie between the four people was, first, that they each belonged to the same group (they were all hungry) and, second, they each had some form of legitimate claim on what was to be to be distributed (the pie). Is it possible to justify social equality on a similar basis? More specifically, we have to ask:

- If, in the above example, $x$ denoted hunger, is it possible to identify a property or quality or characteristic that can be said to belong to all humans?
- Would this common property give rise to a legitimate claim on the part of all humans for a socially egalitarian distribution?

One recent and influential attempt to address such questions has emerged from within the Social Policy literature – albeit in a text which is not concerned with social equality per se. Len Doyal and Ian Gough (1991) have argued that all humans possess certain basic needs, indicating the presence of some form of common human nature. They insist that these basic needs are health and autonomy, those being the preconditions for a meaningful human life, no matter when in history or where in the world that life is being lived. These basic needs can therefore be said to constitute a universal 'core' around which our particular collective and personal identities are then formed. It could be said, then, that Doyal and Gough have identified a possible candidate for the $x$ that we were looking for: the common denominator that we all share and which marks us out as members of the same (human) group. If so, we have addressed the first of the above questions: $x$ denotes basic needs that are universally common to all humans. Indeed, many Social Policy commentators make this kind of association between equality and basic needs (as we saw in section 1.3.4 when discussing welfare).

However, while the existence of basic needs might justify equality in some form, it does not necessarily justify a *social* equality since this requires that all have a legitimate claim on the fair distribution of social wealth. Doyal and Gough do, however, provide a potential link between basic needs and social equality. If humans have needs, they point out, then humans require the means to satisfy those needs: goods such as nutritional food, clean water, housing, non-hazardous environments, health care and education, physical and economic security.[1] And just as basic needs are universal so these 'needs-satisfiers' should also be regarded as universal. In short, the existence of basic needs requires that all societies meet certain standards of social organisation and welfare provision if those needs are to be satisfied. And although we can allow for the fact that differing countries will have different ways of organising themselves and their welfare systems – depending on the level of economic development as well as ideological, cultural and religious factors – an underlying commitment to a fair distribution of social wealth would appear to be a necessary condition of basic need satisfaction. This means that no country can ignore the demands of social equality while claiming to fulfil basic human needs.

So, the work of Doyal and Gough is one potential way of answering the question 'why support social equality?' Just as the pie eaters belong to the same group by virtue of being hungry, so we all belong to the same group, humanity, by virtue of possessing the same basic needs. Furthermore, if basic needs are universal, there must exist corresponding needs-satisfiers that establish a universal claim on social goods: if health is a basic need, then systems of health care available to all are a concomitant requirement. However, even among social egalitarians considerable disagreement remains about what type and level of social equality is preferable.

## 2.3 Social Equality and Individual Liberty

Many of the disputes about equality revolve around disagreements as to the proper relationship between social equality and individual liberty. There are those who consider equality and liberty as a zero-sum game. Imagine two piles of stones, one pile labelled 'equality' and the other pile labelled 'liberty'. Assuming that no other stones are available, the only way we can enlarge the equality pile is by taking some stones from the liberty pile and vice versa. On this interpretation, social equality and individual liberty are regarded as mutually exclusive and the task then is to decide which of the following three options we prefer:

1. A strong commitment to social equality with a minimal commitment to individual liberty.
2. A strong commitment to individual liberty with a minimal commitment to social equality.
3. Some form of trade-off between the two.

The social policy implications of these options are wide ranging. For instance, the first option might suggest a closely regulated economy and society with extensive redistributive welfare services and extremely high rates of taxation. The second option might suggest a laissez-faire economy and libertarian society with few welfare services and very low rates of taxation. The third option might imply any number of welfare systems depending on the nature of the preferred trade-off.

Alternatively, we might think of social equality and individual liberty as being engaged in a non-zero-sum game where we can increase the size of both piles of stones simultaneously. This has long been an argument advanced by many on the Left. R. H. Tawney (1880–1962) famously argued that it is unequal societies which deprive people of much of their liberty. In a capitalist society, people have to spend so much of their lives making money and trying to avoid poverty that they have little time left for anything else. Therefore, it would be a society of socialist equals that would embody the diversity and variety that anti-egalitarians (wrongly) attribute to capitalist societies with their vast inequalities of wealth and power (Tawney, 1931). This idea that social equality and individual liberty can be mutually reinforcing can be identified with two principal theories.

The first of these derives ultimately from the work of the philosopher Jean-Jacques Rousseau (1712–78). Rousseau (1973: 28) was concerned to reconcile 'the equality which nature has ordained between men, and the inequality which they have introduced'. A return to a state of nature is out of the question, he believed. Therefore, the task should be to remodel society so that its institutions no longer hold us in chains. Rousseau thought of society not as a collection of individuals but as an expression of the 'general will': something that transcends the sum of individual wills. So, whereas representative democracies establish their authority on the basis of majority voting, Rousseau (1973: 175) calls for a *direct* democracy where citizens place themselves 'in common under the supreme direction of the general will'. The authority of the common good therefore derives ultimately from the individual consenting to surrender his or her freedom to it, but this 'surrender' is not so much the negation of individuality as its final realisation.

Some have regarded Rousseau as a theorist who gives comfort to totalitarian dictators, from Robespierre to Stalin (Talmon, 1952). A more generous reading suggests that Rousseau's work is complex and even contradictory because, intentionally or not, he was expressing the inevitable contradictions of any democratic and egalitarian society.

The second theory which treats equality and liberty as a positive sum game is more straightforward. This theory treats social equality and individual liberty as establishing a reciprocal, means–end relationship (see Plant, 1984). In the first instance, social equality can be said to promote liberty (perhaps along the lines suggested by Tawney) and, in so doing, individuals come to recognise and promote such equality as a necessary condition of their enhanced freedom. Think of the way in which one of the egalitarian functions of social policy is to redistribute risks both across the life cycle and across the population, providing people with more security and opportunities than sink-or-swim capitalism. Some architects of the welfare state reasoned that as people came to recognise this, support for egalitarian services would grow.

## 2.4 Equality of What?

A crude egalitarianism (where equality does imply uniformity in the manner of Orwell's *Nineteen Eighty-Four*) has little to offer Social Policy given the discipline's emphasis on individual welfare. It is therefore the positive sum accounts of social equality which deserve most attention. Nevertheless, those who are attracted to the principle of social equality have to decide whether they are predominantly liberals (concerned primarily with liberty) or egalitarians (concerned primarily with equality). This is the subject of section 2.5. Before we reach that stage, though, it is useful to delve into a recent debate within philosophical circles.

This debate has revolved around two distinctions. The first of these distinctions is that between opportunity and outcome. Think of the following analogy. For any kind of competitive race to be fair two conditions have to prevail: the first condition is that all competitors should be subjected to the same rules of adjudication; the second condition is that each competitor should be required to compete over the exact same distance as everyone else. Now, there can be little doubt that present-day society fails to embody these conditions. The existence of both direct and indirect discrimination suggests that different rules are applied to different groups. Furthermore, the existence of poverty indicates that, in effect, some competitors have further to go to complete the race than others, that is, the poor are forced to start the race from further back. Applying the principle of equal opportunities is therefore a means of trying to correct these deficiencies: ensuring that everyone is subjected to the same rules of adjudication might imply introducing anti-discriminatory legislation; giving everybody an equal start in life (starting-line equality) might imply introducing a system of publicly funded education so that success in life derives from talents and hard work rather than luck and accidents of birth.

However, there are three reasons for believing that equality of opportunity is insufficient (Baker, 1987). First, subjecting everyone to the same rules now might not be enough to compensate for many of the injustices inherited from the past. Second, equal opportunities cannot, by themselves, eliminate poverty. Finally, the principle implies an equal opportunity for people to become *unequal*, potentially contradicting the very values of egalitarianism (see the discussion of meritocracy in Chapter 6).

Critics therefore propose that equality of opportunity has to be supplemented by a further principle, that of equality of outcomes. This is where we intervene at the end of the race to ensure that any remaining injustices are corrected (finishing-line equality). We might, for instance, impose a substantial tax on inheritances and redistribute the revenue thus raised to the poorest. However, equality of outcome is criticised, in turn, by those who insist that to artificially determine the results of the race is to interfere with something that should, strictly speaking, be left to the determination of individual merit and desert (Barry, 1987). If I work hard to become rich, what right has the state to tax the wealth that I freely choose to leave to my children?

The second distinction we need to be aware of is that between welfare and resources. In the literature we are about to review, 'welfare' means having our preferences and needs fulfilled and satisfied; 'resources' refers to the material resources (income, wealth, savings) and perhaps also to the internal resources (talents, abilities, aptitudes) that we possess and which enable us to attain the things that matter to us. Placing these two distinctions together yields Figure 2.1 and the four versions of equality which are outlined below – see also Cohen (1990) and Sen (1992), both of whom have contributed to and enriched the relevant debate (Callinicos, 2000: 52–64).

## 2.4.1 *Equality of welfare*

This would imply everyone experiencing the same degree of fulfilment or satisfaction and would probably require a strongly paternalistic welfare state. The trouble is that the principle of equal welfare would necessitate the subsidy

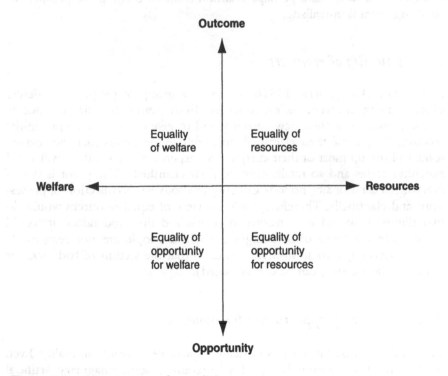

**Figure 2.1** A taxonomy of equalities

of expensive tastes. If I wish to learn how to play the piano, if I would be dissatisfied by not being able to do so and if the state is committed to equality of welfare, then the state has a duty to fund my piano lessons. Yet because I can be held responsible for developing such an expensive taste why should anyone else have an obligation to subsidise it? For this reason, few theorists have supported equality of welfare, although a watered down version of this idea is more plausible, that is, perhaps the state has a responsibility to ensure that everyone experiences an equal *minimum* level of welfare.

### 2.4.2 *Equality of opportunity for welfare*

Those attracted to the welfarist end of the spectrum tend to have preferred an equal opportunities version of the above (cf. Cohen, 1990). One argument is that because people are either entirely or largely responsible for their tastes, the most society can do is ensure that everyone has the opportunity to satisfy those tastes.[2] The state does not have a duty to fund my piano lessons, but it might have a responsibility to provide me with a decent income out of which I can fund my own piano lessons if I so choose. People will therefore be required to adjust their tastes, and perhaps abandon some of them, if the prospect of satisfying them is unrealistic.

### 2.4.3 *Equality of resources*

Ronald Dworkin (1981a, 1981b) imagines a group of people on a desert island. Having to invent their own society from scratch, the islanders decide to use clamshells as their new currency and to give everyone an equal initial amount. People use their clamshells to purchase the things that they desire: some will use up most of their currency on expensive tastes, others will avoid expensive tastes and so retain most of their clamshells. The point is that if everyone acts rationally, nobody can envy anybody else's collection of possessions and clamshells. Therefore, such a society of equal resources would do two things: it would be sensitive to people's desires and tastes; it would compensate for those disadvantages for which people are not responsible (the islanders pay into an insurance fund so that the victims of bad luck, for example a falling tree, can be compensated).

### 2.4.4 *Equality of opportunity for resources*

The trouble is that this ideal is virtually impossible to realise in reality. Even material resources cannot be equalised (except in some imaginary, artificial environment), still less the internal resources or endowments that we all possess. Nor can people be expected to act rationally: we do not have enough information about our social environments to enable us to know what is the most rational course of action and, even if we did, we are all tempted to act irrationally sometimes. Furthermore, some accidents will be so severe that we can never hope to compensate for them completely. Equality of resources might therefore be an ideal that we constantly fall short of achieving, so that the best fall-back position we can hope for is an equality of opportunity for resources.

So, at the risk of oversimplification, we can say the following. Those whose beliefs tend towards welfare equality and resource equality are liberal egalitarians (social equality is the priority), and those who support equal opportunities for either welfare or resources are egalitarian liberals (liberty is the priority). Admittedly, this distinction is far too blunt, as many theorists straddle the distinctions drawn above; even so, it makes for a useful framework as we go on to discuss social and distributive justice.

## 2.5 Social and Distributive Justice

As an example of egalitarian liberalism we shall be outlining the work of John Rawls and as an example of liberal egalitarianism we shall be touching on certain aspects of socialist and Marxist thought. There is, in addition, a third theory that has egalitarian implications, utilitarianism.

### 2.5.1 Utilitarianism and equality

Utilitarianism, which we touched on in section 1.5 when discussing social welfare, is a prescriptive set of ideas encompassing both moral and political philosophy. Originating in the work of Jeremy Bentham and John Stuart Mill (1806–73), utilitarianism is concerned with the question of how to maximise utility. Utility is a notoriously difficult concept to define. As we saw in the last chapter, Bentham took it to mean happiness, or an excess of pleasure over pain (Bentham, 1984). Because Bentham believed that pleasure and pain could be measured, he concluded that utility was quantifiable: something had utility if it could be shown to contribute to the sum of human happiness. The problem (as we saw in section 1.3.1) is that this is only a shallow version of happiness that neglects the more complex pleasures and satisfactions of human life. However, subsequent utilitarians have adopted more of a non-hedonistic account of utility as denoting some form of preference-satisfaction. If I am dining in a restaurant, any of the meals on the menu may have utility for me depending on what my preferences are: if I am profligate, I am likely to value the most expensive meal; if I am a food connoisseur, the most exotic meal might hold the greatest utility; if I am on a diet, the meal with the fewest calories will be most valuable.

Utilitarianism qualifies as an egalitarian doctrine because it states that equal consideration should be given to everyone's happiness and/or preferences. This is partly because equality is held to have an intrinsic value – relating back to Bentham's insistence that each person should count as one and nobody as more than one – but also partly because equality has an instrumental value: treating people equally is the best way of maximising overall utility.

To illustrate this point, imagine a society of 100 people, 50 of whom possess £1 million each, while the other 50 possess nothing. According to a utilitarian, if by redistributing £10,000 from the richest to the poorest the pleasure/ satisfaction experienced by the latter is greater than the displeasure/dissatis- faction experienced by the former, we are entitled to perform such a redistribution. Indeed, we are justified in continuing to redistribute until such time as the increasing utility of the poorest fails to outweigh the decreas- ing utility of the richest. Therefore, a utilitarian approach to social justice is concerned with maximising utility and so has the potential to be strongly egalitarian.[3]

The problem is that utilitarianism might lend itself to what I have called crude egalitarianism because liberty is set to one side. What if our society contained 50 people with two arms each and 50 people with no arms? A strictly utilitarian calculation seems to demand the redistribution of one arm per person from the fortunate 50 to the unfortunate 50. But this hardly seems consistent with the requirements of liberty. That 50 people have been dealt a bad hand (terrible pun, sorry) by life's lottery is certainly regrettable but this does not necessarily justify a compensatory redistribution that trumps the freedoms of others. We could revise utilitarianism so that its anti-liberal tendencies are suppressed, but this would simply undermine the essential rationale of utilitarianism itself. This argument brings us to the work of perhaps the most important political philosopher of the twentieth century, John Rawls.

## 2.5.2 *Egalitarian liberalism*

There are many reasons why Rawls's ideas are significant. For our purposes, we need to be aware of how he has theorised the principle of social justice and why this principle justifies redistributive social policies.

Rawls (1972) asks us to imagine ourselves as a group of people who have to decide what kind of society they would prefer to inhabit. In imagining this scenario, it is necessary to prevent bias, otherwise each of us is likely to prefer only that society which rewards the attributes that we individually possess. Therefore, we have to imagine ourselves as being behind a 'veil of ignorance', which means that nobody can have any knowledge of things such as their intelligence level, skills and abilities, class position and social status, gender, race and ethnicity, age and so on (Rawls, 1972: 12). In this way, fairness and impartiality can be ensured because bias-motivating attributes have been factored out. So, in this 'original position', what kind of society would we choose to inhabit? Rawls insists that we would choose to live in a society that protects our freedoms but also maximises the well-being of the least well off – the maximin principle. Because behind the veil of ignorance people do not know whether they are rich or poor, a rational person will decide to play it safe and support the maximin principle just in case they themselves turn out to be one of the poor when the veil is removed. A Rawlsian society would therefore embody the following two principles of justice:

> First Principle – Each person is to have an equal right to the most extensive total system of equal basic liberties compatible with a similar system of liberty for all.
> Second Principle – Social and economic inequalities are to be arranged so that they are both:
> (a) to the greatest benefit of the least advantaged, and
> (b) attached to offices and positions open to all under conditions of fair equality of opportunity. (Rawls, 1972: 302)

The first principle concerns liberty and Rawls argues that this principle is the most important when it comes to deciding how society should be governed and he insists that a just society cannot restrict liberty in the name of either equality or utility – he is therefore opposed to utilitarianism. The second principle concerns equality and Rawls insists that equality of opportunity must take precedence. However, some equalisation of outcomes is justified in terms of what he calls the 'difference principle': the notion that inequalities should be arranged so that they are to the benefit of the least advantaged.

Consider the following three alternatives. In Blue society Amanda owns 12 clamshells, Bill owns 6 and Carol owns 1. In Yellow society Amanda owns 10 clamshells, Bill owns 5 and Carol owns 3. In Red society Amanda owns 4 clamshells, Bill owns 3 and Carol owns 2. These options are summarised in Table 2.1.

**Table 2.1** Three distributive alternatives

|        | Amanda | Bill | Carol |
|--------|--------|------|-------|
| Blue   | 12     | 6    | 1     |
| Yellow | 10     | 5    | 3     |
| Red    | 4      | 3    | 2     |

Which of these alternatives should we prefer? An anti-egalitarian prefers Blue because this has the most unequal distribution, whereas an egalitarian prefers Red because this is the most equal of the three options. But according to the difference principle we should prefer Yellow because it is the one within which Carol, the least well off in each society, possesses the most clamshells, even though it is less egalitarian than Red. According to Rawlsian social justice, if the wealth and income of the richest do not benefit the poorest, we are justified in redistributing that wealth and income up to the point when such redistribution would no longer work in favour of the poorest. We might, for instance, decide to introduce ever higher levels of taxation and spend the revenue raised on the least well off; but if we reached a point where raising still more taxation only harmed the poor's interests, for example by damaging economic growth, we should stop redistributing. In sum, Rawls's theory of justice incorporates a strong element of social justice (the difference principle) that seems to require redistribution and the equalisation of income, wealth and power, but not equality for equality's sake.[4]

What kind of economic and social policies does this theory of social justice prescribe? Rawls (1972: 274) states that his ideas are biased neither towards capitalism nor towards socialism. More often than not, however, he has been interpreted as giving support to the tradition of Centre-Left social democratic thought. If the object is to improve the material circumstances of the poorest, private ownership and free markets might be required to generate wealth and ensure the *efficient* allocation of goods; but, in addition, redistributive taxation, egalitarian welfare services, (some) socialised ownership of property and limited market regulation are required to ensure the *just* allocation of those goods. In social policy terms, Rawls might be thought of as a supporter of state welfare capitalism.

For this reason, Rawls has come under attack from both Right and Left. The Right charge Rawls with ignoring the role that individual entitlement should play in society (see the arguments of Nozick in the next chapter). The Left charge Rawls with ignoring the value that social equality can have in and of itself (see next section). In addition, some feminists (for example Frazer and Lacey, 1993) have alleged that Rawls's ideas are biased in favour of masculinist principles and assumptions; while communitarians (Sandel, 1982) criticise Rawls's interpretation of the 'self' by insisting that we cannot be regarded as disembodied beings, even for the purposes of an imaginary exercise, because who and what we are depends on the particular social and historical contexts within which we are rooted (communitarianism is dealt with in Chapter 4) (cf. Rawls, 1993). More philosophical objections suggest that it is naive to assume that people in the original position would play it safe and adopt the maximin principle, for example they may prefer an extremely unequal society while taking the risk that they themselves will turn out to be poor.

### 2.5.3 *Liberal egalitarianism*

In order to appreciate liberal egalitarianism we must understand something of the left-wing reaction to Rawls. Cohen (1995), for instance, identifies a possible inconsistency in Rawls's political theory. According to Rawls, a just society is a society that cannot make any reference to what people deserve. We do not deserve our natural talents (such as intelligence) any more than we deserve our social resources (such as inheritances). They are both morally arbitrary because they are both due to accidents of birth. So, a Rawlsian society may allow you to be wealthy, but only if the interests of the poor demand it and not because you *deserve* such wealth. Yet, observes Cohen, if natural talents and social resources really are arbitrary from a moral point of view (and Cohen agrees that they are), Rawls is not entitled to justify inequalities to the extent that he does. Indeed, Rawlsian inequalities would only reinforce the inequalities of talent that Rawls claims are morally arbitrary. On these or similar grounds, some left-wingers insist that radical egalitarians should abandon the Rawlsian approach.

For instance, some Marxist critics (Macpherson, 1973; Nielsen, 1985) believe that it is not possible to be neutral between socialism and capitalism because these systems are based upon incommensurable conceptions of justice. By focusing on the formal characteristics of social and economic inequalities, Rawls ignores what goes on 'inside' the socioeconomic structure. For Rawls, exploitation may well be acceptable as long as the difference principle is observed; but for socialists and Marxists exploitation is never justified, however well off the exploited people might actually be. Welfare capitalism may be rejected on similar grounds. Rather than simply making liberty the priority, we have to ask exactly *whose* liberties are at stake. We may be perfectly entitled to curtail the liberties of the members of the ruling class in order to rid society of the injustices of private property ownership and so enhance the liberties of those who are currently poor and exploited.

Others, however, argue that elements of Rawlsian justice can be incorporated into a radical egalitarianism. For Levine (1998), we must look beyond the tradition of liberal democracy and aim to create a 'democratic equality', where citizenship means more than the formal rights to assemble, be legally represented and vote, and is set within the context of the popular ownership and control of productive property. This might mean enshrining in a constitution not only the right to work but also the right *not* to work, so that time can be freed up for cooperative pursuits.

In essence, liberal egalitarians are those who believe social equality to have a value-in-itself. There might be several reasons why Red society should be preferred, even if Carol were to have less disposable income than in Yellow society. A more unequal society may have hidden costs, for instance. The well-being of those at the bottom of the social ladder could be as affected by how many people are on the rungs above them, and how far the ladder stretches, as it is by how much money they possess. Although Carol owns more in Yellow society than in Red, the fact that the social distance between herself and everyone else is greater may serve to exacerbate any sense of inadequacy and isolation that she feels. Furthermore, it might well be that a society which is unequal, but where even the poor are relatively prosperous, is characterised by undesirable social values and habits: a dog-eat-dog mentality that erodes bonds of trust, community and collective cooperation.

Liberal egalitarians, then, reverse the emphasis of egalitarian liberals such as Rawls. Social equality, they insist, should not simply be bolted onto a formal concern with liberty and freedom.

## 2.6 Social Policy and Equality

One of the most important debates within Social Policy concerns the extent to which the welfare state should or should not be regarded as a set of egalitarian institutions and practices. This question divides into two. First, were the architects and builders of the welfare state motivated by egalitarian concerns? Second, how egalitarian has the welfare state been?

It is undoubtedly the case that social equality was regarded as important by many who laid the foundations of the welfare state. The 'architects' were those intellectuals, academics, policy-makers and politicians who desired a realistic alternative to laissez-faire capitalism. These included socialists such as Sydney and Beatrice Webb, liberals such as J. M. Keynes and William Beveridge and conservatives such as Harold Macmillan. The 'builders' were those social movements which campaigned and fought for welfare reform at the grass-roots level.

What this added up to was a widespread desire for what Tawney (1931) called the 'strategy of equality' (Deakin, 1987: 18–22). This strategy required the establishment of institutions that would guarantee equal access to those goods without which life is impoverished and incomplete. Tawney favoured classlessness as the ultimate goal of social and economic reform and so was a supporter of comprehensive education decades before the corresponding reforms were instituted. Other architects were more lukewarm towards social equality. T. H. Marshall (1893–1981) defended the welfare state as something which equalised status and eliminated unjust inequalities (these being un-deserved advantages and disadvantages), but which could safely leave *just* inequalities alone because these are necessary to a healthy economy and reflective of individual differences and abilities (see section 4.3, when we discuss citizenship rights, and Chapter 6, when we discuss class and meritoc-racy).

We must also remember, however, that support for social equality was not universally shared, even among those who founded the welfare state. Bismarck set up pensions and unemployment insurance in the Germany of the 1870s to forestall the possibility of socialists gaining power and implementing egalitarian reforms. It seems that, although a desire for greater social equality motivated many welfare architects, it would be simplistic to interpret the welfare state as a straightforward strategy of equality.

Consequently, and as we shall see in Chapter 6, the welfare state's record on equalising wealth, income and power is less than spectacular. Julian Le Grand (1982) makes this argument by identifying five types of equality:

- *Equality of public expenditure*: Public expenditure on the provision of a particular social service should be allocated equally between all relevant individuals, for example two state schools of equal size should receive equivalent amounts of public money.
- *Equality of final income*: This implies a vertical redistribution from the rich to the poor.
- *Equality of use*: The amount of a public service used by all relevant individuals should be the same, for example two people who are equally ill with the same condition should receive equivalent medical treatment.
- *Equality of cost*: All service users should face the same private (or opportunity) costs, for example an inequality of costs arises if Jack is able to take time off work to visit his doctor, whereas Jill's employer docks her half a day's wages.
- *Equality of outcome*: This refers to an equivalency in the consequences that a welfare service has for its users.[5]

Le Grand believes that the welfare state has failed to deliver on any of the above. For instance, he insists that the wealthiest receive up to 40 per cent more in terms of health care expenditure than the poorest in Britain. Essentially, this is because the welfare state is caught in a contradiction: it was intended by many to embody an ethos of equality without fundamentally challenging the profound inequalities of capitalist society (Hindess, 1987).

Similar conclusions can be drawn from the work of John Hills (1997). Hills finds that most of the benefits that people derive from the welfare state originate out of the taxes and contributions they themselves have paid; only one-quarter of what the welfare state delivers could be defined as 'Robin Hood' redistribution from rich to poor. For Le Grand, this is not necessarily a bad thing (Goodin and Le Grand, 1987) because if the welfare state were to equalise resources too much, it could easily lose the support of those from whom such resources would be taken. By pursuing only modest redistribution the welfare state has been able to retain the broad support of the middle classes and it is this which enabled it to survive the radical Right onslaught of the 1980s and 90s.

By and large, then, we should think of the welfare state as being mostly concerned with equality of opportunity and as making only occasional nods in the direction of equality of outcome – a conclusion which, for some, should motivate us to initiate welfare reforms that are, at best, weakly egalitarian (Commission on Social Justice, 1994).[6] It is predominantly an egalitarian liberal set of institutions. The debate does not end there, however, for even within the limits set by the principle of equal opportunity there are many different ways of organising welfare services. To illustrate this point let us look at two important debates.

### 2.6.1 Universalism and selectivism

According to Richard Titmuss (1907–73), the principle of universality refers to

> the aim of making services available and accessible to the whole population in such ways as would not involve users in any humiliating loss of status, dignity or self-respect. There should be no sense of inferiority, pauperism, shame or stigma in the use of a publicly provided service; no attribution that one was being or becoming a 'public burden'. (Titmuss, 1968: 129)

Access to universal services is therefore 'triggered' by the demonstration of some kind of need irrespective of one's income level, for example a medical examination might reveal the need for hospitalisation. By contrast, selectivism is usually taken to imply a means test (such as food stamps in the USA) and/or a charge for the service at the point of use (having to pay a fee to consult a doctor, for instance).

Now, from an egalitarian point of view, both universality and selectivity have their attractions. Universal services embody an ethic of citizenship: the notion that we are all part of the same society and should all have access to welfare provision. The trouble is that, apart from being expensive, universal services may also contradict egalitarian aims, for if the Duke of Westminster is entitled to receive the same provision as his chauffeur, this might perpetuate, rather than eradicate, the inequalities between them. Therefore, selective services are more vertically redistributive. Means-tested benefits are funded out of taxation and are provided only to those who fall below a stipulated income level. Selectivism therefore implies that people should be *treated* unequally by virtue of the fact that they have unequal incomes. The trouble is that selectivism, too, can contradict egalitarian aims, for such services divide people into haves and have-nots with a considerable stigma being attached to those who depend on selectivist provision.

During the era of the classic welfare state (1940s–1970s), the debate between universalists and selectivists was academic, as the welfare state usually combined both approaches. However, universalism has been in retreat now for a number of years. Radical Right governments placed a considerable emphasis on the merits of means testing, or 'targeting', as this approach was regarded as a way of cutting social expenditure. In addition, Deacon et al. (1997) observe that selectivism tends to be the favourite strategy of developing countries and of supranational agencies such as the International Monetary Fund (IMF) and the World Bank.

## 2.6.2 Positive discrimination

Policies of positive discrimination are associated largely with the USA. The idea is that where certain groups have been disadvantaged in the past, usually as a result of direct or indirect discrimination, we have a duty to ensure that existing institutions and practices give a preferential form of treatment to those groups so that the injustices to which they have been subjected will be eliminated. We might decide, for instance, that companies and colleges have to employ/admit a certain percentage of women, black people and disabled people.[7]

Critics of positive discrimination allege that such policies ignore merit and are unfair to talented individuals. Let us say that Jeff, who is white, male, able-bodied and has five qualifications, applies for a job which is subsequently given to a black, disabled women with three qualifications for reasons of positive discrimination. Is this fair? Nobody could seriously deny that black, disabled women are not discriminated against in society, but this is not Jeff's fault, so why should he lose out because of some politically correct quota system? Furthermore, positive discrimination may mean that well-off individuals from disadvantaged groups may gain at the expense of poorer individuals from *both* advantaged and disadvantaged groups. It may also mean that talented individuals from underprivileged groups are incorrectly assumed to owe their success to quotas rather than merit. Finally, by creating a backlash against social equality per se, positive discrimination may distract from a more radical egalitarian agenda.

However, defenders of positive discrimination argue that the short-term injustice to a privileged individual such as Jeff is outweighed by the long-term interests of the disadvantaged group. Dworkin (1977: 223–39) goes further and contends that because institutions such as colleges can be thought of as *social* institutions, with duties to the wider society, it is no more unfair to admit someone on, say, racial grounds than it is to do so on the grounds of qualifications and IQ. If black communities need more black doctors, a few less white medical students is a small price to pay.

One possible compromise between these two positions is to give preferential treatment to *low-income* individuals rather than to specific groups. Because economic deprivation is often a consequence of discrimination, actively discriminating in favour of the poor could help the underprivileged without incurring as much of a backlash from the privileged. Somebody with three qualifications might well possess more merit and suitability for the job than someone with five qualifications, if the latter grew up in a mansion and the former grew up in a slum. Restorative justice may be reconcilable with considerations of merit after all.

## 2.7 Recent Developments

Some interesting debates about social equality have been initiated in recent years that take us beyond the more traditional themes that have been addressed in this chapter. The implications of these new debates for the design of, and research into, social policies are still being worked out.

### 2.7.1 Complex equality

Michael Walzer (1983; Miller and Walzer, 1995) draws a distinction between simple equality and complex equality. Simple equality is that which occurs when we impose a single system of distributive justice upon society. In debating social justice we usually pay most attention to the minimum and maximum limits of any desired distribution. This approach to social justice is the equivalent of staking out a playing field within which all the competitors are required to remain. Similarly, all social goods, for example income, wealth, security, education, health, are to be automatically located within this single 'sphere' of distributive justice. But according to Walzer this approach betrays certain weaknesses. For instance, given that some people (especially the wealthy) will try to break out of this playing field, a centralised and extremely powerful agency is required to prevent this from happening, the state. Yet this state-maintained, simple equality may end up stifling diversity, plurality and local autonomy, while leaving the dominant interests of the economically powerful intact.

Walzer argues that we should conceive of complex equality as a viable alternative. Instead of fitting a diverse range of social goods into a single sphere of distributive justice, the theory of complex equality envisages each good operating within its own distributive sphere according to norms that are not necessarily shared by other spheres. This implies that dominance in one sphere would not engender dominance in others. I may be dominant in terms of wealth, for instance, but this should not mean that I am similarly dominant in terms of access to health care or educational opportunities. So, the objective for both theories of equality is the same – the avoidance of monopoly – but whereas simple equality risks substituting economic monopoly (the power of the rich) with political monopoly (the power of the state) if it is to be effective, complex equality would be organised around communal and democratic forms of provision that emerge from within the playing field itself (Walzer,

1990; Miller, 1990). In social policy terms a Walzerian welfare state would seem to require systems of provision that are rooted in civil society (Keane, 1988).

## 2.7.2 Differential equality

Differential equality is, in many respects, similar to complex equality, although the point here is to reformulate the principle of equality at an even deeper level (see also the discussions about citizenship in sections 4.5 and 4.6). Although many egalitarians have acknowledged the importance of plurality and diversity, many egalitarian politics and policies have imposed a conceptual 'blanket' on society, smoothing over and enclosing certain valuable differences. Oppression, it is argued, can often result from benign intentions. For instance, gender equality has long been a goal of progressive movements, but unless such equality is sensitive to the differences between white/black women, straight/lesbian women, Western/non-Western women, able-bodied/disabled women and so on, then gender equality may inadvertently institutionalise subtler forms of discrimination and prejudice.

Differential equality, then, is about breaking down the conceptual difference between 'difference' and 'equality' and trying to develop appropriate social, public, economic and political practices. The theoretical work has been performed largely by postmodernists, often those attracted to feminist theory (for example Butler, 1990; Nicholson, 1990; Young, 1990). The social implications of differential equality can be wide ranging but usually imply a retention of what the welfare state can do best (provision for basic needs) combined with a call for the democratisation of welfare services so that these differential identities can gain a new and powerful voice. Some insist that it is a differential or postmodern social policy, based around the new social movements, that should inspire future welfare reform (for a definition of new social movements see Chapter 6).

## 2.7.3 Equality of obligation

Many Centre-Left political parties no longer treat social equality as a rallying call. As the welfare state project faced what many called a crisis in the 1970s, egalitarian objectives began to be sidelined and replaced by more anodyne terms such as 'fairness'. In Britain, a nadir was reached when the Commission on Social Justice (1994), initiated by the Labour Party in 1993, made its recommendations for future welfare reform on the basis that 'levellers' should be contrasted with 'investors'. The leveller was characterised as being concerned only with the distribution of wealth and with a 'levelling down' of the rich, the implication being that it was old-fashioned egalitarians who fell under this heading. By contrast, investors are supposedly concerned with a form of social justice geared towards wealth creation and economic efficiency. The crudeness of this contrast set the scene for the subsequent policies of the New Labour government and its project of the 'Third Way'.

In practice, this has meant that many social democrats now find deregulated and flexible markets to be desirable. Although initiated by Clinton's 'New Democrats' in 1992, New Labour has epitomised the Centre-Left's drift away from welfare egalitarianism (even of the modest sort outlined in this chapter) towards a concern with social inclusion (Giddens, 1998). Whereas social democratic parties had traditionally thought of the welfare state as that which would help prevent social exclusion in the first place, it has come to be widely regarded both as a source of exclusion itself *and* as a potential instrument for forcing the excluded back into the disciplines of paid employment. This is not so much a 'levelling down' as a 'levelling in'. So the emphasis is now less on equality of rights as on equality of obligations, with differences in class, social background and income no longer being regarded as 'excuses' allowing people to ignore their social responsibilities. Equality of opportunity is still in vogue but the emphasis is very much on the poor having to change their values and habits in order to accommodate themselves to mainstream society, rather than mainstream society revising its values and habits in order to accommodate itself to the interests and needs of the poor.

Readers should now possess a clearer idea as to why the principle of equality has enduring appeal (sections 2.1 and 2.2). Yet the concept is undoubtedly a complex and controversial one, particularly when we consider the adjacent concept of liberty. Sections 2.3 and 2.4 traced some of the main controversies and section 2.5 explained how these translate into competing theories of social justice. As such, we risk misinterpreting social policies unless we appreciate the extent to which welfare services struggle to reconcile social equality and liberty (section 2.6), a struggle that is likely to continue as new theories and perspectives of social equality become influential (section 2.7).

Having reviewed one side of the coin we now need to flip the coin over and review the other, liberty.

# 3
# Liberty

If equality has been one of the principles by which modern societies have defined themselves, the same can also be said of liberty. We therefore understand something about the modern period once we appreciate the tension that exists between these principles, a tension that has sometimes been creative and sometimes destructive. During the halcyon days of the welfare state, equality and liberty were reconciled in a form of creative equilibrium, yet this balancing act began to be severely undermined by the 1970s, and we shall see why this was in the following chapter.

The premise of Chapters 2–4 is that the concepts of equality and liberty are inevitable reference points for one another and that we misunderstand the kernel of welfare theory unless we grasp this basic point. As such, we will be revisiting some of the themes of Chapter 2 below, albeit from a different angle, and anticipating some of the ideas and debates that we shall encounter at greater length later on in the book. Sections 3.2 and 3.3 cover, respectively, the extreme and more moderate theories of liberty that have been proposed. Sections 3.4 and 3.5 explore how and why liberty has been used as a weapon with which to attack social equality and state welfare, but also offers reasons why such attacks can be interpreted as misjudged. Section 3.6 reviews ideas that do not quite fit into a simple Left–Right spectrum of political thought, section 3.7 contrasts negative with positive freedom and section 3.8 explains two of the most interesting developments in recent theorising about liberty.

## 3.1 Introducing Liberty

Like equality, liberty is both a concept and a principle with, in both cases, the central question being: 'How is the freedom of one compatible with the freedom of many?' As we shall see in this chapter, there are many answers that can and have been given to this question (cf. Goodin, 1988: 306–31).[1]

Plato (1955) insisted that freedom could not imply people doing whatever they wanted, for this would lead to chaos and anarchy: the blind dominance of the appetites. Instead, freedom could only pertain when the characteristics of the individual and those of society harmonised perfectly according to the requirements of just principles. Aristotle (1988) also distinguished between ordered liberty and anarchic liberty. He equated freedom with citizenship and, in the ancient world, free citizens were predominantly male, Athenian property owners, thereby enjoying a status that was superior to the non-citizens of slaves, foreigners and women. In short, the ancient Greeks made the liberty of the one compatible with the liberty of the many by restricting the number of people definable as free.

As an organising principle of legal, political, social and ethical reform, freedom would have to wait for the modern period. In contrast to the ancients, however, modern defenders of liberty have increasingly sought to break the bonds of exclusion imposed by our ancestors and make freedom a universal principle. For over the past 200 years, fewer and fewer reasons have been found for restricting the principle to a lucky elite and, one by one, regimes based on slavery, apartheid, limited suffrage, despotism, female subjugation and religious oppression have toppled. But with each extension of freedom the central question noted above has become still more prominent than before. In this chapter we will look at some of the main answers that have been given to that question and where social policy fits into the picture.

## 3.2 Crude Libertarianism

Crude libertarians are not hard to find. Resembling an ancient who has been unwillingly transplanted to modern society, Friedrich Nietzsche (1844–1900) is the most brilliant exponent of crude libertarianism. Nietzsche (1967, 1973) repeatedly affirms the triumph of the will and the ego, at the same time as denouncing the humanism of the modern era. Humanist philosophies are a corruption of the individual will; they are slave moralities that attempt to drown individuality beneath the weight of collective laws, rules, commands and codes. These moralities operate by constructing a truth and persuading the masses to accept this truth as natural and universal, rather than what it actually is: an expression of the particular interests who designed it. In fact, humanisms are the means by which the weak gather together in moral systems of good and evil in order to protect themselves against the strong: those who are capable of recognising those ethical systems as fictional and transcending such life-denying moralities. Humanist systems such as liberalism and socialism (successors to the greatest deceit of all, Christianity) are therefore condemned by Nietzsche for identifying an equality between unequals. Humans, he suggests, are divided into two types: the rule-followers, for whom the herd instincts of morality are perfectly suited as it enables them to evade taking responsibility for themselves, and the *Übermensch*, who is able to transcend the moral and social illusions of the herd and will the power of self-mastery.

Herbert Spencer (1820–1903) similarly proclaims the advantages of egoism. Spencer (1969) was one of the first to combine economics and social theory with biology. As a 'social Darwinian' he insisted that what we call society is a constant process of struggle, a never-ending fight for survival. Not only was this natural, it was perfectly defensible: for if only the strongest survived, humanity as a whole would become stronger. This suggested that people should be left alone to survive (or not) as best they could, as any interference into these natural processes would only leave humanity weaker than it would otherwise be. Spencer regarded a market free-for-all as the ideal medium for this evolutionary struggle with the state having little role to play.[2]

Having divided humanity into two, it is unclear whether Nietzsche has an answer to the question posed at the start of this chapter. At times, he does not seem to care whether an individual's freedom is compatible with that of others, at other times he seems to think that herd moralities are necessary if the strong are to have something to rebel against, and sometimes he enjoins everyone to discover the will to power within themselves. It is therefore difficult to know what role, if any, the state would play in a Nietzschean society. By contrast, Spencer's social Darwinism is attached to a defence of an actual social and economic system – a nineteenth-century capitalism red in tooth and claw. Spencer's arguments therefore represent another version of a familiar position: that capitalism successfully coordinates the actions of many through an 'invisible hand' that harnesses the competitive, dynamic innovations of the wealth-creating free market. In a sense, Spencer was merely taking this position to its logical conclusion by arguing that it ruled out any paternalistic help for the weak and the poor. Our task now is to understand this invisible hand (section 3.3) and to appreciate why new versions of Spencer's draconian philosophy have revived in recent decades (section 3.4).

## 3.3 The Invisible Hand

We have already outlined three definitions of freedom: Aristotle's notion of freedom as a property of exclusive citizenship (definition 1); Nietzsche's belief that freedom lies in the transcendence of moral systems (definition 2); Spencer's idea of freedom as self-interest within a free-market capitalism (definition 3). The popularity of this third definition, especially in recent years, demands that we explore it further.

The problem of how to ensure that a free market remains ordered and harmonious became particularly acute in the seventeenth century. As the power of the aristocracy was undermined, as democratic movements gathered momentum and as the economy became industrialised, so people were faced with the problem of how to reconcile private interest with the public good. There *were* those who insisted that because humans possess a God-given altruism then the two were easily reconcilable. Many, however, identified self-interest as the overwhelming source of human motivation. Mandeville (1670–1733), for instance, insisted that what everyone desired, first and foremost, was wealth and luxury for themselves (Mandeville, 1988). Public benefits could not be the result of *deliberately* trying to create such benefits; instead, if everyone pursued their own private interest, the sum of such interests would inevitably generate the public good. By benefiting themselves the selfish would benefit others also.

David Hume (1969) took issue with this view. He also believed in a system of private property and market exchange but observed that such a system could only exist in the first place if there were certain moral, social and legal rules binding on all. Since these rules *established* the means by which private interests could be translated into public benefits, from where did the rules themselves derive? Hume identifies an altruistic side to human nature. Such altruism does not imply the denial of self-interest but an empathetic process whereby I can project myself into the role of a neutral spectator in order to provide an impartial assessment of my own actions. In a society of purely egoistic selves there would be nothing to stop me from harming others if it were to my advantage to do so; but the system of private property and market exchange would then quickly destroy itself as the same would be true for everyone else! But the capacity to empathise and imagine myself as an impartial spectator means that I can curb any tendencies that I may feel to harm others. The system of rules, which only government can guarantee, is simply a way of formalising this capacity: of ensuring that individuals understand that their long-term interests could be damaged by the pursuit of short-term gain.

Adam Smith (1723–90) extended Hume's political philosophy and virtually invented 'classical' economics with its insistence that the free market was the means by which private interest was translated into the public good and the means by which my freedom is made compatible with yours (Smith, 1970). In a competitive market, hat manufacturers, let us say, will have to lower their prices if they are to attract customers and, by doing so, everyone gains: producers will make a profit and consumers will be able to buy hats at affordable prices. There are two scenarios where this will not be true, however. First, where the supply of hats is too high (or the demand for them too low, which is the same thing). Here, the market will be flooded to such an extent that the low price of hats will not enable everyone to make a profit. Second, where the supply is too low (or demand too high) customers will have to pay exorbitant prices. However, these scenarios should cancel each other out over the course of time. If, for instance, the supply of shoes was too low, those who failed in the hat market would be able to step in and try their luck in the shoe market, supplying that demand and bringing the prices of shoes down while still being able to make a profit. In short, a free and competitive market should always balance itself out over time and achieve an equilibrium of supply and demand; and by producers trying to make a profit and consumers trying to save money then everybody should gain in the long run. Therefore, market competitors are led by an 'invisible hand' to promote the general welfare even though this was not part of their original intention. Like Hume, however, Smith attaches this invisible hand to a visible arm: namely, certain moral and social codes of behaviour that are underwritten by the rule of law and guaranteed, in the last instance, by the state.

All of this means that definition 3 needs to be divided into two. On the one hand, freedom can be regarded as the pursuit of self-interest that translates into the public good without any need for collective intervention (definition 3a). On the other, freedom can be regarded as the pursuit of self-interest that translates into the public good via a free market based on moral, social and legal rules that are actively protected by the state (definition 3b). Definition 3a tends to be attractive to a variety of anarchists, many of whom are anti-capitalist, who often insist that the state can be replaced by direct democracies operating within small-scale communities (see section 3.6.2). It is also supported by market libertarians who imagine that the state can be entirely replaced with market capitalistic relationships (Rand, 1961). Definition 3b is attractive to those whose social and political critiques are rather less one dimensional. The next section outlines the ideas of two of the most important theorists of recent decades: Robert Nozick, who defends 3a, and Friedrich Hayek, who defends 3b.

## 3.4 Nozick and Hayek

Nozick (1974) criticises the stance of pure anarchists and libertarians for their complete rejection of the state. According to Nozick there has to be some agency on which all can rely for their physical and legal security, otherwise we would experience the endless proliferation of private police forces, private armies and private legal systems with irresolvable conflicts constantly emerging between them. Nevertheless, Nozick is certainly enough of a right-wing libertarian to be categorised as defending definition 3a. He starts with the inviolability of individual rights: put simply, he holds something to be just if it derives from the exercise of such rights and unjust if it involves their infringement. This gives rise to an 'entitlement' or 'procedural' theory of justice which Nozick contrasts favourably with what are called 'patterned' or 'end-state' theories.

Imagine that six people are playing poker. Each player starts the game with a certain amount of money and a certain knowledge of the game based on their previous experiences. Let us say that when the game ends Players 1 and 2 have done very well, Players 3 and 4 have broken even and Players 5 and 6 are almost bankrupt. Do we have any grounds for regarding this state of affairs as unjust? According to Nozick we do not. Since each player chose to play, selected a particular strategy and bet a certain way on the cards they were randomly dealt, the result of the game can be interpreted as perfectly fair. In short, *if in a series of exchanges each individual transfer and transaction is just, that is, does not violate anyone's rights, the outcome of that series is also just, even if massive inequalities have been created*. This form of justice can be contrasted with patterned justice as this focuses on the end-state of a series of transactions (the result of the game) rather than the process out of which the end-state was produced. According to Nozick, if we were to take pity on Players 5 and 6 by giving to them some of the winnings of Players 1 and 2, this act of redistribution would violate the rights of the latter and would be unjust. (Note that this has nothing to do with desert as Players 1 and 2 may have been nothing more than incredible lucky: *even though they may not deserve their winnings they are entitled to them and should be able to dispose of them as they wish*.)

Nozick's arguments offer a considerable challenge to all forms of redistributive and egalitarian politics – his libertarian philosophy was partly formulated as a response to Rawls's theory of social justice. Since the entitlement theory is held by Nozick to justify a system of private property then anything that threatens private property, whether it be out-and-out socialism or a welfare state, cannot be defended without violating the rights that Nozick defines as inviolable. Policies based on the principle of social justice are the equivalent of taking away from Players 1 and 2 that to which they are ethically entitled: taxation is therefore a form of theft.[3] Consequently, those who seek to relieve destitution and social inequalities are perpetuating injustice rather than solving it. As such, the dismantling of state welfare systems, and their replacement with market-based forms of security and insurance, would be entirely legitimate.

Whereas Nozick's commitment to free-market liberalism demands the almost complete withdrawal of the state, the commitment of Friedrich Hayek (1899–1991) to the same implies a constitutional reorganisation that would, in some respects, leave the state more centralised and powerful than before. The principle of social justice is also anathema to Hayek (1976). The redistribution of income and wealth is certainly ruled out by his political philosophy, but so too is an equality of opportunity. This is because, like Nozick, he regards justice as something that refers to actions and exchanges, and not to end-states or collective circumstances. In short, there can be just actions and exchanges and unjust actions and exchanges, but justice cannot refer to society and social environments. Society, he insists, should be thought of simply as an aggregate of the unintended consequences of individuals' acts and exchanges, and it is this lack of intention that renders the concept of social justice meaningless. If inequalities are the result of people acting and interacting freely without harming others, such inequalities cannot be morally condemned; in the spontaneous, unconstrained market order there is no one determining who wins and who loses.

Instead, it is only the egalitarian, managerialist state which imposes such patterns on society. Ironically, it is the proponents of social justice who have contrived to propagate injustice: every attempt to equalise material resources and opportunities has led to a worse situation than prevailed before by giving too much power to the state. By handicapping the free market, for instance, the welfare state has created far more destitution than would otherwise have been the case. Imposing some kind of ideal, utopian pattern of distribution on society can only lead to the infringement of individual liberties by a state exceeding what should be its proper role: namely, guaranteeing national security, the rule of law and the rules of just conduct.

Initially, Hayek (1944) imagined that the redistributive state simply needed to be rolled back so that the spontaneous market could be allowed to do its job. Towards the end of his life, however, he came to believe that a liberty-enhancing constitution could only be preserved through political and legal reforms that were even more ambitious than the privatisations and deregulative strategies favoured by most radical Right politicians (Hayek, 1979), hence his support for what we here call definition 3b. In essence, such reform would have to minimise the possibility of the free market being damaged by those who advocated things such as redistribution and the macro-economic management of the economy, for example Hayek recommends the exclusion of trade unions from the political process. He is therefore opposed to a strong state that threatens the market but not to a strong state that bolsters and protects the market.

## 3.5 Equality Versus Liberty?

These criticisms of state welfare are certainly powerful but are they convincing? The last chapter spelt out several arguments which suggest that liberty and equality are mutually reinforcing. We therefore already have recourse to a fourth definition according to which freedom and social equality are inclusive. This definition might suggest that the critiques of Nozick and Hayek are one dimensional and that a welfare state is an indispensable part of an advanced, liberal society. To see why this might be the case, let us revisit some of the arguments of the last chapter by introducing ourselves to four important thinkers who give weight to this fourth definition: Kant, Hegel, Durkheim and Green.

Immanuel Kant (1724–1804) argued that rational actions were those that corresponded to a 'categorical imperative' which demands that we should act only on those maxims that can be willed as universal laws (Kant, 1999). For example, lying is immoral because if everyone were to do it regularly no lie could ever be effective, unlike truth-telling, therefore, lying cannot be

universalised. So, Kantian freedom implies a rational obedience to a moral law
and a recognition that all autonomous beings can similarly obey such laws.
The precepts of universal reason demand that people treat each other as ends
and not just as means: a free society, according to Kant, is a 'kingdom of ends',
a society of autonomous beings acting in accordance with the categorical
imperative. This suggests that in a Kantian society my freedom is only sustainable if I recognise it as being dependent on your freedom: autonomy and
social interdependence are compatible with one another. Kant therefore
initiated a train of thought whose next great exponent was Georg Hegel
(1770–1831).

Prior to Hegel, freedom had usually been defined ahistorically, that is, the
same for all people in all places and at all times. Hegel (1967), however,
regarded freedom as something which evolved with the unfolding of history
and the self-realisation of *Geist*. *Geist* is an incredibly difficult concept to define
but might initially be thought of as absolute spirit or mind. For Hegel, it is not
sufficient to explain the world in material terms, for this is to ignore that which
suffuses and permeates the material, while being somehow independent of,
and superior to, that materiality. *Geist* is that which 'authors' the material
world and historical development can be explained as *Geist* coming to consciousness of itself through three stages.

The first stage is the stage of collective, historical unconsciousness: the
primitive state of humanity. The second stage consists of succeeding periods
of alienation and conflict as humanity comes to recognise itself as an object of
study and the source of its own evolution. The final stage is that of infinite and
endless self-consciousness, the overcoming of alienated being, the reconcili-
ation of dialectical opposites, the transparent union of self and essence. The
meaning of freedom therefore changes with every unfolding 'moment' of
history. During stage two it is articulated within the spheres of the family
and civil society: the former referring to the emotive bonds of kinship, the
latter referring to the contractual bonds of rights and duties. But as we move
into stage three so the opposition between family and civil society is reconciled
within the state. The state therefore represents the transcendence of particu-
larity and universality, of individuality and collectivity, and freedom comes to
mean the realisation of the self within and through the realisation of others.
Despite the density of his philosophy, Hegel is basically reiterating Kant's
point that freedom implies the mutual recognition of interdependent selves.

Hegel's legacy dominates the last 200 years of Western thought. In addition
to the likes of Karl Marx (1818–83), two theorists who stand in the shadow of
Hegel's influence, and whose ideas relate strongly to issues of state welfare, are
Emile Durkheim (1858–1917) and T. H. Green (1836–82).

Durkheim (1984) made a distinction between mechanical and organic
solidarity. In primitive societies the division of labour, that is, the differentiation of society into distinct spheres of activity, is relatively undeveloped and so
marginal to the order and cultural integration of such societies. By contrast,

modern societies are highly differentiated in their activities and institutions: individuals are organically interdependent. Durkheim pointed out, however, that the existing division of labour was a dysfunctional version of this organic solidarity for two reasons: first, because it is 'anomic' and neglects the moral norms that are needed to provide individuals with meaningful ethical frameworks; second, because it is based on the advantages of inherited wealth and class exploitation, so there is a mismatch between individual potential and occupational status. Correcting these imperfections, he argued, would require a convergence of individualistic and collectivist values.

Durkheim was sympathetic to socialism, although it is not always easy to actually describe him as a socialist. He believed that the socialist emphasis on solidarity could supply the moral norms needed to combat anomie while eliminating class inequalities. However, his was at best a non-Marxist socialism that rejected the call for worldwide social revolution and regarded inequalities as necessary for the division of labour, as long as they were not inequalities deriving from accidents of birth. Durkheim's preferred society would be neither capitalistic nor socialistic. He managed to combine an admiration for the medieval guild system with an advocacy of a state that would articulate the collective consciousness and thoughts of society. The welfare state no doubt falls short of these grandiose visions. Nevertheless, even in Durkheimian terms, it can be interpreted as a set of institutions which attempt to correct the existing division of labour: morally, it emphasises social solidarity, reciprocity and mutuality; economically, it reduces market inequalities. Ruth Levitas (1996) has even argued that recent welfare reforms have revived the Durkheimian emphasis on anomie and moral solidarity, while abandoning Durkheim's socialistic emphasis on the dangers of class inequality.

Green (1986) was a seminal figure in the development of social, or welfare, liberalism. J. S. Mill had already done much to divert liberalism away from its earlier commitment to a simplistic individualism and Green now argued that a conception of the 'common good' had to occupy a central place in liberal thought.[4] Individuals, he argued, were social beings and the principle of liberty was implicated within communal forms of association. My well-being is therefore dependent on your well-being and the good of the one is inseparable from the good of all. Therefore, rather than regard the state as a danger to individuality, it could be interpreted as a promoter of the common good and therefore also of freedom. By establishing individuals' legal commitments to the law and their moral commitments to each other, the state enables us to overcome the dichotomy between liberty and equality that those such as Nozick and Hayek regard as irreconcilable. As with Durkheim, Green's ideas enable us to interpret the welfare state as that which establishes strong links between the demands of individual liberty and the imperatives of the common good.

Definition 4 provides us with a basis for answering the criticisms of Nozick and Hayek. Nozick can be accused of ignoring the extent to which individuals are products of their social environments (Dubos, 1998). So, if individuals are not atoms who pop into the world with fully formed rights, procedural theories of justice cannot fully capture what we want justice to mean. The players in the card game are not equal participants: their internal and external resources will have been largely determined by accidents of birth and class inequalities. If so, the exchanges within the game cannot be regarded as fair since some players will have undeserved advantages over others. But if this is the case, even on Nozick's own reckoning the outcome of the game must be unfair also, that is, if the exchanges are unjust, the outcome must also be unjust. Therefore, the principles of social justice and redistributive egalitarianism might well be justifiable and perhaps Rawls was on the right lines after all.

The intriguing thing is that Nozick himself allows for the possibility that existing patterns of distribution may well be unfair due to the illegitimate acquisitions and transactions that have occurred in the past. He therefore indicates that a massive, one-off redistribution of resources may well be warranted: a redistribution, in fact, that goes way beyond anything envisaged by the welfare state that he spends so much time attacking. In conclusion, by ignoring the interdependency of the self, the mutuality of freedom and social equality, and the extent to which liberty is a social construction, Nozick leaves himself with a procedural theory of justice that gets tangled in its own philosophical and ideological knots. His critics point out that the means cannot, of themselves, justify the end.

Similar considerations apply to Hayek's thought. As we saw above, he insists that justice and injustice only pertain when resources have been *deliberately* allocated, that is, market distributions are not unjust because they are the unintended result of millions of small-scale exchanges. Yet this position can be easily criticised: because the injustices of capitalism distort market outcomes in favour of the already powerful, *it is as if* a deliberative mechanism is at work. In short, there are class-specific market *structures* that subtly guide the invisible hand in particular directions, that is, in favour of the wealthy. But whereas Nozick is at least sensitive to the possibility of past injustices, Hayek is not. A Hayekian society would reduce welfare services to a few residual safety nets while introducing an autocratic state to ensure than market losers have a minimal influence within market society. Many, however, struggle to understand why this would be preferable to a democratic welfare state, or even to the communist state that Hayek abhorred. So, *just as Nozick can only dismiss welfarist politics by allowing for the possibility of a redistribution that exceeds anything ever accomplished by the welfare state, so Hayek can only abandon social justice by replacing one kind of centralised state with another.*

In conclusion, the arguments that are raised against the welfare state on the basis of definitions 3a and 3b can be challenged by invoking definition 4. Again we have seen why a Left–Right contrast is important. The latter assert that the freedom of one is only compatible with the freedom of many through the invisible hand of the market (although those such as Hayek imagine that the state has a continuing role to play); the former assert that a state committed to welfare and social equality is a necessary and indispensable part of modern, liberal societies.

## 3.6 More Perspectives on Freedom

This Left–Right spectrum, however, has its weaknesses and does not quite capture every single position on equality and liberty that has been advanced. In this section we will touch on two such positions.

### 3.6.1 Left libertarianism

Nozick justifies private property by reference back to the political philosophy of John Locke (1632–1704). Locke (1960) imagines that in the pre-social 'state of nature' the world was originally unowned. Let us say that the two of us are walking through a forest and spot a large branch that has fallen from a tree. As the branch lies on the forest floor it is unowned by either one of us. However, what happens if I pick up the branch and start working on it with a knife, perhaps shaping it into a carving? According to Locke and Nozick, I have created an item of private property. By 'mixing my labour with the fruits of the earth' I now privately own a piece of wood that was previously unowned: your running off with the carving would be theft, therefore, whereas my appropriation of the branch was not. As long as the natural resources that I leave for you are as plentiful and as good as the ones that I take for myself, you have no cause for compliant. And if the original acquisition of the earth's resources was just, according to Nozick, every freely agreed transaction that follows is also just.

But what if we assume, instead, that the world was originally owned in *common* (as we supposed in Chapter 1 when discussing Hardin)? This would call my acquisition of the branch into question. The common ownership of the world demands that for any system of property to be legitimate it must be framed with the common interests of all in mind; in fact, this might rule out private property altogether (on the grounds that no original acquisition by individuals can be just)! Alternatively, we might assume that the world *was* originally unowned but insist that only an egalitarian acquisition of its resources is permissible: this would justify a system of private ownership and exchange only if it served egalitarian ends. Whichever of these assumptions is preferred, Left libertarians propose that, although priority be given to individual liberty, this must be set within the context of a fair and equal ownership of the earth's resources (Steiner, 1994). This is a libertarian philosophy of equal shares which can have many different implications for welfare reform.

Left libertarians might, for example, require the abolition of most of the existing welfare state due to the constraints that it places on freedom but nevertheless demand an egalitarian replacement. For instance, this could take the form of a 'lump-sum grant' provided to individuals reaching the age of majority; so that rather than being entitled to a chain of welfare services and benefits throughout their lives, people would receive a one-off pot of money to squander or invest as they saw fit. The catch is that if you blew the grant on beer and cigarettes you would have no safety net to fall back on (Ackerman and Alstott, 1999). A more paternalistic version of the lump-sum grant idea is a basic income which would be an unconditional income paid periodically to every man, women and child without reference to employment status, employment record, employment intentions or marital status. This is the option favoured by Philippe Van Parijs (1992, 1995; Fitzpatrick, 1999a) who styles himself as a 'real libertarian'. So Left libertarianism favours some form of extensive welfare system but not necessarily a welfare state as it traditionally has been defined.

## 3.6.2 Anarchism

While Left libertarians can still envisage some kind of state authority and distributive agency, anarchists support a radical decentralisation of decision-making that undercuts our familiar understanding of economic and social policy. With their opposition to all forms of coercion and top-down pre-scription, anarchists favour replacing mass society with small-scale communities based on voluntarism, consent and direct democracy (Marshall, 1993). The ultimate nemesis for anarchists is therefore the state. State institutions, includ-ing welfarist ones, are charged with creating impersonal and distant centres of power that divest ordinary men and women of control over, and responsibility for, their own lives.

However, there are identifiable schools of Right and Left anarchism. Right anarchists are those such as Nozick who believe that the free market can perform the coordinating roles that a stateless or minimal state society will still require to be performed. By contrast, Left anarchists interpret the market to be as dangerous a source of coercion and compulsion as the state, so that a truly anarchist society has to be based on egalitarian foundations that are both non-state and non-market in form. Left anarchists therefore tend to support the abolition of private ownership in the means of production.

Yet the problem for Left anarchists is to explain how private property can be abolished, and social equality maintained, without the countervailing force of the state. Market capitalism might expire if the vast majority of the world's population simultaneously decided to form themselves into self-sufficient, communist associations, but anything falling short of this is unlikely to be effective against the hegemony of capital.[5] Pure anarchism therefore tends be more imaginable on a small-scale than on a large one (cf. Woodcock, 1986). Indeed, some anarchists have adopted a less radical position and have offered a qualified support to the state to the extent that this can operate as an instrument of anti-capitalist politics. This is an approach that begins to look more favourably at welfare institutions (Walter, 1977).[6]

So, Left libertarians believe that individual liberty must derive from some notion of equal shares, which probably implies a continuing role for the state. Anarchists make similar assertions about the virtues of social equality but, because it is not clear how an anarchistic society can be created and maintained without some form of centralised authority, the most promising approach (from the point of view of social policy) is a 'qualified Left anarchism' that effects some form of rapprochement with the state. It could be claimed that Left libertarians and 'qualified Left anarchists' are basically the same.

## 3.7 Negative and Positive Liberty

There is another important debate about freedom that we have touched on covertly but which can now be elucidated: Isaiah Berlin's (1909–97) distinction between negative and positive liberty (Berlin, 1969). Negative liberty is the freedom which we experience when we face an absence of constraints. For instance, if I imprison you in a cell then I am depriving you of liberty in this sense, whether I do so legitimately (as a prison warden) or illegitimately (as a kidnapper). Positive liberty is the freedom we experience when we possess the capacity to pursue some end or course of action. For instance, if you cannot afford to buy a car, your freedom of movement is less than that of a car owner.
   Berlin drew this simple but influential distinction in order to warn against the dangers of defining liberty in the positive sense, because when we start to associate freedom with capacity we may start to support redistribution to those with minimal resources. The problem with this is that redistribution requires the state and the state can represent the greatest threat to liberty in its more fundamental, negative sense. Berlin was not necessarily advocating the abandonment of positive conceptions of freedom; he was, however, suggesting that we proceed carefully whenever the state is called on to perform redistributive and interventionist roles.
   But if Berlin himself warned against treating this distinction too simplistically, his warning has not always been heeded. As has been indicated above, and as we shall see again in Chapter 7, the radical Right have been adamant that positive liberty is chimerical and that the institutions, policies and practices that it inspires, such as those of the welfare state, are a considerable threat to (negative) liberty. Redistribution does not enhance anybody's freedom because *freedom and the lack of it have got nothing to do with the distribution of income and wealth*. A lack of money may lead to a reduction of opportunities

but does not imply a lack of freedom: you are still *free* to fly to Australia even if you cannot *afford* to do so. By contrast, the Left have denounced this reduction of liberty to negative liberty as lacking substance. In a formal sense it true that the beggar is free to dine at the Ritz, just as the banker is free to sleep under a bridge, but this conception of liberty deprives the principle of any meaningful content. For the Left, being prevented from doing something implies more than physical constraints, it also implies financial constraints (so the beggar *is* less free than the banker).

## 3.8 Recent Developments

The debate which has occupied most of this chapter is unlikely ever to be resolved to the satisfaction of everyone. Liberty and equality are both centrally contested concepts and the debates about them are probably endless. Never-theless, recent years have seen the emergence of ideas which may well rival the above debate for attention as they enter the vocabulary of social and welfare theorists.

### 3.8.1 Freedom as anxiety and reflexivity

Originating with Blaise Pascal (1623–62) and Søren Kierkegaard (1813–55), there is an 'existential' tradition of thought which has begun to wield a great deal of influence on social policy by highlighting the ambiguities of freedom. Whereas liberalism largely stresses the benefits of expanding the horizons of liberty, existential thinkers have focused on the ambivalences. Kierkegaard (1992) insisted that humans are faced with a series of choices throughout their lives and that there are no courts of morality to which we can appeal to find out which option is best. We simply have to choose, make a 'leap into the dark' and live with those decisions for better or for worse. This means that freedom is permanently characterised by dread, anxiety and uncertainty.

Of course, we routinely appeal to a variety of courts: God, nature, the state, parents, tradition and custom, the law and so on; but such appeals are inauthentic attempts to strip ourselves of a responsibility that we cannot, ultimately, avoid. Such attempts to flee from freedom and responsibility are what Jean-Paul Sartre (1905–80) referred to as 'bad faith' (Sartre, 1958). If to be human is to be 'condemned to freedom', we are tempted to become thing-like: because the nature of an object is complete and fully determined then simulating this aspect of objectness is one way of coping with the contingencies and incompleteness of freedom. Our societies are founded on such bad faith attempts to be both free and not free at the same time: by adhering to rules, timetables and schedules, the bourgeois citizen is the model to which we are all encouraged to aspire.

Bauman (1987, 1993), too, focuses on the ambiguities of liberty. The exhilaration of being free accompanies a profound anxiousness as to what we should do, but a simple appeal to moral systems is no longer possible. Rules of conduct can no longer be canonised or treated as unquestionable command-ments: to be free is to be an adjudicator and referee of what is right and wrong. This is our initial dilemma revisited: how do we live together while remaining free? Bauman takes two steps in answer to this question.

First, he draws on the philosophy of Emmanuel Levinas (1906–95) to suggest that we have to recognise ourselves and others as free beings rather than as specimens of moral and theological systems. People tend to clothe each other in hierarchies and regulations, and it is only when these systems are 'unveiled' that people can properly recognise each other and the inter-sub-jectivity of freedom. In short, the above question is answered by admitting that there is never a final answer: inter-subjective freedom cannot be contained in moral systems of do's and don'ts.

Second, Bauman disassociates freedom from a crude marketplace individu-alism. In fact, there are two ways in which we try to fly from freedom in contemporary society. We hand our freedom over to market forces and/or we live uncritically according to some collective tradition. Bauman's analysis here accords with that of Tony Giddens (1994) who agrees that neither of these options is available to us any longer. In particular, Giddens suggests that we now live in post-traditional societies, these being societies where we cannot avoid reflecting on all customs, ways of life and traditions of thought if we wish to avoid falling into fundamentalisms of one sort or another. Our reflexive societies must therefore be 'beyond Left and Right' and this implies building systems of 'positive welfare' that are less concerned with the distribution of material resources and more concerned with counselling to the non-material sides of our nature (Giddens, 1998). Bauman seems to agree with Giddens about the virtues of reflexivity as a means of coping with the ambiguities of freedom, but he retains a central place for redistributive welfare institutions as a way of building cooperative and egalitarian social relations. Universal and comprehensive welfare services are needed to reflect and express the 'com-monality of fate' which makes us human and recognisable to one another.

For Bauman, then, freedom implies an irreducible inter-subjectivity rather than a crude individualism; and the welfare state represents not a flight from freedom but a means of easing the sources of insecurity, pooling anxiety and reflecting on the conditions of our existence together rather than in the isolated cells of the marketplace.

## 3.8.2 Freedom as governance

All the above arguments have shared a basic, underlying assumption: that the self is conceptually and ontologically separate from all forms of political, economic and social power. Power is often regarded as something that can act *on* the self, for example as a repression of human nature, but not *through* the self as constitutive of its formation. It was only when Michel Foucault (1979) came along that the self began to be regarded as a site of power, as an unbounded territory of struggle and conflict. Foucault is probably the most influential theorist of the last 30 years and, as such, his ideas will appear in various guises throughout this book. In particular, we will examine Foucault's ideas in more detail in Chapter 5, when discussing power, and Chapter 10, when discussing post-structuralism. However, a preliminary sketch of those ideas' significance for Social Policy can be offered here.

We often use words such as 'normal' in everyday conversation, especially in relation to the behaviour and appearances of those we observe, making an implicit contrast between the normal and the abnormal. Yet our views as to what can be described as normal do not exist in a social vacuum; rather, everything that we see, hear, read and experience subtly communicates to us a cognitive and perceptual 'map' of what should and should not be regarded as normal. I am the bearer of aesthetic and moral judgements that I have inter-nalised in the attempt to appear and act normal myself. In short, we organise our lives in terms of certain norms and expect others to do the same: we strive to remain within a zone of normality and regard everything lurking outside that zone as abnormal, unnatural and disorderly. Admittedly, this description of normalisation is highly simplistic. It is not that the self pops into existence, recognises social norms and gathers itself around them; instead, *the self is a physiological and psychological effect of normalisation*. Foucault draws attention to the ways in which we are not only social constructions, as traditionally understood, but *discursive* constructions: organic signs of the normality/abnormality distinction, signifying and confirming the centrality of this dis-tinction within the social field.

Social practices, institutions and policies can be interpreted as normalising discourses: the means through which we are made as the signs of normality/abnormality. Donzelot (1979), for instance, examines the way in which the modern family is organised so that it both disconnects and reconnects the private and the public. The two must be kept separate in order to preserve the space of the private, economic actor (the individualistic workers and entrepreneurs of market societies); and yet the two must also be conjoined so that the family operates for, and in accordance with, social authority. Social policies are therefore the paradoxical techniques of disconnection and reconnection – the technologies of normalisation – and Donzelot illustrates the way in which the modern family is produced through a barrage of medical, religious, legal, cultural and philanthropic 'interventions', effected by an endless queue of experts, while the apparent privacy and inviolability of the family survives as a necessary ideological fiction.

More recently, Nikolas Rose (1999a, 1999b; Dean, 1999) has argued that rather than regard freedom and power as distinct we should recognise that the one is meaningless without the other: freedom is an effect of power and power is a product of freedom. The two are reciprocally intertwined, so the fact that we live in societies which are arguably freer than any that have ever existed does not mean that there is *less* governance, it means that contemporary freedoms require *new forms* of governance. Welfare systems can therefore be understood as contributions to the governance *of* the self *through* the self as one of a multitude of lines on a grid of power/freedom.

As with Foucault's thought, we shall find ourselves returning to these themes in Chapters 5 and 10.

We have almost completed our tour of equality, liberty and the relations between the two. We have seen that liberty lends itself, as surely as equality does, to crude and simplistic interpretations (section 3.2) but that it is the more moderate conceptualisations which have prevailed (section 3.3). However, by the last quarter of the twentieth century, some of the more extreme models of liberty were back in vogue and we outlined two such theories, those of Nozick and Hayek, in section 3.4. Section 3.5 revisited some of the arguments of Chapter 2 by identifying a common thread that runs through the ideas of Kant, Hegel, Durkheim and Green: namely, that equality and liberty are mutually compatible. If so, it is far too early to ring the death knell of the welfare state. Sections 3.6 & 3.7 presented various ideas and distinctions that our previous account had to leave out of the picture and section 3.8 suggested that, as old as it is, the concept of freedom is constantly being renewed and reinvented.

Our tour of these issues has one more stop to make, however. Many of the greatest controversies concerning social policies in recent years have revolved around the meaning and the application of citizenship. To a large extent those controversies trace back to the kind of creative tensions that we have just spent two chapters dealing with. We have therefore left ourselves in a strong position to appreciate what those controversies imply, both for the subject of Social Policy and for the future of welfare reform.

# 4

# Citizenship

Although its importance has never been denied, citizenship has become particularly crucial to welfare theory over the last 10–15 years. Initially, the concept was revived along with the 'rediscovery' of civil society in the late 1980s. Those on the Right were searching for forms of association that challenged what they saw as the hegemony of the state; those on the Left were trying to challenge what they saw as the new hegemony of the market. For different reasons, therefore, both sides seized on civil society and the principle of citizenship which is said to flow into and out of civil society. As the debate crystallised, it became clear that the Right's emphasis was primarily on liberty and obligations, while the Left's was primarily on equality and entitlements. As we shall see in section 4.6, this division is an oversimplification and yet it is not unreasonable to interpret the 'new Centre', or the 'new social democracy' or the 'Third Way' as an attempt to reconcile the polarities of this division within a new political philosophy.

Although not a historical account, this chapter tells the story of the various debates that have raged back and forth over the past two decades. It also reviews those aspects of the debate that are not quite reducible to a Left–Right opposition. The basics of the debate are covered in sections 4.1–4.5, before we plunge into some of the debate's intricacies in section 4.6. We then mention an important distinction (section 4.7) and say something about the concepts of difference and gender (sections 4.8 & 4.9). As in the previous two chapters, we conclude by outlining some recent interesting developments (section 4.10).

## 4.1 Introducing Citizenship

There are two conditions on which citizenship can be said to depend. First, the state must be plural and democratic, as dictatorial and monarchical states do not have citizens, they have subjects. Second, civil society must be open and free. For citizenship to flourish, then, two extremes must be avoided. The state must not be allowed to absorb civil society, as was the case in the Soviet Union, where the attempt to engineer a perfectly ordered, regulated society strangled the spaces of creativity and disorderliness that citizens require. In addition, however, the state must be retained as the only reliable guarantor *in the last instance* of the rights and obligations of citizenship. In short, state and civil society must counterbalance one another.

If this is accepted, and we will see later that the radical Right are likely to dissent, citizenship can be taken to refer to the status of the members of a polity which is free, democratic and, to some degree, socially egalitarian. It is essential to remember that citizens are both the sovereigns and the subjects of the polity, that is, they abide by the laws and procedures of which they are themselves the de facto authors. The key concept at work here is that of rights.

## 4.2 Rights

Rights were originally defined as natural, that is, as bestowed on humans by nature or 'natural law'. Some, for example Locke, believed that natural law derives from divine law, or the ordinance and will of God. Others, for example Kant, have insisted that natural law cannot be inferred from any divine order. Either way, this conception of natural law and natural rights implies, first, that humans are rights-bearing entities, that is, it is the possession of rights which marks us out from non-humans, and, second, that rights exist prior to legal, political and social systems, that is, we have developed such systems to embody the pre-social rights that we possess. By contrast, some have maintained that rights are constructed, consensual or institutional (Dworkin, 1977). Basically, this means that rights are not natural or pre-social; rather, they are constructs *of* society and its institutions: the means by which social beings agree to recognise each other as objects of respect. But whether rights are natural or otherwise, the concept must imply certain basic characteristics:

- Rights must be universal across time and space: they must belong to all regardless of class, sex, race and so on.
- Rights must be inalienable: they cannot be surrendered, stolen, sold or traded.
- Rights imply autonomy, that is, they confer on people the liberty to determine desirable goals and pursue those goals as long as the harm principle is not violated.[1]

- Rights are possessed by individuals.[2]
- Rights protect and empower people against the illegitimate and arbitrary use of power by others, for example the state, and are in this sense 'negative': as in the doctrine of habeus corpus which prohibits the non-judicial arrest and incarceration of the person.
- Rights enjoin public authorities to allocate resources and goods fairly to individuals.
- Rights must be enforceable.
- Rights are attached to considerations of justice rather than charity, patronage or benevolence.
- Rights are attached to duties.
- Rights may be regarded as foundational (I am entitled to have my needs fulfilled and interests recognised because I possess fundamental rights) or as 'second-level claims' (I bear rights because I have fundamental needs and interests).

The debate about rights is vast and complex (for example Freeden, 1990) but, for social policy students, the essential controversy centres around the concept of *social* rights. A key figure in the debate about social rights is T. H. Marshall.

## 4.3 Marshall and Social Rights

Marshall identifies three elements of citizenship (Marshall and Bottomore, 1992). Civil rights define the liberty to form contracts and own property (and so imply equality before the law) as well as freedom of assembly, speech and thought; these emerged in the eighteenth century with the development of the legal system. Political rights define the right to participate in the political process (to vote and stand for election); these emerged in the nineteenth century with the development of the parliamentary system. Social rights define the right to experience minimum levels of economic and social well-being as participants in society's way of life; these emerged in the twentieth century with the development of welfare systems.

Marshall's chronology is not intended to be set in stone. In reality, the evolution of the civil, political and social components of citizenship was far more complex. For instance, by being perfectly consistent with the rationality of a market society, civil rights were promoted by the rising middle classes of the eighteenth and nineteenth centuries as rights that would facilitate the growth of industrial capitalism and challenge the entrenched interests of the aristocracy and landed gentry. But once the bourgeoisie has achieved its objectives, the claims that it had made to enfranchisement and empowerment began to be replicated by those lower down the social food chain. By the late nineteenth century, the labour movement was gaining in influence and, in many respects, social rights began to develop *before* political rights as a means of subduing the working class's political impact and diverting it away from more revolutionary courses.

Political and, in particular, social rights are therefore less compatible with a free-market society than civil rights and this led to an important strain in modern society: on the one hand, we have markets with their propensity to create *inequalities*, on the other, we have political and social conceptions of citizenship that demand and require *equality*. This has led, according to Marshall, to a 'hyphenated society' where the capitalist, democratic and welfarist elements of society exist side by side in an uneasy, although ultimately productive, tension. In short, Marshall says that a hyphenated society is preferable either to one organised purely according to market forces or one organised purely by the state and public sector. As we noted in section 2.6, this means that social policies should aim to eliminate not inequality per se but *unjust inequalities*, that is, those deriving from undeserved advantages and disadvantages. Such policies are likely to prescribe a 'baseline' of equality, for example the equalisation of educational opportunities, but nothing more radical. The welfare state's aim is not to create a classless society but a society where merit and social mobility are more important than income divisions: a society of citizens rather than a class society (we return to these ideas when discussing meritocracy in Chapter 6).

Marshall is now as important for the critiques that have been made of his ideas as for the ideas themselves and we do not have the space to adequately summarise the relevant debates here (for example Turner, 1986, 1993; Barbalet, 1988; Bulmer and Rees, 1996; Mead, 1996). However, there are four criticisms that are worth mentioning:

- Marshall tries to squeeze too much into his three sets of citizenship rights. For instance, he treats industrial rights (to form trade unions, bargain collectively and strike) as a subset of civil rights, yet civil rights strengthened the grip of employers over workers that industrial rights began to loosen once they had been won by workers' organisations (Giddens, 1982).
- Even a moderate class-based analysis therefore allows for the possibility of forms of citizenship that go beyond Marshall's triumverate of civil, political and social rights. We could, for instance, define a set of economic rights that entitle workers to either the full or partial ownership of capital or productive property.
- Qualifications aside, Marshall's chronology suggests that social rights are the most recent addition to citizenship and this has allowed critics of social rights to suggest that they do not constitute a *real* category of citizenship rights.
- Marshall has been accused of being both too Anglocentric and of ignoring other dimensions of citizenship that have grown more and more prominent over the post-war period, for example gendered and racialised dimensions.

*Welfare Theory*

Yet whether or not we accept Marshall's account of social rights, the concept has wielded enormous influence over Social Policy. Recently, however, it has come under sustained attack from the radical Right.

## 4.4 Social Obligations

The radical Right have alleged that social rights threaten civil rights by enhancing the role of the state and undermining the system of private property, for example through state ownership and high levels of taxation. Rights should therefore be negative, they contend, and so impose strict *limitations* on state activity. A related criticism is that social rights are not rights at all because they can be neither universal nor enforceable. Since the introduction of welfare systems requires a large degree of wealth, the effectiveness of social rights is conditional on the degree of economic development, a condition that contradicts the entire purpose and rationale of rights.

Social democrats, however, have made various counter-arguments to these criticisms. For instance, it can be claimed that, because rights can be potentially undermined by the market as well as by the state, we need a set of rights that balance out public and private forces. In addition, it can be claimed that the design and enforcement of *all* rights, and not just social ones, requires at least some degree of economic development, because every right has to be embodied in an institution and this implies a substantial commitment of resources.

Despite such counter-arguments, the radical Right's attack on social rights has proved influential in one particular area (Roche, 1992), the main allegation being that social rights eclipse the obligations that people owe to one another (Mead, 1986, 1997; Green, 1996). By concentrating on entitlements, the welfare state has produced a destructive, possessive and passive form of citizenship. As people become more dependent on the state, they become less willing to look after and do things for themselves and for others (see the discussion of the underclass in section 5.3.2). At the bottom end of the income scale this generates a welfare dependency, whereby whole generations of families cut themselves off from the world of work, an underclass forms that has little respect for authority and the rule of law; single, never-married mothers effectively 'marry the state' and biological fathers absent themselves from their children's lives. By giving people a safety net to jump onto, the state has only increased the likelihood of people doing so and therefore failing to stand on their own two feet.[3] The social rights of the welfare state have led us to a society of takers rather than givers.

Social rights can be defended from such attacks in a number of ways. First, it can be pointed out that the likes of Beveridge and Marshall did not fail to emphasise the importance of duties and responsibilities, as even a casual reading of their key texts reveals. Second, we can remember that social rights were often promoted by social democrats and socialists who believed that a welfare state was the stepping stone to a new form of society, whether a radically transformed capitalism or a post-capitalist socialism. Either way, social rights depend for their efficacy on a solidaristic context: in an environment of mass unemployment, underemployment, market insecurity, low wages and poverty, social rights perhaps become less effective as a means of individual empowerment, but *it is free-market capitalism which is ultimately to blame for this state of affairs*. Finally, it can be claimed that the radical Right critique is based on a crude individualism which unfairly disregards the many undeserved advantages and disadvantages that people face. To insist that what is wrong with society is that people, especially the poorest, have *too many rights* is to ignore the extent to which we are interdependent, to overlook the effects that socio-economic structures have on our talents and opportunities. In short, it could be said that duties correlate not to rights per se but to powers, that is, one's ownership of resources and property.

Nevertheless, radical Right arguments worked their way into the vocabulary and assumptions of many Centre-Left political parties in the 1990s. We therefore need a much longer consideration of this question: what is the proper relationship between rights and duties and to what extent should people be coerced into performing the latter? We can best review the possible responses that can be given to this question by examining the debate between liberal and communitarian ideas (Goodin, 1988: 74–118).

## 4.5 Liberalism and Communitarianism

We have already encountered communitarianism in Chapter 2 and will deal with it again in section 10.2. However, it is important that we mention it in this context also as communitarianism offers a perspective on citizenship that has been increasingly influential.

Liberal ideas pretty much dominated political theory in the 1970s. Rawls and Nozick may have disagreed about which social philosophy is the correct one to follow, but they are both liberals because they both give priority to the interests of individuals. A reaction to liberalism emerged in the 1980s in the work of those who would come to be called communitarians. The ideas advanced initially by Macintyre (1981, 1987), Sandel (1982, 1996), Walzer (1983) and Taylor (1989) represent the latest chapter in a debate that dates back centuries and concerns the possible relationship between the individual and the community (Dagger, 1997).

According to Kymlicka (1990), liberalism is ultimately based on two premises. The first relates to the 'good life' and liberals insist that individuals should be able to decide for themselves what is and is not the good life. For some, the good life implies caring for people, for others it implies making lots of money, for others it implies being creative and artistic and so on. The point is that there are many possible versions of 'the good' and individuals should be free to choose between them. But communitarians disagree. There are, they say, only a limited number of versions of the good because the good derives from established communal traditions and contexts, and we can therefore 'choose' the good only in so far as we identify with those contexts. Indeed, we have to talk ultimately of a *common* good that we must *discover* rather than *choose*. It is this common good that makes freedom possible and actions are virtuous or otherwise in terms of their contribution to the common good. According to the communitarian, belonging to a community of the good (whatever that might be) is more important than the right of individual choice.

The second premise of liberalism is that the individual self is distinguishable from the ends that the individual chooses to pursue (as we saw in section 2.5.2 when discussing Rawls). I may become a moneymaker or a caregiver but these are contingent identities that I can potentially change at some future date. It is the capacity to choose that defines me rather than the particular choices that I make, meaning that the self is conceptually distinct from its ends. But the communitarian alleges that this is an empty interpretation of the self. My ends *must* substantially constitute who I am: they are constitutive identities rather than contingent ones. The self is not an abstract, free-floating entity, but something that is shaped and defined by the goals of an individual's life, goals that have in turn been formed within a community of the good.

The debate between liberals and communitarians is important in terms of this chapter because it relates to the fact that citizenship has both passive and active elements. The passive aspects correspond to what Habermas (1994) calls 'received membership': in this context, a citizen is a bearer of a prescribed legal status and the individual contributes relatively little to the institutions, relations and practices that ensure the maintenance of that status. The active elements correspond to what Habermas calls 'achieved membership', where citizenship implies active participation by, and integration of, individuals into the societies that constitute their identities. Of course, there are few theorists who focus exclusively on either received or achieved membership, but it is undoubtedly the case that liberals emphasise the former and communitarians the latter. To gain some idea why, let is concentrate on liberal and communitarian views of the state (the state is analysed more comprehensively in Chapter 5).

Liberals believe that, by and large, the state should be neutral between the various conceptions of the good that are on offer to its citizens (Barry, 1995). For example, if some people wish to pursue a religious life and some do not, the state should be neutral between the two. If the state forces religion on its citizens, it discriminates against the non-religious; if it prevents the formation of churches, it discriminates against the religious. A neutral state, therefore, is that which permits religion but is dissociated from the church. However, other liberals argue that the state cannot be built around a pure neutrality. First, this is too idealistic an aspiration (as the state is run by those who hold certain beliefs and are likely to favour those beliefs in the making of policy); second, because the state must reproduce the conditions of its own existence it cannot do so without preferring some versions of the good over others. Therefore, the liberal state should not aim at neutrality per se but should aim at fostering the autonomy of its citizens, that is, their capacity to be self-determining. Communitarians, by contrast, demand that the state should embody and sustain the common good. For example, where a society has historically held to Christian principles, the state is perfectly justified in promoting the culture and the practices of Christianity.

It is not difficult to see where social policy fits into the picture (Rothstein, 1998: 30–55). If the state should be purely neutral (liberal neutrality) then so should social policies. In terms of education, this could require a system that exposed pupils to the greatest number of ways of life without any bias on the part of teachers. If the state should foster autonomy (liberal autonomy) then the education system should teach its pupils to cultivate their powers of self-determination and respect those of others – which may mean warning students about conceptions of the good that are not based on the principle of autonomy. But if the state should embody and promote a common good (as communitarians demand) then so must social policies. Here, education should imply an induction into the way of life of the community within which that education system operates, as well as instruction about the nature of the common good as it is interpreted by that community.

We are at last ready to return to the debate about rights and duties. Liberalism favours rights and entitlements. If individuals are defined as free beings, if being a citizen means having to choose between competing conceptions of the good, and if the state should be neutral and/or prefer autonomous ways of life, then citizenship must be grounded in individual rights. This does not necessarily mean ignoring duties: it means that rights are more fundamental. Communitarianism favours duties and obligations. If individuals are defined as communal beings, if being a citizen means identifying with the good of one's community, and if the state should embody and aim to promote the common good, then citizenship must be grounded in communal duties. This does not necessarily mean ignoring rights, it means that duties are more fundamental.

## 4.6 Four Ideals of Citizenship

Something very interesting happens if we now cross-reference the discussion of the last two chapters with the liberal/communitarian distinction that we have just drawn. In order to avoid terminological confusion, the equality–liberty axis is rendered here as a Left–Right axis.

Figure 4.1 yields four ideal types of citizenship corresponding to the four quadrants. These ideal types are outlined below.

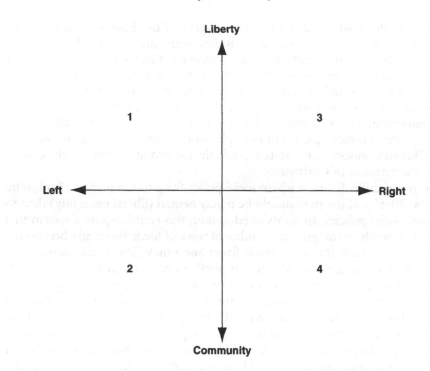

**Figure 4.1**

1. This ideal type is based on the liberal prioritising of rights and the egalitarian prioritising of needs. In short, individuals have a right to the fulfilment of their basic needs and social welfare systems must be geared, first and foremost, to the achievement of that aim. This quadrant belongs to the 'liberal Left'.

2. Here, what is distinctive is the egalitarian prioritising of needs and the communitarian prioritising of duties. The individual is defined as a social being, the fulfilment of whose needs is dependent on the performance of their duties. Welfare systems must be organised around the communal bonds of mutual obligation, but it is needs that remain fundamental rather than desert or entitlement. This quadrant belongs to the 'communitarian Left'.

3. This ideal type is based on the liberal prioritising of rights and the free-market prioritising of entitlements. Individuals have inviolable rights to private property, to exchange their property within a stateless economy and are therefore entitled to whatever the outcomes of such market transactions may be. Citizens must stand on their own two feet with, at best, only the barest of safety nets to fall back on. This quadrant belongs to the 'liberal Right'.

4.  The final ideal gives a communitarian emphasis to duties and a conserva-
    tive emphasis to desert. Citizens are 'duty-bearers' who are characterised
    in terms of what they owe *to* their community rather than any
    rights that they may receive *from* it. Desert is more important than either
    needs or entitlements. State welfare systems are only justified if they
    enforce responsibilities and shore up familial and civic forms of mutual
    assistance. This quadrant belongs to the 'communitarian Right'.

If these ideal types are to help us to understand how and why rights and duties
interrelate, we first need to discuss the issue of reciprocity.

## 4.6.1 Reciprocity

At a philosophical level it is obvious that rights and duties tend to go together.
If I have a right to remain uninjured then you have a duty not to harm me.
However, what holds at the philosophical level does not necessarily hold at the
political one. That is, although there must be some kind of *society-wide*
reciprocity between rights and duties, for example a society consisting of
nothing but rights is unimaginable, does it follow that rights and duties
must reciprocate *at the level of the individual?* It is possible to think of
examples where they do not, for example a baby has rights but no duties
because it is incapable of performing duties. For the most part, however, we
want to say that to be a citizen is to characterised by some degree of rights–
duties reciprocity, of which it is possible to identify the following four categories.

1.  *Unbalanced reciprocity.* This implies that whereas rights and duties reci-
    procate the balance between them is tipped heavily, but not exclusively, in
    favour of one or the other. There are therefore two sets of unbalanced
    reciprocity:

    (a) We might prefer to make rights fundamental but the implications for
        duties alter depending on whether we favour needs or entitlements.
        If, like the liberal Left, we favour needs, we might argue that in an
        inegalitarian society more duties should fall on the privileged than
        the disadvantaged. To suggest that all citizens should possess rights
        and duties in equal measure is tantamount to arguing that the state
        should not correct market inequalities. However, if, like the liberal
        Right, we favour entitlements, we might argue that duties only
        derive from the exercise of rights within a marketplace. To be a
        citizen is to be a market actor who only bears responsibilities that
        he or she has freely contracted to bear.

(b)   We might prefer to make duties fundamental but the implications for rights alter depending on whether we favour needs or deserts. If we favour needs, as does the communitarian Left, we might argue that rights do not exist in a social vacuum but derive from a communal condition. Inequalities of power and privilege are certainly unjust but egalitarian objectives can only be met if everyone pulls in the same direction according to an ethos of mutuality and solidarity. But if we favour desert, like the communitarian Right, we might argue that rights only derive from the exercise of obligations as both family members and members of civil associations. We are therefore entitled to take only if we have substantially demonstrated our propensity to give.

2.   *Balanced reciprocity.* This means that rights and duties balance out evenly, establishing an equilibrium where entitlements bestow obligations and vice versa. However, there are two sets of balanced reciprocity:

(a)   There is *specific reciprocity* where rights and duties reciprocate at the level of the act. In short, if I make a claim on the basis of an entitlement, I simultaneously agree to perform the duty which accompanies the claim. For example, if I claim the right to live in a peaceful neighbourhood, I cannot myself disturb that neighbourhood. Or, if I pay my taxes, I cannot be expected to forgo the rights and entitlements that those taxes help to guarantee. Specific reciprocity therefore follows the model of a contractual exchange: just as my purchase of a drink requires me to hand over the money, so my claiming of a right or performance of a duty requires my possession of reciprocal duties and rights. However, specific reciprocity can take many different forms. It can take an egalitarian form where citizenship rights and duties feed into one another as we progress towards the goal of social justice. It can take a marketised form where the citizen and the consumer become indistinguishable. It can take a civic/familial form where, for instance, my right to bear children accompanies a long-term commitment to any children that I have.

(b)   There is also *generalised reciprocity* where rights and duties balance out at a more general level. This means that, if I perform an act of entitlement, I may not necessarily be subjected to a corresponding and immediate obligation. My right to live in a peaceful neighbourhood may still allow me to disturb that neighbourhood from time to time as long as I remain within tolerable limits, for example by throwing a party. Or, my payment of taxes does not always generate a reciprocal entitlement, for example a car tax may be used for the benefit of society (through pollution abatement) rather than for my immediate benefit as the taxpayer. So, generalised reciprocity establishes a looser equilibrium between rights and duties. As with specific reciprocity, however, generalised reciprocity can take many different forms, depending on whether egalitarian, marketised or civic/familial relationships are preferred.

So, as intricate as these arguments are, the basic conclusion is that we have four ideal types of citizenship and at least four ways of arranging the reciprocity of rights and duties. We can now address the question as to whether the enforcement of duties is justified.

## 4.6.2 *Coercion*

The enforcement of certain duties is always justified. In any society there will need to be some means of enforcing the observation of basic 'negative' duties: principally, the duty not to harm others. The controversy arises when we consider more 'positive' duties, that is, participation in one's social way of life. It would take too long to examine all positive duties, even those most relevant to social policy, but we can gain some idea of the debate's terrain by focusing on an important contemporary question: should unemployed claimants be required to work and/or train for their benefits?

The liberal Left argue that such 'workfare' is unjustified. Since one of our basic needs is the need for a minimum income and since we have a right to have those basic needs fulfilled, then attaching conditions to benefit receipt is unwarranted. The communitarian Left, however, may well advocate workfare measures on the grounds that social justice requires both a needs-based redistribution and a society-wide mutuality of effort; so that while the employed have an obligation to help claimants, claimants must reciprocate with an obligation to help themselves. The liberal Right are usually ambiguous towards workfare. On the one hand, an individualist-entitlement version of citizenship is likely not to support a state benefit system in the first place; on the other, where a benefit system operates, the degree of state intervention required to run a workfare scheme is probably not justifiable. Finally, the communitarian Right gives unequivocal backing to the workfare principle as embodying a set of responsibilities that we owe to the community and a means of proving that we deserve the community's help. So, the ideal types offer distinct responses to the above question: duty-based approaches tend to favour the workfare proposal, whereas rights-based ones do not. The issue becomes more complex, however, when we introduce reciprocity arguments into the picture.

If we prefer an unbalanced reciprocity based on the prioritising of rights, workfare will not be to our liking. Egalitarians will continue to argue that workfare is anti-redistributive in that what it gives with one hand (benefits) it takes with the other (benefit conditions). Entitlement theorists, as noted above, will disapprove of the state's coercion of free individuals. However, those who prefer an unbalanced reciprocity that is based on duties are likely to be split. Inegalitarians will support workfare on the grounds that benefits are entitlements that must first be earned. But egalitarians may well feel that workfare is an obligation too far, that is, although a communitarian approach correctly emphasises duties, these should fall most heavily on the employed and the most affluent. Those preferring specific reciprocity will probably support workfare, although, as before, some egalitarians and anti-statists may well dissent, albeit for different reasons; those preferring generalised reciprocity will probably dislike workfare, although, this time, it is those wedded to a civic/familial ethos who may well dissent.

In conclusion, the liberal Right and Left will probably *not* support attaching conditions to the receipt of benefit, although the former may be more split on the issue than the latter, whereas the communitarian Right will do so. The communitarian Left will also be somewhat split. On the one hand, a strong vein of duty and reciprocity runs through the communitarian Left's view of citizenship (White, 1997); on the other, many will agree with Arneson (1997) that attaching strong conditions to claimants is a harmful diversion from more radical matters. In short, there are numerous positions that can and have been taken regarding the relationship between rights and duties and the extent to which people can be coerced into performing the latter.

## 4.7 Inclusion and Exclusion

Before moving on, it is worth noting why citizenship is both a widely supported *and* a widely contested concept. Citizenship is a sign of belonging, of inclusion within a political community, and it is this sense of belonging which acts as a source of identity, making the world a less frightening and alien place. Yet 'inclusion' only has meaning as the opposing term to that of 'exclusion', just as an inside implies an outside. Therefore, citizens are included members in that they are distinguished from those who are excluded from membership. We saw this in its starkest form in Chapter 3 when I noted that in ancient Athens women, slaves and foreigners were defined neither as free nor, therefore, as citizens. Yet any form of citizenship must have both inclusive and exclusive components: British citizens are British citizens in contradistinction to American citizens and vice versa.

The exclusive aspect of citizenship has become more problematic the closer our societies have moved to the ideals of liberty, equality and democracy. We cannot consistently proclaim the rights and freedoms of all while maintaining systems of subordination and social repression. Yet even when such inconsistencies are ironed out, it would be a brave person who claimed that the distinction between first-class and second-class forms of citizenship has anywhere been eliminated. In our formally free and equal societies, divisions of class, gender, ethnicity, dis/ability, age and sexuality usually accompany status differentials of one form or another.

A key question for students to consider is this: can second-class citizenship be abolished or is this too idealistic an aspiration? Those on the Left and the liberal Right are all likely, although to varying degrees and for different reasons, to suggest that citizenship can become a truly universal category. For the liberal Right the market is the arena within which this will occur as everyone becomes a citizen-consumer; but according to the Left some form of strong social equality is needed if social exclusion is to be abolished. The communitarian Right, by contrast, suggest that since citizenship refers to the demonstrable membership of particular communities it should always possess exclusionary characteristics.

## 4.8 Equality and Difference

We have already noted the contrast between equality and difference (in section 2.7.2 under the heading of 'differential equality'). In terms of citizenship we can contrast a citizenship of sameness with that of diversity. The former is the equivalent of saying that there is a core of sameness lying beneath all the 'surface' differences of gender, ethnicity and so on, and this core identity is what people remark on when they claim that we are 'all the same underneath'. A citizenship of equality, then, prescribes similar treatment for all on the basis that we are all similar and has been vitally important in virtually all modern struggles against oppression and injustice: it posits a universalism that has a strong intuitive attraction and appeals to most, but not all, citizenship theorists in one form or another.

However, some allege that, by supposing an essential sameness, such an equalisation suppresses the importance of difference and so is itself potentially oppressive, for example given the dissimilar histories and life opportunities between black and white people, it is misguided, insulting and possibly even racist to imagine that these differences can be subsumed under, and by, a banner of equal citizenship. Difference citizenship is therefore based on disparity and divergence rather than the essentialisms of sameness and identity. It, too, has a strong intuitive appeal although, traditionally, it could be most closely associated with the communitarian Right: if different communities have different characters, and if citizenship is a property of community, the nature of citizenship alters depending on the nature of the community to which the term refers at any one time. Paradoxically perhaps, and when taken to its extreme, an emphasis on difference can actually lead back to a homogenised sameness and inspire the exclusion of others who are different.

More recently, difference citizenship has influenced the broad range of social thought as sensitivity to gender differences, ethnic differences and so on has grown. The problem with this conception, however, is that it seems to abandon universalism in favour of the local and the particular (if we are all different there is no common denominator) which seems to contradict what citizenship is about in the first place. Furthermore, and as just indicated, an ethos of difference risks lapsing into its own version of essentialism (homogenised sameness), where difference is equated with separation and irreconcilable division.

In order to avoid this lapse into essentialism and communitarian exclusion, many have sought to draw on both these elements in order to develop a citizenship ethic that goes beyond the dichotomy of equality and difference. In order to illustrate what this can mean, let us examine that side of the debate which focuses on gender citizenship.

## 4.9 Gendered Citizenship

A gender dimension has traditionally been lacking from social and political debates, including theories of and about citizenship. This is due to the following implicit combinations repeatedly being made: the citizen = the public = the masculine; the non-citizen = the private = the feminine. With women being located inside the private sphere their perceived connection to citizenship virtues and characteristics has been tenuous at best. Consequently, the civil, political and social emancipation of women has historically lagged behind that of men and can still be said to be incomplete in many respects. Given the extent to which paid employment represents the single most important access to full citizenship, and the extent to which the duties of caring and parenting still fall on women, it is hardly surprising that the citizen-worker continues to be defined in masculinist terms. Of course, formal citizenship rights are accorded to all individuals and are, strictly speaking, gender neutral; but it is the inequalities (of opportunities and power) deriving from the sexual division of labour which continue to ensure that women are more likely to be second-class citizens than men, notwithstanding improvements in women's social position since the 1960s and 70s.

This bias in citizenship theory, discourse and practice has come under sustained attack over the past 15 years from many feminist commentators (for example Pateman, 1988, 1989; Vogel, 1991; Walby, 1997; Lister, 1997; Bussemaker and Voet, 1999). Indeed, some have gone so far as to insist that the concept of citizenship carries an irretrievable male bias so that feminism is wasting its time if it tries to inhabit this essentially male terrain. Others have argued that whereas the politics, policies and practices of citizenship require altering, the concept itself can be left alone. For the most part, however, a lot of time and effort has been expended in trying to reconceptualise citizenship, with some trying to render the concept gender neutral and with others insisting that, while citizenship cannot be 'degendered', feminine and masculine versions of it can be brought together in a mutually creative relationship. In fact, once this latter approach is taken, room has to be made for all forms of difference.

This means that feminism has helped to revolutionise the terms of the debate to the extent that a fifth ideal type can be identified over and above the four dealt with earlier. To gain an idea of what this might involve we need to revisit some of our earlier discussion.

Feminists have appealed to both rights and duties (Okin, 1979): the former as an important means of empowerment and self-determination; the latter as a means of emphasising the extent to which all societies depend on the unpaid and undervalued work mainly performed by women – thus turning the tables on employment-centred conceptions of social obligation which risk under-estimating the importance of caring. Feminists have also appealed to both the 'received' and the 'achieved' ingredients of citizenship, with the definition of the latter being extended beyond the world of paid work to include non-employment forms of social contribution. However, the distinction between inclusion and exclusion has presented feminists with more difficulty. An 'inclusive feminism' (that which tries to include everyone as citizenship members) has trouble in employing a term that seems to depend conceptually on the systematic exclusion of non-members; an 'exclusive feminism', by contrast, may admit most women into the citizens' club yet continue to bar those who cannot or will not pass the test of membership, and so not offer much of an improvement on the older traditions of citizenship. One possible solution is to say that, by broadening, to the greatest extent desirable, our definition of what constitutes a valuable social contribution, we can minimise the number of those who do not pass this test.

Feminists such as Ruth Lister (1997) therefore call for a 'critical synthesis' of the above kinds of distinction in the belief that a gendered perspective on citizenship can overcome the limitations of traditional ones. Let us return to the equality/difference distinction. A citizenship of equality would seem to require a gender neutrality: gender is regarded as an 'outer layer' that is of secondary importance to a 'core' which is more fundamental than any male/female distinctions, and it is in respect of this gender-neutral core that we should be thought of as citizens. The difficulty with this conception of citizenship, as far as women are concerned, is that the societies in which we live are far from being gender neutral; rather, they have been shaped over the course of centuries by male interests, needs and attitudes. Therefore, an 'equal citizenship' might make equality between the sexes conditional on women becoming more like men, that is, adopting the same behaviour, aspirations and values.

By contrast, a citizenship of difference interprets gender as being essential to the nature of citizenship: citizenship is gender specific through and through and there is no gender-neutral core that belongs equally to men and women. Indeed, once we allow for gender difference then we have to allow for a multiplicity of differences structured along the lines of ethnicity, sexuality, age and dis/ability. The trouble with 'differential citizenship' is that it might lead to a plurality of 'identity groups', none of which are held to share anything in common with any of the others. In addition, differential citizenship might essentialise these groupings so that, for instance, women become identified as caregivers who are essentially different to the male group of breadwinners. In seeking a critical synthesis, feminists such as Lister wish to utilise the best and most progressive aspects of equality and difference, focusing on the extent to which the terms are mutually reconcilable.

An important example of this kind of critical synthesis is to be found in the work of Nancy Fraser (1997) vis-à-vis the public/private distinction. Historically, men have been identified with the public world of politics and paid work, and women have been identified with the private world of domesticity and unpaid work. This has left women in a socially inferior position, with less access than men to economic resources (jobs and income) and to the centres of political power. Fraser suggests that three models can be devised which might correct this imbalance between the sexes.

The 'universal breadwinner' model would encourage women to enter the public sphere by becoming equal wage earners with men; citizenship is interpreted here as an equality of wage earning. The 'caregiver parity' model implies that women should continue to identify with the private sphere but that this should be as highly valued as the masculine sphere of the public. Fraser is critical of both of these models: the former commits the error of equal citizenship, that is, requiring women to resemble men, while the latter commits the error of differential citizenship, that is, locking women into non-masculine caring roles. Her preference for a 'universal caregiver' model is because it embodies the critical synthesis that most feminists desire. This model suggests that both men and women have access to the public and the private and so share out the responsibilities attached to paid and unpaid work more equally. In short, the difference between the public and the private is maintained but men and women are more equal in respect of the rights and duties attached to both spheres.

# 4.10  Recent Developments[4]

## 4.10.1  Global citizenship

The development of citizenship rights was coterminous with that of the nation-state. However, if we are entering a world in which the role of the nation-state is shrinking (see the discussion of globalisation in Chapter 9), what happens to citizenship rights? If we now live in an era of post-national globalisation, what happens to rights and entitlements? Do we cease to be citizens in this globalised environment or can rights, too, become global in their meaning and scope? Some have argued that citizenship rights are incompatible with globalisation and that it is only as market actors that we can exert an influence on the global economy (Ohmae, 1995). Others have held out the possibility that civil and political rights can be and are being globalised (Held, 1995), for example we can construct institutions to guarantee rights which individual nation-states are unable or unwilling to guarantee. Of course, the enforcement of such global rights is difficult to guarantee (precisely because it is nation-states that have to sign up to, and enforce, them) but this does not necessarily undermine the validity of the concept. The main problem arises when we consider social rights. Can there be a globalised form of social citizenship that defines all humans as having rights to at least minimum levels of welfare and security?

There are those who answer 'no' to this question, for example Mishra (1999) (see also section 9.3.4). Mishra is of the opinion that, already threatened by the shift away from the Keynesian/Beveridgean consensus, social rights are inconsistent with a globalised environment. Whereas many post-war supporters of social rights held out the prospect for the welfare state to transport us either to a post-capitalist society or at least to a society in which private capital is substantially tamed, Mishra argues that this is no longer possible. Market capitalism is the only game in town and the only thing we can do is to fight for the best version. As there is no popular support for social *rights*, we must formulate social *standards* as they emerge from a communal consensus and use those standards in constructing the most humane form of capitalism possible. So, global capitalism can and should be regulated but social rights are not relevant to this project.

However, others insist that social rights are an essential aspect of maintaining *universal* social standards in an era of global capitalism (Deacon et al., 1997). The arguments against *global* social rights in a globalised era are similar to those, in the nineteenth and early twentieth centuries, against *national* social rights in an era of the nation-state; namely, that there is no alternative to the economic laws of gravity which dictate that collective interference with the unrestrained market is undesirable, unnecessary and counterproductive. Therefore, the question as to whether we should design and institutionalise global social rights is not so much an economic question about the future as a political question about the past: those who criticise the idea of global social citizenship are usually those who are convinced that our experiences with social rights provision to date has been a failure. So, it may be that the issue of global citizenship is not really about globalisation after all.

### 4.10.2 Ecological citizenship[5]

Ecological citizenship could be thought of as another form of global citizenship (Steward, 1991; Oliver and Heater, 1994; Van Steenbergen, 1994;

Newby, 1996). A global ecological citizenship could be dated back to 1968 when Apollo 8 photographed an 'earthrise' while in lunar orbit. At its simplest, this aspect of citizenship expresses our consciousness that we are all members of spaceship Earth and have an obligation to look after the planet both for its sake and for ours. However, this universalist interpretation rests, sometimes uneasily, with a more 'particularistic' one: ecological citizenship is that which is embodied in, and promoted by, Green social movements and political parties.

Part of the problem is that citizenship denotes an anthropocentrism, that is, an emphasis on the human, whereas environmentalism makes substantial room for a biocentric or ecocentric ethic that holistically emphasis the environment of which humans are only one part. On this basis, some insist that the concept of citizenship has no relevance to environmentalism. Others argue that an ecological perspective has to make room for citizenship to some extent, for instance, if citizenship implies obligations and if we possess obligations to both present and future generations of non-human life forms, 'citizenship' is somehow expressive of the relationship that we hold towards the natural world. It has also been argued that animals possess rights, meaning that the orbit of citizenship is wider than that of the human realm (Cavalieri and Singer, 1995).

### 4.10.3 Cultural citizenship

Rights have usually been thought of as attributes of individuals. However, as the world has shrunk and become more interdependent, some have insisted that cultures (ways of life) require legal protection if they are to be preserved and nurtured. It could be argued that we are all cultural citizens who possess rights in respect of the particular culture that we inhabit and which has substantially made us what we are.

This idea that groups can possess citizenship rights easily offends against the individualist approach that citizenship theories have traditionally preferred. At the extreme, they could prescribe a cultural separatism with little room for the cross-fertilisation that prevents cultures from atrophying. However, some have insisted that 'group rights' are consistent with the traditions of liberal democratic thought. Kymlicka (1995a, 1995b) has defined what he calls the collective rights of minority cultures, which he regards as essential to any multicultural politics and pluralistic society. This means that while ethnic groups cannot inhibit their members from claiming the rights and freedoms available in a wider society, such groups can make claims that it would not be legitimate for other groups, especially majority ones, to make.

We have now completed what, in effect, is the first part of this book. Sections 4.1–4.5 laid the groundwork by demonstrating that the contentious issue about citizenship is the question of how rights and duties relate to one another. For students of Social Policy, the problem is about deciding when we are justified in coercing people into performing moral and socially useful acts, and what forms of coercion might be called for. Section 4.6 tackled the intricacies of this issue, identifying four ideal types and four ways of conceptualising the rights–duties relationship based on competing notions of reciprocity. Section 4.7 underlined the point that at stake in all these apparently abstract arguments is the human sense of belonging, of home, identity and inclusion. We examined the philosophical problems that occur when 'difference' is introduced into the picture and how feminist theorists have addressed those problems (sections 4.8 and 4.9). We concluded by reviewing some recent developments (section 4.10).

The last three chapters have endeavoured to show that a Left–Right political division explains much, although by no means all, of the controversy that the concepts of equality, liberty and citizenship generate. Equality and liberty are undoubtedly the opposite sides of the same coin, but this is a coin that can be spun in any number of ideological directions. The metaphor is apt, since citizenship might be thought of as a currency which can take a number of forms depending on how the coin is spun. In this chapter we saw that there are four ideal types, from the liberal Left to the communitarian Right, and that these types adopt complex and intricate views on the issue of coercion and obligation. There is little doubt that these controversies will continue into the distant future, establishing new lines of thought and argument that can only be guessed at here. In the next two chapters, we move on to examine a series of concepts that lie at the political and sociological heart of Social Policy, beginning with the political concepts of the state, poverty, power and human nature.

# Key Political Concepts

What does 'politics' or 'the political' mean? To some extent, the political is the means by which the interests which we possess as members of society become recognised, articulated and, in cases of conflict, reconciled. Yet the political is also the means by which interests and identities are formed and constructed in the first place – think of Schmitt's friend/enemy distinction that was mentioned in Chapter 1 and, in the previous three chapters, the extent to which principles such as equality, liberty and citizenship are contested and argued over. This is precisely because what is at stake in these debates are human interests and the flourishing of individuals and groups as they attempt to live and work together. Therefore, the theories that we are reviewing in this book are themselves the means by which humans attempt to shape themselves and understand what they do and do not have in common with those with whom they share this planet.

Having established the importance of a Left–Right distinction, we will now be examining four political concepts that, while of crucial importance to welfare theory, we were not able to touch on at any length in the previous chapters; these are: the state (section 5.1), power (section 5.2), poverty and social exclusion (section 5.3) and human nature (section 5.4). So in this chapter (and the next) we begin to tidy up some of the threads that have been left loose and prepare ourselves for the discussion of welfare ideologies in Chapter 7.

## 5.1 The State

The state consists of three components: a legislature (which makes the laws), an executive (which applies the laws) and a judiciary (which interprets and upholds the laws). In Britain, the Houses of Parliament are the legis-lature, the government is the executive, the courts are the judiciary, with the crown or the monarch as the head of state. Theoretically, the legislature should be the dominant partner, although since the mid-nineteenth century the executive has taken over many of the legislature's powers and functions.

Political theorists have asked two basic questions: 'what *is* the state?' and 'what form *should* the state take?' To a large extent the responses which have been given to one question correspond closely to those which have been given to the other. At the risk of oversimplifying, but in order to provide an effective starting point, we can identify a distinction between individualistic and organic theories of the state (cf. Jordan, 1985; C. Pierson, 1996).

The individualistic theory interprets the state as that which serves the interests of its citizens. Individuals reside in civil society and, as the origin of its political authority, the state's job is to protect that civil society against both internal and external threats. This theory seems to prescribe a system of limited government lest the state itself becomes a source of danger to civil society, although definitions of 'limited' can change and mean different things to different generations. The organic theory interprets the state as a holistic entity, as that which must inevitably shape the interests of citizens. Civil society and the state are interdependent rather than separable so that the state is not the alien, remote, potential source of danger that the individualistic theory portrays it as being, but the necessary condition of social stability and human flourishing. This theory seems to prescribe a system of 'corporatist' government where the state's job is to preserve the interconnections between the social parts. It would be a mistake to regard the individualistic theory as right-wing and the organic one as left-wing: both sides of the political spectrum can draw on either theory, or a mixture of the two. Indeed, many of the most influential theorists subvert the distinction just drawn.

## 5.1.1 A brief theoretical history

The ancient world would not have recognised the distinction just made as theories of the state derived more from competing philosophical ideas about the nature of virtue and good character. It was really only with the growth of the nation-state that the relationship between state and civil society became problematic in a way that we continue to recognise in the twenty-first century. Niccolo Machiavelli (1459–1517) was the first to suggest that our conception of the state cannot derive from theological presuppositions about the nature of the divine realm (Machiavelli, 1984), but it was Thomas Hobbes (1588–1679) and John Locke who set the terms of the modern debate.

For Hobbes (1973), the state of nature implied a war of 'all against all' so that avoiding this conflict required a sovereign whose power and authority over society would be absolute; in return for their obedience people would thereby receive a degree of security that can never pertain in the state of nature. So, Hobbes defends a state which possesses near absolute power over its citizens.[1] By contrast, Locke (1960) insists that the state's legitimacy derives from its protection of the 'pre-social' rights to 'life, liberty and estates', so that the consent of individuals must be constantly sought and respected. A limited form of governance is therefore called for, implying a political system of checks and balances based on what Montesquieu (1689–1755) called a 'separation of powers' in order to ensure that the state remains within its legitimate boundaries (Montesquieu, 1989).

Although it has wielded a limited influence on actual policy-making, the Marxist theory of the state offers an interesting alternative to the above. Marx opposed Hegel's notion that the state stood over and above civil society, unifying its disparate parts (see the discussion of Hegel in section 3.5). According to Marx, the nature of the state derives from the nature of the economy within which it is to be found: a feudal state is not the same thing as a capitalist one because the economies of these systems are different. In a capitalist society, the capitalist state is itself a player in the struggle of class against class, constantly favouring property owners over the propertyless. Originally, Marx held a very simplistic interpretation of the state, believing that it was nothing more than an organising committee for the bourgeoisie; he subsequently refined this view but nevertheless maintained that the capitalist state acts *in general* in the interests of the ruling class to maintain the accumulative cycle of the capitalist economy (Marx, 1977) – see the longer discussion of Marxism in section 7.4.

Max Weber (1864–1920) in turn criticised what he regarded as Marx's economic determinism and suggested that the state be thought of as just one type of authority which can be set against other types (Weber, 1991).[2] In short, social power is not simply economic in nature. The rational-legal authority of the state derives from the formation and application of impersonal rules within hierarchical structures of decision-making.[3] The state is therefore the closest approximation we have to a pure bureaucracy – regardless of whether we are talking about a capitalist, democratic, authoritarian, socialist or communist state – and the growth of the state is perhaps the most important manifestation of the increasing 'bureaucratisation' and 'disenchantment' of the modern world: the confinement of the spirit within an 'iron cage' of impersonal and spiritless rationality.

This idea that the state's influence was becoming ubiquitous in the modern world helped to promote the further and not unrelated idea that the state could be used as a means of advancing individual and social well-being, that is, it could be a humane tool of progress and not just a bureaucratic instrument of impersonal rationality. Justifications for a welfare state proceed from that point on.

## 5.1.2 *The welfare state*

There are economic, social and ideological justifications for the welfare state. Since we shall be looking at the ideological arguments in Chapters 7, all we need do here is review the economic and social ones.

The economic justification of the classic welfare state is essentially Keynesian. J. M. Keynes (1883–1946) argued that the state can and should secure the conditions for stable economic growth (Keynes, 1954). Prior to Keynes orthodox opinion held that the state should not intervene in the economy, as this would be damaging at best and counterproductive at worst. This was because free markets were thought of as the only means of maximising well-being, both individually and collectively, due to the invisible hand that we discussed in Chapter 3. So, whereas critics pointed to high levels of unemployment as examples of market failure, the defenders of laissez-faire capitalism argued that unemployment was the result of workers pricing themselves out of jobs, that is, asking for wages higher than those the market can afford to pay. Therefore, the solution to unemployment was for everyone, although especially the unemployed, to reduce their wage demands. If I hire four workers at £5 per hour each, I pay out £20 in wages every hour; but if those workers reduce their wages to £4 per hour, I can afford to take on another person and, if this happens across the economy, unemployment will be 'soaked up'. By contrast, state interference with the economy only upsets the balancing act of the invisible hand: for instance, if people are financially compensated for being out of work, they will have little incentive to reduce their wage levels.

Keynes agreed with the textbooks that unrestrained markets could balance themselves out in the long run. The trouble, he argued, was that in the long run we are all dead: by the time market supply and demand has corrected itself the social consequences might well have been devastating. For example, by the time falling wage levels have created additional jobs, unemployed workers may no longer be available to fill them as they will have died of starvation in the interim. Some degree of state regulation and control is therefore justified, although Keynes disagreed with socialists in their call for the full-blown socialisation of the means of production. At the domestic level a Keynesian approach requires the state to manage the level of demand, for example by lowering taxes, printing money or creating jobs through public works programmes, in the expectation that the beneficial effects of doing so will multiply and reinvigorate an ailing economy. At the international level, it requires the formation of 'interstate' agencies whose remit would be the maintenance of stability within the global economy, for example the IMF and the World Bank. Keynes therefore believed that an economy could be run at or near full employment as long as the correct monetary and fiscal policies were pursued.

So, Keynes established a central economic justification for the post-war welfare state: *to save capitalism from itself*. Without state intervention, market

capitalism and liberal democracy would be unstable and vulnerable to authoritarian takeover (as had happened in Germany in the early 1930s). The welfare
state was not, for Keynes, a stepping stone to a socialist society, it was about
making capitalism work better by generating levels of investment and economic activity that laissez-faire markets could not deliver. The logic of Keynes's position was widely accepted for about a third of a century after his
death. But once the radical Right had regrouped, with their preference for pre-
Keynesian economics, this argument about saving capitalism from itself began
to be undermined. Consequently, once full employment slipped down the list
of political priorities, one of the conditions of, and arguments for, the welfare
state also fell away.

   Understanding the social justification for the welfare state refers us to its
redistributive and justice-enhancing properties (Glennerster and Hills, 1998).
Having covered justice in previous chapters let us concentrate here on redistribution. The main instrument of welfarist redistribution was always intended
to be the running of the economy at full employment, so that benefiting from
the welfare state has always been dependent on a large degree of participation
in the labour market – explaining why women have traditionally not benefited
as much as men. In short, the redistribution effected by the welfare state has
always been about the amelioration of market conditions rather than a prelude
to a post-capitalist society. Without deeper changes in the political economy,
welfare state redistribution is always going to be about rearranging the furniture rather than changing the shape of the room. Whatever the problems
with his normative assessment, T. H. Marshall at least recognised the rationale
of post-war reform: to reduce class resentment while leaving intact many of
the market inequalities out of which the class system is generated in the first
place.

   The empirical evidence seems to back up these conclusions. As we noted in
section 2.6, when discussing equality of opportunity, three-quarters of what
the welfare state does consists of horizontal redistribution with vertical redistribution being relatively unimportant.[4] In other words, the welfare state is
much more of a saving's bank than it is a Robin Hood figure (Hills, 1997). So
the social dimensions of the welfare state are profoundly ambiguous. Piachaud
(1997) estimates that the welfare state reduces by half the numbers that would
otherwise be living in poverty: so what is, on the one hand, a cause for
celebration is, on the other, a cause for concern that so many continue to be
left in poverty. The social justification for state welfare has come under more
and more strain as the era of full-time, male employment fades into memory
and the system has been left to cope with economic conditions for which the
likes of Keynes and Beveridge never designed it.

   The social justification for the welfare state can be stated as the attempt to
ameliorate but not eliminate the poverty and deprivation of market capitalism.
This social justification remains stronger than the economic justification that
we have just reviewed. In what many interpret as a globalised economy (see

Chapter 9), state welfare must be more concerned with the future, that is, with the competitive restructuring of the labour force, and less concerned with rights and entitlements that derive from past economic activity. According to such arguments, capitalism no longer needs to be saved from itself or, if it does, state welfare is no longer an appropriate instrument.

Has the welfare state been an individualist or an organic state? In fact, the welfare state is actually consistent with both theories. It can be regarded as a means by which private individuals enter into a mutualist contract to protect each other against common risks and dangers. The social insurance principle can be interpreted in these terms, with the welfare state as a collectivist instrument of individual and family security. This 'individualist welfare' state is perhaps most clearly embodied in English-speaking countries, especially America, given the Anglo-American emphasis on the separateness of state and civil society. However, the welfare state can also be thought to resemble the more organic conceptions outlined above, in its ability to bind social groups and economic classes together into some kind of solidaristic whole. In these terms it can be seen to provide a coherence and integrity to the miscellany of civil society, bringing family, workplace, church and voluntary sector together under the tutelage and authority of the statutory sphere. The 'organic welfare' state is more about the holism and interdependency of state and civil society and probably corresponds most closely to conservative-corporatist nations such as Germany. However, reiterating a point already made, most welfare systems incorporate to some extent both individualist and organic characteristics.

## 5.1.3 A post-welfare state?

Few imagine that we still live in an era of the classic welfare state but what, if anything, has succeeded it? Do we still live in an era of welfare capitalism or have we moved into a post-welfare society? Let us outline and critique three ideas which say that we have surpassed welfare state capitalism.

The first and most obvious theory insisting that the welfare state is effectively dead comes from the radical Right. Since we will be returning to those ideas in Chapter 7 we need not say anything more here.

The second post-welfare theory is one that has just been mentioned and derives from the globalisation debate that we shall examine at greater length in Chapter 9. Some contributors to this debate (for example Ohmae, 1995) have argued that we can no longer talk about national sovereignty, as nation-states are now sinking beneath the rising tide of the global economy. Globalisation refers to those processes and flows that are making national economies increasingly interdependent and indistinguishable. Therefore, our task should be to let ourselves be carried away by the ever-accelerating currents and streams of global flows on the basis that 'there is no alternative'. Economic, public and social policies should be primarily framed with the interests of international capital and competitive market forces in mind; consequently, this school of thought regards the post-war welfare system as either dead or dying (Graham, 1994). Nations, now integrated into the world economy as 'inward investment sites', place themselves at a competitive disadvantage if they maintain public expenditure and social regulation at too high and restrictive a level. Therefore, the level of welfare spending should be scaled back drastically and governments should divest themselves of their roles as welfare providers and financiers.

The third theory which questions the relevance of the welfare state derives not from political and economic changes, but from changes in our theoretical understanding of ourselves. Post-structuralists challenge any conception of the state and political power as something which is centralised and visible, and so founded on sovereignty and consent (see next section). For Foucault (Hindess, 1996: 131–6), we ought to focus on 'governance', as that which *makes and forms* subjects/selves, rather than government per se. Concentrating on the state in the way that the traditional (law-making) model of government requires distracts us from the ways in which power flows through the veins and arteries (the capillaries) of the social body via non-state agencies. Ultimately, post-structuralism rejects both the individualist and organic models that we have applied above. The welfare state is not that which is concerned with the welfare of autonomous citizens residing within civil society, but a series of discursive disciplines that construct the very subjects who experience levels of welfare in the first place. The 'welfare state' is therefore something of a misnomer and what we should analyse instead is the way in which 'technologies of power' operate throughout the formal and informal sectors of society.

However, there are also three arguments which suggest that the welfare state is not redundant, either as an institution or as a concept. The first of these returns us to the globalisation debate. According to some, the suggestion that the best thing that government can do is to get out of the way of the wealth-creating entrepreneurial sector is contradicted with reference to the developmental states of the East Asian Pacific (Goodman et al., 1998). The governments of Japan, South Korea, Taiwan, Hong Kong and Singapore have not 'stepped back', as the apologists for laissez faire recommend; instead, they have adopted various forms of 'system building'. East Asia has undergone a period of rapid industrialisation with the state providing the long-term investment strategies that have delivered high levels of economic growth. Social welfare provision has been of central importance to this economic strategy, in that funded social insurance systems provide a level of national savings that many in the debt-burdened, consumption-oriented West have envied. In Singapore, for example, the Central Provident Fund not only provides resources for housing, health care and benefits, but is also an important tool of macro-economic regulation, that is, a means of combating recession and facilitating long-term investment projects. In short, the experience of 'developmental states' has been taken as evidence that the globalisation argument is too simplistic.

Second, not dissimilar arguments can be made in relation to the West. Neo-Keynesians such as Layard (1998) and Marquand (1988) believe that a Keynesian approach can be adapted and reapplied. Governments can still act to create jobs through a variety of direct and indirect measures: they can rebalance the relations between capital and labour, encouraging a culture of cooperation rather than of conflict; they can facilitate low levels of inflation without accompanying levels of high unemployment and social inequality. In other words, something resembling the classic welfare state remains vital if welfare capitalism is to survive. In particular, the benefit system can be made more 'active', that is, more concerned with job provision and retraining, and the education system can be improved to ensure that all possess the basic skills that are more essential than ever to both individual and national prosperity.

Finally, there are those who draw on post-Fordist theories (also reviewed in Chapter 9) to argue that the power of the welfare state has augmented in many respects (Jessop, 1994). The power of the nation-state has declined due to globalisation, so that the job of the state is to manage the integration of the nation into the streams of international competitiveness. This means that it must ensure that workers are both skilled and flexible, public services approximate to commercial enterprises, the benefit system subsidies low wages and discourages idleness, and a certain amount of insecurity and casualisation is created because this can be economically beneficial. For Marxists such as Jessop, the welfare state is alive and well due to its more authoritarian and disciplinarian qualities coming to the fore.

## 5.2 Power

### 5.2.1 Power as quantitative capacity

Several famous definitions of power have been suggested over the years. For Bertrand Russell (1872–1970) it implied the 'production of intended effects', while for Robert Dahl *A* has power over *B* to the extent that *A* can get *B* to do something that *B* would not otherwise do (Lukes, 1986). Steven Lukes (1974) is attracted to the notion that power basically implies a capacity to change one's environment in some way. This is a 'quantitative' capacity as it implies something which is measurable and physical in terms of both processes and outcomes, and it was this conception of power that dominated political science from the 1950s to the 1970s, especially in America. As such, analyses of political power that dominated the debate can be sorted into three categories: pluralist, elitist and radical. Let us look at these in turn and say something about the welfare state in each case.

A pluralist theory says two things: political power is not the same thing as economic power and political power is distributed among a plurality of actors, agencies and groups in society (Dahl, 1961; cf. Dahl, 1985). Pluralism says that power is decentralised and that, through mechanisms of political representation and participation, everyone has the opportunity to contribute to important decision-making processes. An election is the most obvious example of such a mechanism. This does not mean that the specific outcome of decision-making processes will satisfy everyone; individuals and groups conflict about the right way to do things, with some individuals and groups being successful and others not. The point is that political resources are dispersed so that political conflict and debate is not dominated by one side or another. This means that the state should be interpreted as a neutral umpire of the political game, facilitating the competition but not intervening in favour of any one team. Of course, crude and sophisticated versions of pluralism exist. Crude versions propose the perfect dispersal of political power, the perfect equality of social actors and the perfect neutrality of the state. Sophisticated versions treat pluralism as an ideal to be aimed for but one which, admittedly, we often fall short of in the real world.

According to a pluralist reading, we can say two things about the welfare state. First, the particular social institutions of the welfare state could be thought of as the outcome of past and ongoing political conflicts between, for instance, capital and labour: with capitalists wanting to reduce social expenditure, taxation and regulation and with workers wanting to increase them. Second, the welfare state in a more general sense could be interpreted as a neutral arbiter, refereeing conflicts over the production and distribution of social resources without favouring one outcome over another.

The advantage of pluralism is that it proposes an optimistic evaluation of politics, where power is available to everyone, and it focuses on the complexity of policy-making processes. The disadvantage is that it may well offer an overoptimistic appraisal of political power, papering over the distinction between the powerful and the excluded, and fails to analyse processes that take place 'behind the scenes' of observable phenomena. To understand what this means we have to outline elitist theories of power.

Elitism states that political power and economic power are closely related and the former is nowhere near as decentralised as pluralists seem to imagine (Mills, 1956). The mechanisms that pluralists treat as open and undominated are, in fact, skewed in favour of already-powerful actors, groups and agencies. Elections and lobbying are both dominated by the interests of the wealthy, precisely because the wealthy can afford to buy more political influence from parties and governments than can the disadvantaged. The idea that decision-making processes are open to everyone is regarded as triumphantly naive, as it is the powerful who set the agenda whereas the needs and interests of the non-elites are pushed down that agenda's list of priorities. In a conflict over the building of an out-of-town hypermarket, whose interests are most likely to prevail: the corporation with an annual turnover of millions (perhaps billions) or the local protestors whose financial resources are modest? According to elitism, the state is itself a player in the political game, intervening on behalf of one team (the elite) to the detriment of the others. As with pluralism, crude and sophisticated versions of elitism can be imagined.[5] Crude versions regard the interests of elites as always being dominant, whereas sophisticated versions acknowledge the complexity of political power, for example once in a while the state will favour the arguments of the local protestors. Elements of elitism can therefore overlap with elements of pluralism.

An elitist reading of the welfare state suggests that it favours one particular form of production and distribution. However, whether it is capital or labour that is favoured depends largely on your ideological starting point. The Left are likely to see the welfare state largely as a pro-capitalist institution: something that helps the market economy to run more efficiently and forestalling the likelihood of riot, social dissent and anti-capitalist revolution. The Right are likely to see the welfare state as a gravy train for the undeserving, giving social benefits to unemployed people that they have not earned and which the economy cannot afford.

The strength of elitism is that it offers a structural reading of society that understands the extent to which political power operates 'behind our backs', setting agendas that do not represent the interests of all, but primarily the interests of selected, elite groups and individuals. It suggests that policy-making is as much about what is omitted from consideration as what is included. However, elitism can be accused of promoting a pessimistic approach to politics: if a minority of elites dominates the process, why bother engaging with that process? It can also be accused of not being susceptible to empirical analysis: if elite influence is largely a hidden phenomena (as it has to be to be effective), how can we ever really identify and study it?

A radical interpretation of political power agrees with elitism on many key points but there are two main differences (Lukes, 1974). First, elitists propose a multidimensional view of the nature of elites, so that labour is as capable of forming an elite as capital. By contrast, Marxists argue that in a capitalist society elites are always *capitalist elites*; at its simplest, Marxism has proposed the existence of a ruling class whose ideas and interests are almost always socially dominant. However, some versions of feminism also buy into the radical view, offering a gendered interpretation that regards the dominant elites as male dominated, masculinist and patriarchal. Second, radicals argue that not only are the interests of non-elites pushed down the political agenda but that, in important respects, non-elites are kept in ignorance of their interests in the first place. According to Marxism, for example, capitalism tries to keep workers in a state of 'false consciousness' where they may not even recognise the extent to which they are being exploited.

On these grounds the welfare state can be thought of as a means by which a dominant elite maintains itself in a position of power by preventing the non-elites from recognising their real needs and interests. For instance, a long-term aim of the socialist movement has been the freeing of workers from the source of their enslavement, that is, the wage contract; but the welfare state ensures that paid work continues to be valued over all other forms of actual or potential activity and the identity of citizens as workers is maintained through a series of ideological and disciplinary measures.

The strength of the radical explanation is that it overcomes the vague subjectivity of both pluralist and elitist accounts in focusing on the objective and essential dynamics of social development and organisation. It looks at the structural contexts within which action takes place and the constraints that the dispossessed non-elites must struggle against, and it examines the role that ideology plays in the operation of power. However, radical theories are potentially guilty of oversimplifying the complexity of society, reducing power to one type of thing and not being able to explain how social power systems perpetuate when 'non-elites' are often victorious in the struggles they pursue. Radicalism risks ignoring the importance of action and agency altogether, that is, our ability to shape the world we live in by overthrowing dominant ideas and interests.

## 5.2.2 Power as authority

Hindess (1996) warns against the danger of ignoring an older tradition in political theory that introduces more of a qualitative dimension to the debate. This dimension rests on the notion of consent and so draws a distinction between legitimate and illegitimate uses of power. So, whereas the definition of 'quantitative capacity' focuses on the exercise and function of power, 'legitimate capacity' focuses on the moral and social justifiability of power: the latter looks not only at governance but also at the governed.

An interesting way of illustrating the difference is by thinking of an educational setting. On one level, lecturers obviously have power over students to set and mark assessments and award degree grades, a power that can strongly affect the rest of students' lives. And yet it would be simplistic to interpret this power as merely a quantitative capacity, given that students have *chosen* to submit themselves to the hierarchies and academic standards of higher education. The power that lecturers possess, therefore, is a quantitative capacity on one level only; on another, perhaps more important level, it is an authority. In short, the power of lecturers exists only in so far as students consent to recognise it and abide by the judgement of those teaching them: a lecturer's authority ultimately derives from the freely given consent of those over whom power is wielded. This means that we need to talk about qualitative or legitimate capacity, that is, authority, in addition to quantitative capacity.

According to Hindess, unless we make this fundamental distinction we miss what is distinctive about the modern period: present-day states may or may not correspond to one of the interpretations outlined in section 5.2.1, but the modern ideal has been one of government by consent, an ideal that should not be cynically disregarded. As far as the welfare state is concerned, this notion of power offers a necessary corrective to those theories, proposed by both Left and Right, that take a deterministic view of the development of state welfare. An emphasis on consent reminds us that the welfare state was, and continues to be, consented to by those who are its clients/customers/citizens, even if we can argue over how much actual consent there is to be detected within state welfare systems.

## 5.2.3 Power as production

Chapter 3 gave a preliminary sketch of the ideas of Michel Foucault and we have added to this in section 5.1.3. We have noted how Foucault considers the self to be formed in and through practices and discourses of normalisation. On these grounds, freedom is a form of governance, and vice versa, rather than something that either prefigures or succeeds governance in a simplistic sense: freedom and power are intertwined as a 'discursive technology'. To concentrate on sovereignty and consent, as the previous two subsections have done, is therefore to cling to an infantile and premodern 'kings and queens' notion of political power; whereas if we, metaphorically speaking, cut the sovereign's head off, we will be able to recognise the real nature of power.

But what is this exactly? Traditionally, power has been thought of in negative terms, as something that distorts, deceives, represses, controls and oppresses. Yet, following in the footsteps of Nietzsche, Foucault insists that this is too narrow and myopic a view:

> If power were never anything but repressive, if it never did anything but to say no, do you really think one would be brought to obey it? What makes power hold good, what makes it accepted, is the fact that it doesn't only weigh on us as a force that says no, but that it traverses and produces things, it induces pleasure, forms knowledge, produces discourse. It needs to be considered as a productive network which runs through the whole social body... (Foucault, 1984: 61)

Sexuality, for instance, is a product of power in that sexuality is a discourse concerned both with control of the population, for example family planning strategies, and of the human body. However, this discourse is not simply repressive but also productive: we might think of the ways in which attempts to prohibit and criminalise same-sex relationships have shaped the liberatory and celebratory politics of today's gay and lesbian movements. Foucault's notion of power undercuts the more conventional accounts that we have reviewed in this chapter: if power is political and if power is everywhere then everything is political in some sense.

Foucault's insights in this respect have been influential across the social sciences, for just as pluralism, elitism and radicalism risk ignoring the legitimacy of power as authority, so the emphasis on consent risks ignoring the formation of the self who then does the consenting. However, the potential problem with this idea of power as production is that it devalues power as a useful concept, rendering redundant the distinction between legitimate and illegitimate uses of power. The power that I have to make you read the footnote at the end of this sentence (go on, you know you can't resist it forever) is hardly the same as the power which in a patriarchal society, say, men wield over women.[6] But Foucault's argument that truth is itself a 'regime of power' means that analyses of power become indiscriminate: if power is everywhere then, in a sense, power is nowhere, and it becomes harder to form a progressive politics which wants to concentrate on the repressive characteristics of power such as that wielded by capital over labour, by men over women, and so on.

## 5.3 Poverty and Social Exclusion

### 5.3.1 Defining poverty and social exclusion

Poverty is not a force of nature. The poor may always have been with us, as the famous adage says, but this does not necessarily mean that they must always be with us. Certainly, poverty and social exclusion embody important economic and sociocultural dimensions but each must be understood, first and foremost, as a *political* construct.

Poverty is undoubtedly the oldest of the two concepts. The simplest way of defining poverty is to regard is as a lack of even a minimum level of subsistence, or a lack of the basic needs of food, safe drinking water, shelter and physical health. This 'absolute' definition is largely applicable to developing nations. According to the United Nations Development Programme (1997), about one-quarter of the world's population lives in absolute poverty, with 1.3 billion subsisting on less than $1 per day, and 800 million do not have enough to eat. Absolute definitions tend to be contrasted with the notion of relative poverty. According to this definition, someone is or is not poor relative to those around them, that is, in comparison to the standard of living of others. Relative poverty implies an exclusion from the kind of living standards generally prevailing in society due to inadequate resources, especially income. According to Gordon et al. (2000), approximately 26% of the UK population was experiencing relative poverty at the end of 1999.

And this is precisely where the ideological disagreement begins to kick in. According to the notion of relative poverty, it might be possible for someone to own a TV, a washing machine and other consumer goods and yet still be defined as being relatively poor. So whereas it was absolute poverty that was operationalised by the earliest researchers into poverty, by the 1950s many on the Left were arguing that, although the welfare state had significantly reduced absolute poverty, relative poverty remained at unacceptably high levels (Abel-Smith and Townsend, 1965). In short, although relative poverty and social inequality are not the same, the poverty lobby argued that inequalities of income and wealth were still too high.

To some extent, the anti-welfare backlash of the post-1970s period can be explained as a reaction to this idea of relative poverty. In order to counter the influence of the best research (Townsend, 1979), the Right argued that what was needed was less state welfare provision, not more, as the welfare state only undermined individuals' willingness to help themselves. This gave birth to the debate about the 'underclass' and 'welfare dependency' that we shall examine below.

However, even some of those sympathetic to the poverty lobby argued that this new concept of relative poverty was too vague. As we noted in section 1.4.2 when discussing the meaning of welfare, Amartya Sen (1983) agrees that relativist definitions are relevant, but also insists that any coherent definition of relative poverty had to refer back to, and draw on, the definition of absolute poverty as well. Poverty means lacking a capacity to realise a goal or achieve a set of goods, although what this 'lack' actually consists of will vary from society to society.

The concept of poverty is still a key element of the political vocabulary, yet it has to some extent been superseded by that of social exclusion (Room, 1995; Oppenheim, 1998; Askonas and Stewart, 2000). The definition of social exclusion we adopt depends heavily on how we see it relating to the concept of poverty. First, we might regard social exclusion as capturing nothing more than the idea already expressed: that material deprivation cuts a person off from social networks and contacts and reduces that person's stock of social capital. In other words, social exclusion is another way of saying 'relative poverty' and, for Townsend (1979), we must not lose sight of the importance of material deprivation and the maldistribution of social resources. Second, we might treat poverty and social exclusion as denoting different aspects of the same social phenomena. The latter is a process of detachment from the labour market, social communities and organisations; the former is the lack of an adequate income, an indicator rather than a process. The latter is about participation, whereas the former is about distribution. The advantage of this approach is that it reminds us that policies to address poverty and exclusion must be sophisticated and multifaceted: boosting incomes is a necessary but not sufficient condition of promoting social inclusion. Third, we might think of social exclusion in more individualistic terms. Exclusion from social norms and networks occurs because of the actions of the excluded, with certain people perversely choosing to absent themselves from normal society. As such, we might need to reject the notion of poverty altogether. For instance, many might lack an adequate income, but this is of secondary importance if the cause of that deprivation is immorality or laziness. It is this individualist interpretation which turns some on the Left against the concept of social exclusion altogether. The suspicion is that poverty is gradually being abandoned as an explanatory concept in order that cost-cutting governments can blame the poor for their poverty and implement supply-side policies that coerce and control the weakest members of society.

Since the debates about definition clearly interact with those about explanation, the next section outlines the five main political theories of poverty and takes a brief detour into the underclass debate.

## 5.3.2 *Explaining poverty and social exclusion*

As we saw in Chapters 2–4, a Left–Right political spectrum is of considerable importance to welfare theory and nowhere is this more apparent than in competing theories of poverty and social exclusion (cf. Alcock, 1997; cf. Jordan, 1996). Each of the following is distinct, although each explanation overlaps to some extent with those that are adjacent to it.

The first perspective belongs to those on the Right for whom poverty is behavioral or pathological. This can mean either that the poor are deliberately lazy and indolent, or that they are genetically predisposed to being poor, or a bit of both. So, this is an explanation where the source or causes of poverty are located squarely within poor individuals themselves. The notion that the poor are lazy is one that stretches back millennia and underpins the long-standing distinction between the deserving and undeserving poor, with the former being regarded as virtuous, for example people disabled from birth, and the latter as immoral. The idea that the poor are genetically inferior is more recent, originating with advances in biology towards the end of the nineteenth century. There is a tension between these two pathological accounts, for one seems to be claiming that the poor are responsible for their situation, whereas the other attributes our social positions to our biological inheritance. Charles Murray (2000) has recently welded these accounts together by insisting that while poverty has genetic causes so it also has genetic *consequences*, leading to a deterioration in the genome of the poor.

The disadvantage of the pathological explanation is that it oversimplifies the many causal factors of poverty and is too reductive by singling out one factor and magnifying its significance. The importance of our social environments in shaping our identities and our social status is too well documented for this individualistic and/or biological explanation to carry us very far.

The second main explanation of poverty is also one that belongs to the Right, except here environmental factors are introduced. The 'cycle of deprivation' argument recognises the importance of socialisation but adds that if the social environment is dysfunctional in any way children will grow up accordingly. So if, as a child, my family and immediate community are lazy, indolent, prone to criminality and so on, I will grow up with similar values and expectations. Consequently, I will demonstrate behaviour and attitudes which are likely to leave me poor. Therefore, the cycle of deprivation explanation says that there exists a 'culture of poverty' which is inherited from one generation to the next. This explanation is also long standing, although encapsulated most recently by Murray (1984; cf. Mead, 1986), who argues that a dysfunctional environment is one of the effects of the welfare state which first helps to create poverty and then to perpetuate it by engendering a 'culture of dependency' where people lose the habits of work, responsibility and self-help. It is such arguments that underpin the underclass debate.

The 'underclass' is a term that has been widely used on the Left also, for example it approximates to Marx's notion of the lumpenproletariat, but it was the American right-wing who appropriated the concept and gave it a meaning consistent with an anti-welfare state critique (Morris, 1994). Concerns about the underclass and the 'culture of dependency' revived in the early 1980s and flourished in a fertile political climate with the Reagan administration in America and the Thatcher government in Britain. Murray alleged that overgenerous benefits in America had led to the emergence of a significant underclass of several million people. By encouraging neither marriage nor independence within the labour market, assistance benefits had created a generation of unemployed and unemployable black youths, as well as a generation of lone mothers who expected to be 'married to the state'. For those such as Murray, therefore, the term 'underclass' does not refer to an extreme of poverty, that is, the poorest of the poor, but to a different *type* of poverty: the value system (culture) possessed by those who expect society and the state to do everything for them without having to contribute anything in return. These kinds of argument have given a theoretical justification for the expansion of disciplinary workfare programmes where claimants are compelled to work or train in return for their benefits, in order to remotivate the habits that they have allegedly lost.

However, the cycle of deprivation argument betrays a number of weaknesses. Although it acknowledges the importance of social environments, it only does so in order to bolster the pathological explanation that seems to underpin it, by using the 'environment' as a stick with which to beat the welfare state. Therefore, the explanation risks ignoring the reasons why people become poor in the first place. Can it be a coincidence that some social groups are constantly more prone to poverty than others? As we shall see in Chapter 8, people from ethnic minorities are consistently more likely to experience poverty. Yet if we apply right-wing explanations this can only be because of their inherent failings, bolstered by a dependency-creating welfare system. Murray, in particular, has run into trouble on this score, being accused of racism due to his claim that black people are less intelligent than white (and therefore more likely to be poor) (Herrnstein and Murray, 1994).

Similarly, research has shown that there is no general culture of dependency (Walker with Howard, 2000). Dean and Taylor-Gooby (1992) concluded that terms such as 'underclass' and 'dependency culture' are not so much objective phenomena 'out there' as symbolic and discursive constructions which indicate a widespread tendency to blame the victims for the very disadvantages which have been perpetrated against them. For example, benefit claimants are not culturally separate from 'normal' society: if anything, claimants cope with their situation by adopting and internalising what they see as the norms and values of non-claimants. Far from requiring the additional motivation to work, claimants might actually have unreal expectations about what the job market can deliver.

The third explanation focuses on the failures of policy. It is not the poor who are to blame but the policies and institutions, which were set up to eliminate poverty, having either failed completely or having not succeeded sufficiently (depending on who you read). This is an explanation which attracts support from across the political spectrum, although for differing reasons. The main disagreement lies between those who emphasise the failure of particular policies and those who insist that even the best designed and implemented policies have a limited horizon of success. Take benefits, for example. Benefits, at least in the UK, are generally regarded as being inadequate, yet there are two reasons why this might be so. On the one hand, perhaps governments have lacked the political will to commit a sufficient level of social expenditure, compounding the failures that Beveridge made in estimating the level of a minimum income standard (Veit-Wilson, 1992). On the other, perhaps benefits will always be inadequate, due to the flaws inherent within any social security system; for example, the more universal a benefit is, the less it is going to be worth in monetary terms, yet the more selective a benefit is, the lower the take-up of that benefit and the more likely it is to impose poverty traps.

Just as this explanation can attract support from across the political spectrum, so it can attract criticism. Many on the Right would still insist that policies fail when they do not take account of the failings of the poor. For instance, giving a hand-out rather than a hand up to the poorest allows them to define themselves as passive, as possessing rights but few duties. Many on the Left insist that policies fail when they do not take account of certain structural constraints, for example the welfare state redistributes a certain amount of income but leaves untouched the vastly unequal system of capital ownership.

The fourth explanation belongs more to the political Left and focuses on 'structural constraints'. This says that society is largely determined by forces beyond either individual or collective control. Imagine that a radical government comes to power and announces that it is going to eliminate poverty by raising general taxation, corporate taxation and by socialising the means of production. International investors and multinational companies would run a mile, the currency would sink, interest rates would have to rise and therefore unemployment would begin to rise. For many voters this might be reason enough not to vote for radical parties, but for the Left it is evidence that the needs of the affluent always come first. Therefore, poverty is a result of the limits of collective action.

The final explanation is a refined version of the fourth which says that poverty is functional for capitalism. This Marxist explanation suggests that the poor are required as a reserve army of labour, that is, a pool of labour out of which employers can draw during periods of economic growth and back into which workers can be thrown during periods of economic contraction. Furthermore, poverty disciplines the rest of us. Because it is such an undesirable condition, the non-poor are effectively required to adapt themselves (their beliefs and values, their behavior and appearance, even their very identities) to the imperatives of capitalism. In short, poverty is a strategy that exists in order that capitalist affluence can exist (Jones and Novak, 1999).

The disadvantage of the fourth and fifth explanations is that they might encourage passivity and fatalism. If capitalism places very narrow limits on collective action, why should we bother trying to change anything? Perhaps we can make marginal improvements here and there, yet it might also be the case that these explanations reinvent the notion that the 'poor are always with us'. Of course, Marxism anticipates a social and economic revolution, but that option is surely now less realistic than at any time in the past. So the danger with these explanations is that we underestimate the impact which collective action has already had – in the form of a welfare state – and leave ourselves with no clear policy agenda. It is easier to blame poverty on the evils of capitalism than to devise realistic, if imperfect, alternatives.

## 5.4 Human Nature

These considerations bring us neatly to our final section. Why should human nature be thought of as a key political concept? Part of the answer lies in a debate that Foucault once had on television with the American political commentator Noam Chomsky (Foucault, 1984). Chomsky argued that there is such a thing as a human nature, for if there were not, (a) scientific understanding would be impossible, and (b) political critiques could not be formulated (if there is no human nature to be repressed, we have no grounds on which to criticise repression) (cf. Geras, 1995). Foucault, however, insisted that we should not ask questions about human nature per se, the existence of which he doubted, but investigate how the concept of 'human nature' has been defined and utilised within a variety of discursive regimes. Chomsky asks the question 'why?' (why should we struggle against injustice?) and concludes that without some notion of a human nature we have *no* reason to do so. Foucault asks the question 'how?' (how does power operate?) and concludes that by ignoring this question, by concentrating on the 'why?', we risk perpetuating what we call injustice rather than being able to struggle against it.

Human nature must therefore be of central importance to Social Policy (Hewitt, 2000). Indeed, it could be claimed that all political, economic and social ideas depend on some prior conception of human nature. But rather than engage with the kind of metaphysical debate just outlined, as this would take us too far away from welfare theory, I propose to briefly discuss the following questions and then say something at greater length about needs.

### 5.4.1 Key questions

*Is human nature given or constructed?*
Relating back in part to the Foucault/Chomsky debate, there is the question of whether human nature is pre-social or social. A pre-social nature implies something that is biological and/or psychological in essence, whereas a social nature implies something that is assembled through the processes of socialisation. In the former case, society is thought of as a reflection of human nature; in the latter case human nature is thought of as a reflection of society. The debate is an important one because it is here that we determine the extent to which we are able to shape ourselves and our environment. If human nature is fixed and pre-social, this might indicate the existence of certain natural limitations that restrict the scope of social reform and so of social policy, but if human nature is constructed (constructivism) this might indicate that social reform is potentially limitless.

*Are humans atoms or social beings?*
Of related concern is the question as to whether human nature denotes an atomism, that is, a rigid separation between selves, so that society resembles a billiard table whose members interact like the billiard balls, colliding mechanically according to strict laws of motion; or whether the boundaries of the self are blurred, indistinct and indeterminate because human nature is social through and through, implying that we, as social beings, are profoundly interdependent.

*Are humans perfectible?*
Some have insisted that appropriate social policies can remove the flaws and defects from human nature. If the latter is a social construct, human nature is as good or bad as the society which shapes it. This may mean that if we can design and engineer the perfect society we can also design and engineer the perfect person. Others believe that such utopianism is dangerous, for example witness the attempts at widespread social engineering in Nazi Germany or Stalinist Russia. Conservatives such as Edmund Burke (1729–97) have argued that human nature is inherently imperfect and that society has developed in

such a way that the negative effects of these imperfections are minimised (Burke, 1968). Social reform should therefore be tentative at best, otherwise the balance of society could be upset and the imperfections of human beings could emerge in full force.

*Is human nature universal?*
Constructivists believe that because human nature is malleable we cannot talk about it in the singular: rather, there are as many potential human *natures* as there are potential social environments. Therefore, human nature is always relative to the society within which it is formed. However, critics argue that if there is no such thing as a *universal* human nature, that is, something which is constant across *all* societies, there is little sense in talking about human nature in the first place. A related matter concerns the extent to which human nature can be said to be gendered and racialised. Can it be said that men and women have different natures? Do different 'races' have different natures? Or are any such suggestions playing on dangerous territory, potentially leading us down the road towards bigotry and dogmatism?

*Are humans self-interested or altruistic?*
This is one of the perennial questions of Social Policy and one that has revived in recent years (Goodin, 1988: 113–18). Social democrats and socialists have traditionally thought that humans are either naturally altruistic or else have the capacity to become so once a socially just environment is in place (Page, 1996). The classic argument in this respect belongs to Titmuss (1970) and his finding that a blood donation service which is based on altruistic gift giving is both more reliable and welfare enhancing than one which is based on monetary exchange. Yet the radical Right tend to view humans as essentially self-interested (Smith, 1970; cf. Field, 1995). This is often the basis of their support for laissez-faire market economics (so that the invisible hand can coordinate individual acts of self-interest into a state of affairs that is in the best interests of all) and/or moral conservatism (so that there are ethical constraints on our non-market actions). Of course, constructivism suggests that humans are not *essentially* one thing or another, as there is no essence underlying the layers of the self that are deposited by social processes.

Yet it is a compromise between the above positions for which I suspect many people would opt. Human nature is undoubtedly a social construction to a large extent, yet there must be a pre-social core that enables us to speak of human nature in the first place. This core might then be said to contain both self-interested and altruistic characteristics, either or both of which may be activated by the social environment we have assembled according to our notions of well-being. In a mundane sense this implies that what prevails is either an 'enlightened self-interest' or a 'qualified (reciprocal) altruism', with most humans occupying the middle ground of the selfish–altruistic spectrum. In a more profound sense, it means that human nature is as much an effect as it

is a cause of social policies. The fact that this conclusion has complex philosophical and practical implications is precisely why the above question can be
said to be perennial.

*Should we talk about* human *nature at all?*
Why draw the line at humanity? If both humans and non-humans are conscious and sentient, should we not rather be discussing *animal* nature to
include both categories? Even elements of those qualities traditionally attributed to humans alone – such as rationality and language – can be detected in
many non-human species; as such, thinking about sentient nature in human
terms is a very anthropocentric thing to do (see section 4.10.2 and the
discussion of ecological citizenship, and Chapter 10).

## 5.4.2 Needs

We can illustrate some of these debates at greater length by returning again to
the subject of needs (Bradshaw, 1972; Goodin, 1988: 27–50; Ware and
Goodin, 1990). As indicated in Chapter 1, Social Policy is concerned, first
and foremost, with *basic* needs, whose lack of fulfilment means that human life
can neither flourish nor perhaps even survive. However, Social Policy may also
take an interest in the means by which individuals can fulfil their *non-basic*
needs. Social Policy is additionally concerned with needs which are social in
nature. The problem, of course, is in deciding where the dividing line between
basic/non-basic and social/non-social actually resides.

How can we try to determine which needs are basic and social? One answer
to this question is that we should try to do so objectively. For instance, we
might take a scientific approach and base our determinations on the fundamental material resources that a person requires simply in order to live. We can
work out the daily intake of food and water that the human body requires and
so define as being in need those who are not achieving this daily intake. Such a
method allows us to determine the level of deprivation that has to be present
for someone to experience absolute poverty. Although there is a satisfying
tangibility to defining needs in this fashion, the problem with it is that we risk
ignoring the less tangible, non-material needs which may also qualify as both
basic and social. If human beings need to belong and be recognised as worthy
in the eyes of their fellow citizens, surely this can be thought of as a basic,
social need as well.

The most famous attempt to relate the material to the non-material was
made by Abraham Maslow (1908–70). Maslow (1954) defined a hierarchy of
needs: at the bottom are the physiological needs whose fulfilment we require
for sheer survival, next are needs related to physical safety and security, next are
needs concerned with our relationships with others (especially ones of emotional and sexual bonding), then the need for self-esteem, while at the top of

the hierarchy is the need for creativity and self-actualisation. Maslow believed that once each level of need has been fulfilled the next level up the hierarchy becomes important. Maslow's theory is ultimately one of social development, with a society's position on the hierarchy denoting its degree of development and progress and, on these grounds, social policy is crucially important in securing the material needs at the 'bottom' and enabling people to secure the non-material ones at the 'top'. The problem now, however, is that, although we have introduced a more sophisticated dimension into our analysis, we risk losing the specificity of a purely scientific approach, for example how can the fulfilment of self-actualisation be scientifically determined?

Are there any other ways of objectively determining basic social needs? We could be brutal and say that, rather than trying to define them in the abstract, basic social needs are whatever the available resources allow us to afford. So, rather than define a society's development according to its fulfilment of needs, we define needs according to a society's development. The problem with this approach is that we lose the universalism which an objective approach seems to offer, that is, we begin to think of basic social needs as constructed and relative to a particular society rather than as essential and universal across all societies. A slightly different approach is to define needs according to the opinions of certain professionals and experts. This implies bringing together a universalist conception of what needs are in themselves, with a resource-driven approach that determines what types of need we can afford to recognise and fulfil.

What becomes very clear, then, is that objectivist and universalist approaches quickly shade into relativist and subjectivist approaches. Might we therefore be better off ignoring objectivity and universalism altogether? Perhaps needs should be defined as 'felt needs' which refers to whatever individuals and groups feel themselves to need. Needs are, after all, states possessed and experienced by *people*, so why should individuals' perception of needs be ignored? One possible reason is that felt needs can be too subjective and so may be misleading and unrealistic, for example I may have a need to play the piano (see Chapter 2) but this does not necessarily generate a responsibility on the part of the state to fund my piano lessons. Concentrating on felt needs, then, may obscure the basic/non-basic and social/non-social distinctions that we wished to draw in the first place by confusing a need with a desire.

An alternative is to focus on 'expressed needs' which are those needs that people express in terms of their political and economic contexts. This avoids the pure subjectivism of felt needs in that expressed needs submit themselves to a political adjudication: the most important expressed needs are those which survive the passage of time and around which some form of social consensus is built. The problem, however, is that such expressed needs are really 'demands' that inevitably relate back to the subjective interests, power and resources of those who make them.

We seem to have reached an impasse. On the one hand, an objectivist and universalist approach risks compressing the concept of needs down to its materialist core; on the other, a subjectivist and relativist approach risks being too vague.

Before we conclude, there are two further distinctions that we ought to mention. The first is that between real and false needs. A radical view of power suggests that disadvantaged, discriminated and exploited people are not allowed to know and/or formulate what their real interests are: they are led to identify their interests with those who oppress them (workers with capitalists, women with men). This implies that people develop, or are made to develop, false needs which do not reflect their real interests. A Marxist, for instance, might say that workers conspire in their own exploitation because, rather than overthrow the system that exploits them, they prefer to buy into the capitalist dream and waste their lives trying to own the goods and consumables that they themselves produced (Marcuse, 1964). Advertising and the entire ethos of commercialism are therefore important sources of instilling false needs in people.

A second distinction is that between discursive and non-discursive needs. This returns us to post-structuralist theory (Hewitt, 1992). Are needs discursive or not? Do they exist independently of, and prior to, the process of discursive construction? Or do needs only exist in so far as they are named and appear within a certain discourse: liberal, Marxist, feminist and so on? Such questions may look esoteric and yet they articulate a point which has been at the heart of this chapter: if politics is both about how *we* make the world and how the world makes *us*, state welfare systems must be of essential importance and we make a serious error, as welfare theorists, if we ignore them. We will explore theories such as post-structuralism and postmodernism at greater length in Chapter 10.

The point just made seems like an appropriate place at which to finish. We make the world and the world makes us. Theoretical debates about political concepts such as the state, power, poverty and exclusion and human nature are therefore useful because they establish a kind of prism which first focuses and then scatters the relevant ideas, offering insight into how we both reflect and construct the world around us. Social policies are a crucial part of that process of reflecting and constructing and welfare theory enables us to appreciate the crucial role that welfare institutions play in this respect.

However, there is one concept that we have not yet touched on systematically or at any length. This is because while it contains substantial political characteristics it also links the political with the sociological – sociology being the other principal foundation of welfare theory. It is this concept which is the key subject of the next chapter, class.

# 6

# Key Sociological Concepts

Class is perhaps the concept within which sociology, politics and Social Policy come together most clearly. All welfare systems have operated within a class structure and if we understand the latter we do much to understand the former. Furthermore, all welfare systems have altered the hierarchies of class to varying extents: both the composition of the classes and the relations between them. Therefore, if we understand those changes, we are able to chart the effects which welfare systems have on their social environments and we can begin to say something about welfare reform. Should a welfare state aim to eliminate the injustices of a class society? To eliminate class society itself? If so, to what extent has the welfare state been successful in this respect and what are the implications of this for the future of the welfare state? These are not questions to be addressed systematically below, but questions for both of us, author and reader, to consider and reconsider long after this book is back on its shelf.

We lead into the discussion of class by sketching the two main theoretical interpretations of society: atomism and holism (section 6.1). Section 6.2 deals at some length with the principal questions that we must ponder. What is a class society? What changes has that society been subject to in recent years? How does the concept of class help to illuminate Social Policy? Yet, important as it is, class is certainly not the final word on society and social relations. Indeed, many insist that, as a sociological concept, its day is almost done. Therefore, section 6.3 looks at a more recent concept whose relationship to class is sometimes conflictual and sometimes more harmonious: social movements. This will act as a prelude to Chapter 8 when we examine the 'new' social divisions of gender, race and ethnicity, dis/ability, age and sexuality.

## 6.1 Society

It would be presumptuous to imagine that society can be adequately debated within the confines of a book, let alone, as here, the fragment of a chapter. However, we need to say something about society as an introduction to the main subject of this chapter.

Basically, society can be defined either holistically or atomistically.[1] The holistic view conceives of society as more than the sum of its parts, as an integral unit which can be analysed separately from the parts that are bound within it. Society is therefore a system which cannot be reduced to its parts. For instance, and as we saw in Chapter 3, Hegel (1977) gave an 'idealistic' interpretation of society, regarding it as the historical manifestation of *Geist*, or absolute spirit. The parts of society, individuals and families, are no more than lower-order 'moments' of a higher unity. In his political writings, Hegel conceived of this unity as the national state but in his more philosophical work the unity signified a 'world mind' that was coming to self-consciousness through successive stages of alienation. In short, the social world is the coming to consciousness of itself, a process of endless becoming through dialectical self-reflection, and individuals are the means through which this consciousness emerges on the stage of history. At the other extreme, the atomistic view conceives of society as nothing more than the sum of its parts. Essentially, this means that individuals are the only social reality and that holistic theories are guilty of treating philosophical abstractions as real. Atomism is therefore a materialistic philosophy that regards individuals as sovereign and social phenomena as immediately visible.

It is, however, rare to find either holists or atomists not making at least some concession to the other. Sociology, therefore, is founded not on a choice between the two philosophies of holism and atomism but on a recognition that society contains both structural and agentive features. Structures cannot be understood without reference to the individuals who, consciously and unconsciously, maintain them; actions and identities are only possible and meaningful in terms of the enduring structures that both enable and constrain them. Society therefore consists of a reciprocal interplay, and social change involves complex feedback mechanisms between the two poles. Society is not a *thing* but an ever-evolving *process* of spatial and temporal relations: a network of networks that contextualises everything that we are and everything that we say and do.

Of course, the problem for sociology is that it is difficult to find the exact balance between structure and agency. Theories often tip into one camp or the other and the most influential sociologists tend to be those who at least establish some theoretical equilibrium (Giddens, 1984). The main problem is that the emphasis on structure intimates that *we* are determined by our environment, whereas the emphasis on agency suggests that our environment is determined *by us*. Neither proposition seems complete without reference to the other, and yet synthesising the two has proved difficult. Marx (1977: 300) seemed to imply that humans *are* their environment when he famously stated that: 'Men make their own history, but they...do not make it under circumstances chosen by themselves, but under circumstances directly encountered, given, and transmitted from the past.' This is a laudable expression of a subtle idea and yet Marx, too, can be accused to leaning into the structural camp (see below).

Most sociologists have directed their attention towards 'class' as a means of thinking through this social equilibrium, for class seems to occupy a midway position between individuals and families on the one hand, and structures and systems on the other.

## 6.2 Class

Class is perhaps *the* key concept of sociology. Indeed, there are very few non-sociologists who claim that developed, Western societies are not stratified in terms of class. The central controversy is not whether we do or do not inhabit class societies but the extent to which individuals and families are or are not socially mobile within the class system. We will address this question, with special reference to Social Policy, in section 6.2.3 after we have reviewed the main theoretical concepts of class and the changes within the class system that have occurred in recent decades. In the final section (6.3) we will examine whether 'social movements' should replace class as the key concept of both sociology and welfare theory.

### 6.2.1 *What is a class society?*

Marx never got round to theorising class at any length, yet the concept undoubtedly lies at the heart of Marxism and socialism. At the beginning of the Communist Manifesto (Marx, 1977) he claims that history must be understood as the history of the class struggle between those who oppress and those who are oppressed. In the feudal era the former were those who owned the land (lords) and the latter were those who did not (serfs). Each historical epoch is characterised by a series of implicit and explicit battles between these two camps and one epoch gives way to another when society is reconstituted and each class mutates into new forms. In the capitalist era the essential conflict is between those who own capital (the bourgeoisie) and those who do not (the proletariat). Marx, writing in the mid-nineteenth century, was certainly aware that there was a wider variety of classes, subclasses and other significant social groups, but he anticipated that the *industrial* conflict between bourgeoisie and proletariat was becoming the main driving force of *social* conflict.

In Marxism, class is both a sociological concept that enables us to describe and explain the stratifications and inequalities of capitalist society (Engels, 1969) and also a political concept that drives society towards first socialist and then communist forms of organisation. The grave diggers, not only of capitalism but all class struggle, would be the proletariat. Gradually immiserated and made destitute by the need of capitalists to monopolise the increasing wealth of society through profits and exploitation, members of the proletariat would come to recognise (a) their common condition, (b) the causes of that condition, and (c) their power to change the socioeconomic order through revolutionary action. Therefore, Marxists theorise class as bearing both objective and subjective components. Class is an objective phenomenon in that we all belong to a class whether or not we recognise ourselves as such. But class also has its subjective dimension because people can be mistaken about their objective class positions, for example a worker who believes that capitalism is in the best interests of the working class is guilty of false consciousness. So, in order to overthrow the system that oppressed them, the proletariat needed to develop a class consciousness through both ideological and practical emancipation (a combination known as 'praxis'). The eventual victory of the working class would also be a victory for *all* humanity, since it would place capital under common ownership and so eliminate the basis of all class oppression. For Marx, then, a class society is any society based on the unequal ownership of productive property and a classless society therefore requires the establishment of common ownership through socialism (the state control of capital) and then communism (where the state withers away because it is no longer needed).

One of the problems with this analysis is that it effects an uneasy balance between deterministic and non-deterministic interpretations of historical progress – with Marx swinging from one to the other and back again throughout his intellectual career. Is historical progress from feudalism to capitalism to socialism to communism inevitable or not? If it is, why should any one individual organise for the revolution when the revolution is coming anyway? If it is not, again, why should any one individual organise when it seems more realistic to create just and humane forms of capitalism, for example through a welfare state? In short, the problem with Marxism is the same problem at the heart of all sociological and political theories (Bourdieu, 1977; Giddens, 1984): how do we adequately incorporate both social structural determinants and the non-determinisms of human agency? If we emphasise the former, we risk neglecting the latter and vice versa.

Just as he opposed Marx's theory of the state (see the previous chapter), so Weber (1978) also proffered an alternative account of class. He argued that the economic dimension of production and ownership was only one aspect of the inequalities in social power. In addition to class (the economic), 'status' (the social) and 'party' (the political) are also important elements of stratification. As far as class is concerned, Weber agreed that a major influence at work was the ownership of property and that each person's class position coincides with their position in the social hierarchy. However, he did not believe that the social and the political could be reduced to the economic, or that class was simply about property. Instead, class position is also about the market capacities that we do or do not possess, that is, the skills and education each of us has attained. Therefore, our class position can alter even when our ownership of property remains the same. Marx is also accused of neglecting the importance to class of consumption and lifestyle (see below) and of homogenising the concept. Unlike Marx, Weber believes that the intermediate classes that lie between and among the bourgeoisie and proletariat are also significant and he draws attention to important divisions and distinctions within each class itself. For Weber, classes are less historically and politically important than Marx believed, being only one of a number of sources of social identity and interaction.

As such, Weber claims that social status is also crucial. What we consume and how we live are related, but not reducible, to our economic position, meaning that an individual's self-image and standing in the eyes of others are also an essential source of their identity and communal role. Status is, then, as important as class in shaping a person's 'life chances'. Finally, Weber also treated political power as an important form of stratification that could not be reduced to economic class. For instance, when Centre-Left parties form a government their members are thereby able to wield power over those who may own more economic resources. In Weberian terms, state welfare could be interpreted as one such form of power.

Therefore, Weber did not talk of a class society, as such, but of modern societies being stratified along a number of dimensions of which class was just one. The advantage of this analysis is that it chimes more harmoniously than Marx's theory with the contemporary experience of Western nations. The emphasis on status and consumption, in particular, offers a multifaceted reading of social developments that treats them at face value and does not subject them to an elitist opinion whereby consumerist values are interpreted as nothing more than false consciousness. However, Weber is also something of a pessimist who regarded the stifling bureaucratisation of modern society as irreversible. In recognising the pluralism of class divisions, status groups and political alignments, he abandons any notion of a social dynamic that can drive progress and emancipation. This combination led Weber to support nationalist forms of charismatic power which, taken to extremes that would have horrified him, lead to demagogues such as Hitler.

The theories of class that emerged throughout the twentieth century are little more than footnotes to Marx and Weber. A rapprochement between Marxists and Weberians was to emerge gradually although not a complete synthesis (for this is impossible to imagine). Starting from within the Marxist camp, Wright (1985) has arguably come closest to doing so by looking not only at the ownership of productive property but also at the importance of 'skills assets' and 'organisational assets'. This allows him to theorise those 'contradictory class positions' consisting of individuals who are neither exploiters nor exploited. This generates a schema comprising 12 class locations, most of which have contradictory characteristics, that begins to resemble the famous occupational scale developed by Goldthorpe et al. (1980).

Used widely throughout sociology, Goldthorpe et al.'s hierarchy is as follows:

1.  Professionals, managers and supervisors in large enterprises (higher service class)
2.  Semi-professionals, managers and supervisors in small enterprises (lower service class)
3.  White-collar workers
4.  Farmers, small employers and self-employed workers (petty bourgeoisie)
5.  Low-level technicians, supervisors and skilled workers
6.  Semi-skilled and unskilled manual workers
7.  Agricultural workers.

However, an even more famous and simpler schematic is that used by the advertising industry and, inevitably, by politicians, opinion-formers and journalists:

A   Upper middle class
B   Middle class
C1  Lower middle class
C2  Skilled working class
D   Semi-skilled working class
E   Unskilled.

From a Weberian perspective these classifications may still neglect the differences of life chances that can be found *within* each strata, as well as the similarities that can be found *between* strata; from a Marxist perspective they can be criticised as conveniently ignoring the continued dominance of the capitalist and land-owning classes who can be thought to sit above the upper middle class, or higher service class. Nevertheless, it is on the basis of such schematics that research into recent changes to the class system have been conducted.

## 6.2.2 Changes within the class system

The pyramidal structure of class – with the upper, middle and working classes occupying the successively descending layers of the pyramid – has long been superseded, largely due to changes in the nature of work. Previously, it was typical to define the working class as manual employees, the middle class as small employers, managers and non-manual employees, and the upper class as large shareholders and employers. However, the decline and extinction of many manufacturing industries and the concomitant rise of the service industries have effected changes to this traditional picture. Commentators disagree, however, as to what the new picture actually resembles.

It may well be that, with the shift from manual (blue-collar) to non-manual (white-collar) work, the middle class has expanded and the working class has shrunk so that the pyramid's midriff has fattened out into the oval shape of a rugby ball. This interpretation plays particularly well with politicians as it is easier to appeal to the political Centre ground if 'we are all middle class now'. The most persuasive evidence for this kind of change lies in the fact that, whereas in 1911 and 1951 manual jobs accounted, respectively, for 74 per cent and 64 per cent of all jobs, by 1991 the figure had dropped to 37 per cent; by contrast, the numbers of clerical, professional and managerial jobs multiplied by a factor of four over the same 80-year period (Gallie, 2000: 287–9).

Consequently, many have characterised this 'middle-class society' as containing two key features. First, the 'embourgeoisement' of the working class, where workers adopt the values, habits and aspirations of the traditional bourgeoisie, a thesis that Goldthorpe et al. (1969) proved to be a gross overstatement of demonstrable trends and one which is now rarely advanced (cf. Gorz, 1982). The second, more enduring, thesis concerns the disaggregation of the working class (decline in trade union membership, increasing individualism) leading to a disalignment in voting behaviour: in short, Centre-Left parties can no longer depend on working-class support alone, as shown by the defection of the C2s (skilled workers) to the Conservatives in the 1980s. The evidence for at least some degree of class disalignment seems to be strong but has been qualified by those who insist that class is still the determining factor in voting behaviour by an overwhelming margin (Heath, 1987).

However, and as we shall see below, the rugby ball interpretation may be an oversimplification of the available evidence by confusing changes to the industrial structure with changes to the class structure. Therefore, it may be wiser to regard the boundaries between the working and middle classes to have blurred, with some leakage from the former to the latter, but not on the scale discussed by Pakulski and Waters (1996; cf. Meiksins-Wood, 1985). Perhaps we have not experienced the death of class so much as the growth of the 'white-collar working class'.

It is also worth mentioning gender in this context. The manufacturing jobs that have disappeared were predominantly those belonging to men, whereas the non-manual service jobs that have replaced them are usually taken by women – partly explaining the significant rise in women's participation in the labour market. Therefore, rather than the shift to non-manual service work signalling the death of the working class, it may merely indicate the feminisation both of the labour market and the working class, where women's class position can no longer be read off the class position of their breadwinning husbands.

Yet the principal evidence for the continuing salience of class emerges from comparisons of class origins and destinations (cf. Dean with Melrose, 1999). Gordon Marshall (1997) shows that across all comparable nations the pattern of social mobility remained remarkably similar throughout the twentieth century. The class structure may have evolved away from the pyramidal shape but the degree of openness has stayed more or less constant. The multiplication in the numbers of clerical, professional and managerial jobs may have opened up more 'room at the top' but it is the children of parents who already hold privileged class locations that have grown up to work in them. The *opportunities* for upward mobility have enlarged but the *distribution* of those opportunities across the classes has remained pretty much the same. For instance, those children coming from the salariat (the middle classes) are five to six times more likely to achieve salariat jobs than are their peers in working-class homes. Heath and Payne (2000) broadly concur, demonstrating that social mobility has increased in absolute terms but only slightly in relative terms.

So, we are left with two competing interpretations of how the class system has changed. For those such as Clark and Lipset (2000), social stratification can no longer be equated with class stratification: class identity has fragmented into so many shards that a class analysis no longer applies. This kind of reading emphasises the importance of lifestyle, consumption and status. However, those such as Scase (1992) and Edgell (1993) insist that this only captures the social surface, underlying which are the kind of structural inequalities that always accompany the capitalist mode of production. As we shall now see, the future direction of social policy alters depending on which of these interpretations we adopt.

### 6.2.3 *Class and social policy*

There are basically four ways of theorising the relationship between class and social policy: pluralist, elitist, functionalist and conflictualist.[2]

Following on from our discussion of it in the last chapter, pluralist theory interprets the welfare state as a compromise between classes, an accommodation or alliance between competing class interests negotiated within a liberal democratic framework. Ideally, each class would prefer to see a distribution of social resources which is heavily in its favour but knows that this would be resisted by the other classes. Modern social policies, therefore, represent a necessary retreat from each class's ideal and a settlement with which each class can live.

T. H. Marshall, as hinted at in Chapter 4, offers a version of pluralist theory (Marshall and Bottomore, 1992). The welfare state, he argues, is partly a product of class abasement as differing economic interests reconcile themselves to a form of welfare capitalism; it is also a cause of future class abatement with people recognising themselves as citizens who possess equality of status, rather than as class actors. In a meritocratic society of social rights and entitlements, class distinctions would not fade away altogether but they would become less significant to the organisation of the polity and economy. We shall return to this notion of meritocracy below.

According to elitist theory, a class is thought of as an interest group which mobilises itself in competition with other groups for state power. Here, state welfare is regarded less as a compromise between classes and more as a victory for one form of class interest over others. This may either involve a winner-takes-all view of power or one that makes some concessions to the pluralist case – as noted in the last chapter, a compromise between pluralists and elitists is possible. So, elitist theory focuses not on the actions of classes but on the political/economic structures within which classes are trying to act.

The specific implications of elitist theory alter, however, depending on who is taken to be victorious. If it is the working class that has gained a privileged access to the state, modern social policies could be interpreted as the gradual reorganisation of social wealth and institutional practices in favour of the most disadvantaged and least empowered. This would correspond to aspects of the conflictualist theory (see below). But, if it is the middle and/or upper classes that are able to define the terms of collective action, social policies could be read as a masquerade for the perpetuation of class oppression and social inequality. This would correspond to aspects of functionalist theory.

Functionalist theory states that social policies must be interpreted as functions of modern socioeconomic organisation. This means that, in order to understand what welfare services do, we must understand what role they play within a bigger picture. A conservative such as Parsons (1961), for instance, argues that the function of schools is to instil in their pupils the values and capacities that they will require as working adults. The education system inserts individuals into the roles on which society is structured and so has to be explained in terms of the wider social division of labour. Through formal education we are socialised into the national culture and integrated into a system of norms and rules. The problem with this reading is that it potentially overlooks the inconsistencies and self-contradictions of the education system, for example the way in which it foments rebellion and social conflict (or is rebellion, too, functionally necessary for society?). Functionalism can only offer neat explanations of social phenomena by homogenising the objects of its analysis. Marxists have also developed a version of functionalist theory but since we review this in section 7.4.1, when discussing welfare ideologies, we shall detour around it here.

Essentially, functionalism regards state welfare as that which helps to secure the integrity and cohesiveness of the social order. Conservatives welcome this as a means by which class interests are reconciled for the common good; Marxists condemn it a means by which the working class is seduced into the comfortable cages of welfare capitalism.

Finally, the conflictualist theory focuses on the struggle for empowerment and interprets the welfare state as a partial victory and a partial defeat for the working class. We will outline some of the principal ideas in section 7.4.2. Here, it is worth mentioning the 'power resources model' of Korpi (1983) in this context. The power resources model identifies the political sphere as possessing some autonomy from the economic sphere: the character of political power does not simply reproduce that of economic power. The former is therefore gained through the mobilisation of collective interests, a mobilisation that has historically favoured the working class. Initially, modern social policies were used to 'demobilise' and fragment the working class but, over time, came to be ideologically appropriated by the labour movement and Centre-Left governments, and made to serve the interests of the poor and exploited. State welfare provision is both a testament to the organised working class and the consolidation of the power of labour against that of capital and the free market.

The power resources model is an appealing picture that reminds us of the radical potential of social democracy to reorder capitalist society. However, it is mainly applicable to those countries where the Centre-Left has been in government for extended periods of time, namely Scandinavia. It may also overestimate the political determination and influence of the working class. What if the working class is not aware of its best interests? And what if, as Przeworski (1985) observes, state action is based on a middle ground coalition of middle-class interests and the interests of the relatively affluent working class? This would imply that state welfare has little radical potential after all. Esping-Andersen (1990; cf. Baldwin, 1990) warns that focusing on class mobilisation is too simplistic and that it is necessary to look at structures of class coalitions and how these alter from country to country. This forms the basis of Esping-Andersen's famous threefold distinction between liberal (UK, USA), conservative (Germany, Austria) and social democratic (Sweden, Denmark) welfare regimes, as well as his important observation that welfare retrenchment is most likely to occur in those countries with the *least* generous welfare states, as it is here that the middle classes will have been only marginally integrated into the welfare state settlement and so will have little to defend when radical Right parties gain power.

Before we can appreciate the potential future implications of pluralism and so on for welfare reform, we need to understand what happens when we draw in some empirical evidence regarding class and social policy. Let us touch on the UK education and health systems.

For some, it is clear that social background is the determining influence on educational success or failure and there is little that even an egalitarian education system can do in an environment of entrenched social inequality (Bourdieu and Passeron, 1977). For others, it is clear that a well-functioning system of education can help to correct any imbalances in the social environment by providing an equality of opportunity where pupils ultimately succeed or fail based on their own efforts and commitments (see Halsey et al., 1997). Finally, there are those who believe that educational inequalities reflect the natural inequalities of intelligence which are written into our genes (Herrnstein and Murray, 1994).

What is clear is that there are considerable variations in the educational experiences of different socioeconomic groups. Evidence collected over 50 years and across a number of countries suggests that this is the case and, furthermore, the picture has remained fairly static across time (Marshall, 1997). For instance, in the early 1960s, 33 per cent of the children of professional fathers possessed a degree and only 7 per cent had no qualification at all; by contrast, only 1 per cent of children with semi-skilled/unskilled fathers had a degree, with 65 per cent having no qualification whatsoever. By the late 1990s, 66 per cent of the children of professional fathers possessed a degree and only 2 per cent had no qualification at all; by contrast, only 1 per cent of children with semi-skilled/unskilled fathers had a degree with 56 per cent having no qualification whatsoever (Smith, 2000). By and large, qualifications are more prevalent now than they were 40 years ago (more 'room at the top') but relative inequalities have remained remarkably stable, for example it is children from wealthier households who have gained disproportionately from the expansion of higher education.

The possible reasons for this inequality are many. Those on the Left cite factors such as inequalities in both economic resources (books, computers) and cultural capital (articulateness, hegemonic confidence), the fact that anxiety and insecurity within poorer households transmits itself to children, the geographical segregation of the classes (with the housing market effectively excluding poorer children from the best schools), the lower expectations of poorer children, and the division between academic and vocational qualifications. Those on the Right point to things such as the relative powerless of parents as opposed to teachers and liberal educationalists, the misguided egalitarianism of state-run or state-directed education, and the naturalness of such inequalities (the poor are not uneducated and therefore stupid because they are in a lower class, they are in a lower class because they are stupid).

The prescriptions which follow on from these competing interpretations are therefore at odds. The Left focuses on school structures, collective effort and *social* context. This is to prescribe an egalitarian policy where greater resources are directed towards the poorest, albeit within a universalist system, and where schools are regarded as social institutions with redistributive responsibilities. Since the 1960s, at least, this has implied support for comprehensive and non-selective education, with any failures of comprehensive education being attributed to the persistence of fee-paying schools in the private sector, de facto 'secondary moderns' in the public sector, and the cumulative influence of housing and education policies that favour the well off. The Right focuses on educational standards, personal responsibility and *family* context. This view prescribes a private system of education where parents are allowed a free choice of school, perhaps being empowered with a voucher scheme, and where schools have a responsibility to maximise the differing potentials of their pupils with little concern for the effects on social equality. The Right has therefore resisted comprehensive education, and the decline in teaching standards and respect for authority that it accuses such schools of embodying, and liberal family policies that have led to the decline of the nuclear family, with children from one-parent households being particularly disadvantaged.

The debate about class and health is not dissimilar to that about class and education. Townsend et al. (1988) and Wilkinson (1996) show that health inequalities basically mirror the pattern of class inequalities, with mortality rates being especially illustrative. In 1910 the mortality rate for working-age men was twice as high in the poorest social class than in the wealthiest; by 1991 it was *three* times higher. Overall, mortality rates have improved but they have improved for the richest classes much more than for the poorest, especially since the Second World War, and similar findings have been found for morbidity rates.

Again, however, commentators disagree about how these figures are to be interpreted. For the Left, class position determines health. A low income means a poor diet, adverse housing conditions and physical environment, debt and stress (and therefore a greater tendency to smoke and drink); a lack of skills, education and employment prospects increases the risk of depression, illness and suicide. However, for the Right, it is health which determines class position. It is a lack of morals rather than a lack of money which inspires the poorest to lead unhealthy lives: it is hypocritical to complain of a low income at the same time as wasting what money you have on booze and fags (not to mention gambling and drugs). Again, therefore, the social policy prescriptions diverge considerably. The Left favours egalitarian policies that counterbalance the inequalities of social class; the Right favours an emphasis on personal freedom and responsibility, one that rejects the state provision and finance of health care.

The dilemma for the Left is that, within a health system, one form of equality can contradict other forms. For instance, should equality imply provision on the basis of need or should those with lower incomes go to the front of the queue (see Chapter 2 and the discussion of the hungry pie eaters)? The former approach might end up favouring those with the time, knowledge and authority to use health services effectively. Le Grand's (1982; cf. Goodin and Le Grand, 1987) classic study concluded that the NHS is of greatest benefit to the middle classes – explaining the NHS's popularity and its relative immunity from right-wing cuts. Yet the latter approach might only stigmatise the least well off and lead us partly down a privatised road where the affluent are required to pay for all or most health services while safety net health care is reserved for the poor.

Whatever the details, it seems clear that there are basically four ways of relating class to the future reform of social policy, two which can be quickly dismissed. First, the conjecture that we now live in a classless society contradicts the wealth of evidence that is at hand, so that, one way or another, we have to accept that class stratification is a social fact. Second, there is the argument that class inequality is merely genetic inequality writ large. According to Herrnstein and Murray (1994), the human race can be catalogued into the genetically superior and inferior, with various strata running in between. Class is nothing more than the social manifestation of these natural inequalities, a veil beyond which egalitarians and sociologists perversely refuse to peer. This, however, is a spurious argument on several counts. For instance, if the poor are poor because they are genetically inferior to the rich, this would imply that ethnic minorities are genetically inferior because of their greater vulnerability to poverty. In short, the argument crosses the border into racism and invokes the Nazi ideology of Aryans and non-Aryans. Furthermore, there is no scientific evidence for the thesis, for example differences in educational attainment can easily be attributed to well-documented environmental factors.

However, there is another version of the classless thesis which is harder to dismiss. This involves the proposal not that classes have vanished but that it is the individual's effort which determines their class position (Saunders, 1996). Those who work hard will prosper, those who choose not to apply themselves will not prosper. Society is now so open that our class origins no longer determine our class destinations, meaning that social mobility is more important than social stratification. Because of the educational and employment opportunities that exist, because most people are less concerned with class than they used to be and because of greater individualism, we now effectively live in a meritocracy. A meritocratic society is not an egalitarian one but one within which inequalities derive from individual efforts of will and are therefore just. Such arguments are popular with politicians fearful of upsetting affluent voters who believe that they deserve their affluence and have no intention of voting for anyone who insists that things are not so simple. Often, it is a one-class or middle-class society (rather than a classless society) which we are held to live within: as talents and abilities come to matter more than social background so the great mass of people squeeze into the social middle.

This idea of a middle-class meritocracy draws on pluralist and conflictualist theories. According to pluralism, meritocracy is a product of class rapprochement and a mutual desire to end the class war; according to conflictualism it is an effect of increased working-class power and the overcoming of socio-structural disadvantages. The hypothesis, however, bumps up against the evidence that we reviewed in the last section, for example the continuing close link between class origins and destinations. Yet is a meritocracy the kind of society for which we *should* strive through appropriate social policies?

T. H. Marshall thought so, believing that the welfare state was a crucial step on the road towards a meritocracy; more recently, the Right have argued that only a free market and the dismantling of state welfare can generate a meritocracy. Whatever the ideological starting point, however, there is a serious problem with such arguments. Even if we assumed that everyone was equally talented, a meritocracy would still contain social inequalities, for example some people are generally luckier than others and some may choose to underuse their talents, for whatever reason. Inequalities, however, have a habit of ossifying into rigid intergenerational structures, as those who prosper are able to offer a multitude of advantages to their offspring: in other words, a meritocracy would soon revert back into a class system, even if it contained more open forms of social mobility than we experience at present. How could this be prevented from happening? Either we would have to be constantly intervening in this meritocratic society, eliminating any hints of class as soon as they appeared (but how can this be done without also eliminating all social inequalities as well?), or we would have to accept a compromise between merit and class determination, where we acknowledge that social policies will only ever be partly successful in breaking down class barriers.

Of course, we could also reject the whole ideology of meritocracy as too individualistic and blind to the inherent class nature of capitalism. Here, we draw on elitist and functionalist theories of class power, so that radical forms of social policy are needed if class inequalities are ever to be completely overturned. As we shall see in the next chapter, both Marxists and democratic socialists envisage that only the common ownership of productive resources can create a truly classless and egalitarian society. For democratic socialists, state welfare provision takes us the first few necessary steps down that road, while Marxists believe that this may be wishful thinking and that only engagement with capitalism at the workplace and within civil society can be effective in the long term. The problem here is that these are ambitious aims that were barely achievable during the high watermark of welfare capitalism (1945–73) and now seem farther away than ever.

On the whole, then, the subject of Social Policy has reached an impasse as far as class is concerned. Two options for the future seem to stretch before us. First, we may prefer the 'compromise' option whereby we loosen up the class structure and effect some degree of social mobility, but accept that we can do little more. This is certainly a feasible option, yet one that is also modest and uninspiring since the implicit admission at work here is that classes, like the poor, are always with us. Second, we may prefer the 'radical' option where social policies are geared towards a long-term shift in the ownership of productive property. This approach, however, seems arduous, unrewarding in the short term and so undesired by a large majority of people. Could there be other alternatives after all?

## 6.3 Social Movements

Perhaps the alternative is to widen our analysis beyond that of class. Some sociologists have argued that society is best understood as a complex of social movements. For some, this implies that society consists of social movements rather than classes; for others, a class is one of many forms of social movement that exist.

Defining a social movement is difficult (Eder, 1993; Tarrow, 1994; Della Porta and Diani, 1999) but seems to refer to a *process of collective action*, where the emphasis on *process* contrasts dynamically with the sclerosis into which class analysis often falls. This means that as well as encompassing grand social phenomena such as classes, social movement theories can also focus on the specificities of crowds, mobs, gangs and other smaller scale associations. A more ambitious definition might state that:

> A social movement can be a formal, semi-formal or informal network of interrelated actors who share similar values, identities and objectives in a given sociohistorical context.

In these terms, interest in social movements predates the Second World War when theories of mass society became influential. However, social movement theories really only gathered speed in the 1960s when a host of non-class-specific movements arose to challenge both old forms of injustice and new forms of politics. The civil rights/liberties movement, the women's movement, the students' movement, the gay and lesbian movement, the Green movement, the peace/anti-war movement and the anti-nuclear movement all signalled an evolution in political consciousness and organisation that did not fit neatly into the sociological categories of the time. More recently, the anti-racist, anti-Communist, nationalist, religious and indigenous peoples' movements have confirmed such developments.

Social movements are often taken to be concerned with:

- Particular issues that are conceptually broadened out into universalistic values and concerns
- Civil society, culture and lifestyle rather than state institutions and political power
- Openness and flexibility rather than with forming rule-governed hierarchies.

So whereas the 'party' and the 'union' were the archetypes of the early twentieth century, by the end of the century these were considered too bureaucratic and implicated with the unjust use of power to be vehicles of progressive change. Some theorists believe that it is society itself which has altered: classes used to be the foundations of society but now it is social movements. This is a rather crude interpretation that slips back into the classlessness thesis that we have already questioned. For the most part, theorists believe that it is *sociology* which has changed rather than the social realities with which the subject deals. This means that social movements have always existed even if the sociological recognition of their significance came late in the day. It could then be claimed that classes are old social movements that have been, to whatever degree, superseded by the 'new social movements' listed above. Alternatively, it might be that classes are in a constant process of evolution, having new as well as old forms, and that the so-called new social movements have their roots deep in industrial society. By this time, of course, we are combining class analysis with social movement theory, a combination that we shall explore below.

There are two main ways of theorising social movements: resource mobilisation theory (RMT) and new social movement theory (NSMT).

RMT originated within American academia and leans towards liberal individualism (Zald and McCarthy, 1987, 1988). Its premise is that collective behaviour must be explained in terms of the motivations and decisions of individual actors. If a coherent link between the two can be established, collective action can be thought of as rational, if not, it must be regarded as dysfunctional in some way. RMT is therefore concerned with 'how' questions: how do leaders mobilise participants and how are resources (money, media attention, public support) mobilised? In fact, it shares many assumptions with the RCT that we outlined in Chapter 1 and can therefore be criticised on many of the same grounds, especially for an emphasis on individualistic self-interest which tended to suggest that collective action was, indeed, dysfunctional. It was partly in order to avoid such criticisms that RMT expanded in the 1980s, becoming more interested in the cultural environments of collective action; an interesting development but one which presumably undercuts the original intentions of RMT.

Others have therefore insisted that an alternative approach is required. NSMT originated on the European continent and relates social movements to wider sociohistorical developments. Whereas the labour movement had tried to effect change through the state and electoral politics, and had been eventually coopted into the institutions of bureaucratic capitalism, the new social movements were concerned more with the values to be found within civil society. For Touraine (1981) it is this coopting of the working class which partly explains the transition he observed to a post-industrial, knowledge-based society (see Chapter 9). This signifies that the key struggle no longer takes place between capitalist and proletariat over the means of production but between technocrats and new social movements over the conditions of representation and self-determination. The new social movements are therefore drawn from a multiplicity of class positions. The 'new middle class' is especially significant, consisting of relatively affluent and educated professionals, often working within the public sector, in addition to a range of actors concerned about gender, ethnicity, dis/ability and sexuality. The new social movements are therefore defined by a cultural or 'identity' politics that constructs new meanings and forms of identification with which to challenge dominant power relations. For Melucci (1989), theirs is not a direct struggle but a set of practices within everyday life whereby 'submerged networks' resist the dominant cultural signs and open up new public spaces.

How might social movements be related back to class (Maheu, 1995)? Of course, there are those who believe that this is a theoretical enterprise that should not be undertaken. For some, social movements either do not exist or else are subjectivist, bourgeois distractions from 'real' politics, for example struggles over economic resources (Meiksins-Wood, 1985; Lavalette and Mooney, 2000); for others, classes have been superseded and a class analysis fails to capture the organising principles of contemporary society (Pakulski and Waters, 1996). Obviously, these interpretations present quite different challenges for Social Policy. If the concept of social movements should be rejected, social policies and welfare reforms can be assessed purely in terms of their effects on the class system; if, however, it is class that should be rejected, Social Policy has to develop a completely new analytical paradigm.

However, might it be more productive to reconcile the two concepts in some way, so that both class analysis *and* social movement theory are taken to capture important aspects of contemporary society? This could mean accepting that society is objectively and demonstrably structured into the kind of class strata that we studied in the last section, but that there is also an additional dimension consisting of social movements that 'drift' in and between these strata, bearing both class-specific and non-class-specific characteristics. For instance, the women's movement has recognised the relevance of class in determining the subjection of women (with women being regularly economically disadvantaged in terms of income, wealth and employment) but also of issues that cannot be explained solely in terms of class (sexual violence, for instance). So there are three possibilities: (1) sometimes class will be more important than social movements, (2) sometimes social movements will be more important than class, and (3) sometimes there will be a 'complex equivalence' between the two. It largely depends on what we are debating and when. The labour movement corresponds to (1), the gay and lesbian movement corresponds more clearly with (2), while the Green movement seems to correspond to (3). Perhaps the key message, however, is that this approach allows room for flexibility and variation across time and space, and avoids the closed dogmas of those who insist that 'it's all about class' or, alternatively, that 'class is dead'.

What happens to Social Policy if we adopt this middle-way position? First, we need to appreciate the extent to which welfare systems are themselves responsible for the rise of new social movements. According to Offe (1987), the latter can be explained as a consequence of rising prosperity, educational opportunities and the growth of the public sector: the successes of welfare capitalism enabled the new social movements to emerge and the failures of welfare capitalism (and, more recently, the threat of the anti-welfare Right) gave them something to struggle against. For Habermas (1987a), new social movements are the main defenders of the 'lifeworld' against the encroachments of the economic sphere of money and the political sphere of power, and so offer welfare capitalism the potential for democratic renewal.

If this is the case, how have the new social movements been influencing welfare systems? On one level they have offered new perspectives on citizenship and citizenship rights and entitlements that defend Marshall's triumvirate of civil, political and social rights, yet also attempt to apply these to new areas of experience and interaction. On another level, many social movement groups have experimented with new forms of welfare provision that potentially offer radical models of welfare reform. Since we shall we exploring the social and welfare critiques relating to gender, ethnicity, dis/ability, age and sexuality in Chapter 8, there is little need here to anticipate this later discussion.

What of the future for Social Policy, if class and social movements are both relevant to that future? Inglehart (1990) believes that the welfare state is a victim of its own success and has made itself redundant by satisfying the basic needs of income, shelter and so on. State welfare is therefore the source of a post-materialist society within which state welfare itself struggles to flourish. This suggests that future social policies should continue to address the materiality of basic needs through the traditional redistributive instruments that are inspired by a class analysis, but that it should also address the non-materiality of needs through the formation of new forms of social interrelationship, that is, those pioneered by the new social movements. As we saw in Chapter 4, for Fraser (1997) Social Policy must be concerned with the redistribution of economic resources between class strata but also with 'recognition', that is, the redistribution of cultural standing, from dominant to non-dominant status groups. Therefore, in addition to its familiar concern with the state-centred policy-making process, the subject must be more sensitive to the ways in which cultural changes within civil society, for example the vocabulary which people choose to relate to each other, are capable of affecting that process.

In short, the future of Social Policy may be both Weberian *and* Marxist. For those who prefer the compromise option, the addition of social movements into the welfare equation may ameliorate the failure of social policies to substantially erode the bases of the class system; for those who prefer the radical option, social movements may offer a means of reformulating the post-capitalist society towards which we should be working. As always with Social Policy, the future is there to be written.

This concludes our review of the key political and sociological concepts with which the subject of Social Policy deals. We are now ready to return to the Left–Right spectrum that Chapters 2–4 began to make visible and understand the main perspectives around which ideological ideas cluster. Chapter 7 reviews four ideologies whose influence on Social Policy and, indeed, on social policies has been considerable. We have visited some of these ideas before, of course, but we are now in a position to complete the ideological map that we tentatively started to explore at the beginning of Chapter 2.

# 7

# Welfare Ideologies

There are many books that deal with ideologies of welfare (for example George and Wilding, 1994; George and Page, 1995). As indicated in the Introduction, this book attempts to tell a somewhat different story about the theoretical aspects of Social Policy; and yet, as was made clear very early on, it is a story that never strays very far away from debates and disagreements inspired by the political ideologies of the modern era. So although only one chapter is devoted to a summary of the main welfare ideologies, the reader should be able to appreciate by now that the following ideas flow across a much wider theoretical landscape than might sometimes appear to be the case. The most obvious omission from this chapter is that of feminism. This is because Chapter 7 really needs to be read as a companion to Chapter 8 where more recent ideas are reviewed, ideas that fall outside the ideological framework adopted here. A discussion of feminism is therefore postponed for the reasons explained in the next chapter itself.

For now, our task is to sketch the following four welfare ideologies: the radical Right (section 7.1), social conservatism (section 7.2), social democracy (section 7.3) and Marxism (section 7.4).

## 7.1 Radical Right

By the 'radical Right' we mean those who combine a commitment to economic liberalism with a commitment to a moral conservatism (cf. Barry, 1987). The former implies a preference for free markets operating with minimal state interference, while the latter implies a preference for family values, traditional authority and a strong work ethic. What unites both wings of the radical Right is a hostility to state welfare as this is thought to weaken the economy and sap the morality of society.

Essentially, the radical Right identify a contradiction in the classic welfare state between what it promised and what it has delivered. The promises consisted of assurances by vote-buying politicians that state welfare could achieve some very ambitious objectives: the maintenance of full employment, high levels of redistributive equality, the fulfilment of basic needs through legally guaranteed entitlements, an ever-expanding public sector, state control of the macro-economy, and corporatist arrangements between workers and management. Yet in setting out to implement these promises, post-war governments gradually undermined the ability of the economy to finance them. By emphasising public spending rather than public savings, crowding out the private sector and taxing people excessively, the welfare state only undermined its own moral and financial conditions. Consequently, these contradictions had to be removed by the radical Right revolution that virtually all Centre-Left parties have come to accept. The emphasis in social policy is now on employment levels consistent with low inflation, supply-side reforms, incentive-preserving social inequalities, desert and responsibilities rather than needs and rights, an entrepreneurial and risk-taking private sector, deregulation and privatisation, labour market flexibility, the rights of managers and shareholders, and consumer sovereignty.

The specific criticisms that the radical Right makes of the welfare state can be summarised under the following six points (cf. Pierson, 1998). First, a welfare state is held to undermine the disciplines of the market by reducing the rewards for success and lightening the burdens of failure. Capital has little incentive to invest due to high levels of taxation and regulation, and people have little incentive to work hard because, if they do, they will themselves be taxed heavily or, if they do not, they will receive generous benefits from the state anyway. The welfare state therefore undermines competition, between individuals and between companies, and encourages people to be lazy, to expect the state to do everything for them. An ethos of self-help and personal and civic responsibility is gradually eroded, leading both to real violence and a 'symbolic' violence as social manners and courtesies vanish. It is from the competitive dynamics of free-market capitalism that we have received the growth rates and ever-rising living standards of the modern world. By subduing such competition the paternalist state merely invites a depressed and stagnant economy of high unemployment and high inflation, an analysis that the radical Right insists was confirmed by the recessions and crises of the 1970s.

Second, the more the public sector is allowed to expand the more the private sector is squeezed out, deprived of the resources that it requires to flourish. This means that entrepreneurialism is undermined and the economy is left with too many non-producers taking wealth out and too few producers left to put wealth in. As noted above, therefore, the welfare state undermines the economic conditions of its own existence, as if perversely sawing away at the very branch on which it is sitting. Some allege that post-war reforms always made it likely that the growth in social expenditure would outstrip the economy's ability to finance such growth (Barnett, 1986). Governments have attempted to generate high levels of growth in an attempt to plug this gap, but this only had the effect of stoking the economy with inflationary pressures, with damaging consequences for employment levels.

Third, the welfare state effectively holds a monopoly on the delivery of welfare services. But whereas monopolies in the marketplace can be challenged, the invulnerability of a state monopoly leads to a distortion of the market, a neglect of consumer choice and widespread inefficiency. Public sector leaders have all the 'voice', while clients have little freedom to 'exit' from the state and purchase other forms of welfare provision. According to public choice theory (Buchanan, 1986), political parties have an interest in expanding the public sector and raising social expenditure, in order to buy the votes of the electorate, while special interest groups form to lobby and consume scarce resources in the name of whatever cause they purport to represent. All this adds up to an overloaded and ailing welfare system where the state is incapable of adequately performing the many tasks that it has given itself.

Fourth, some of this might be forgivable if the welfare state actually achieved the objectives that are set for it, but this is not the case. The defenders of state welfare misidentify the nature and causes of poverty, the nature of which should not be confused with inequality and the causes of which should not be attributed to abstract, structural phenomena (see the discussion of the possible causes of poverty in section 5.3). Instead, we need to focus on the culture of the poor, their beliefs and values, and recognise that what is important in the formation of deprivation is the attitudes and behaviour of poor individuals themselves. The welfare state may reduce levels of income inequality but it also generates a 'dependency culture' where people are effectively encouraged to throw themselves onto the overgenerous and comfortable safety nets on offer (moral hazard). So, not only is there a category of the undeserving poor but the numbers of those belonging to this category increase due to misguided social policies. What we end up with is an underclass: those who exclude themselves from mainstream society and often indulge in semi-criminal lifestyles (Murray, 1984, 1990).

Fifth, at best collectivism and paternalism give rise to a nanny state which insists that it knows what is good for us more than we do ourselves. At worst, the welfare state can lead us towards an autocratic and dictatorial society down a road which, in Hayek's (1944) famous words, is the 'road to serfdom'. Either way, an egalitarian politics of the common good causes the space of individual freedom and self-determination to shrink. Autonomy becomes less and less possible as civil society becomes subsumed within the public sphere, with citizens subject to the dictats of the centralised, top-heavy, autocratic state. By contrast, market reform implies the decentralisation of decision-making and so rolls back the boundaries of the coercive state.

Finally, by being based on an ethic of needs, the welfare state stresses rights and entitlements rather than duties and responsibilities which derive more from an ethic of desert. It embodies a something-for-nothing attitude that pervades society, helping to undermine all forms of moral, cultural and social authority (Mead, 1986). The ethics of community, mutual responsibility and desert are weakened because the welfare state does not ask enough of us: the affluent think that paying their taxes is all that making a social contribution requires, while the poor sit back and wait for their benefit cheque. Collectivism therefore encourages a general dependency where we expect the state to do things for us and we no longer look to the family or the local community as sources of well-being. Consequently, the ties of family and of civic association begin to unravel. People are no longer held to account for the consequences of their actions.

## 7.1.1 *Criticisms*

These arguments have attracted an enormous amount of commentary and criticism (Levitas, 1986; King, 1987; Gamble, 1988; Gilmour, 1992; Miliband, 1994). There are six critiques that are particularly important (see also Chapter 1, and the criticisms of Nozick and Hayek in section 3.5).

First, there is a potential contradiction between the liberal/libertarian and conservative/communitarian wings of radical Right thought. The free markets favoured by liberals are not always conducive to the conservative emphasis on tradition, authority and family. Unrestrained, deregulated markets have a habit of introducing insecurity and instability into society by eclipsing all values and relations that have nothing to do with profit, gain and success (Gray, 1993). By ignoring social outcomes a libertarian economy tends to undermine the very things that enables markets to work in the first place: civility, trust, mutual respect and long-term commitment. For example, because free markets require both workers and investors to be geographically mobile, there is a limit to which this mobility is compatible with the immobilities and stabilities required by family life. Of course, the contradiction is resolvable by opting either for a pure libertarianism or a pure conservatism but this is not what most radical Right theorists have done.

Second, scrapping the welfare state does not eliminate the 'contradiction' between accumulation (economic growth) and legitimation (social expenditure), it merely displaces it. If we slash social expenditure, we *may* secure the conditions of economic prosperity (although there is scant evidence for this) but we also produce another set of social problems deriving from the inequalities that lower social expenditure brings, for example rising crime rates, low wages, unemployment, casualisation and a generalised insecurity affecting all social strata.

Third, rather than unleashing an entrepreneurial ethic that benefits every-one, free-market reforms merely consolidate existing structural inequalities: those that *have* get more, those that *have not* get less. The welfare state's war on poverty is transformed into a war on the poor with individual failings being blamed for continued disadvantage; if the free market is theoretically open to everyone, it stands to reason that those who lose out are the authors of their own fate. So, the radical Right cause a deterioration in the social position of the poorest and then set about blaming the victims of their policies for the resulting social problems.

Fourth, the radical Right assert a simplistic dichotomy between markets and states: the more we have of one the less we can have of the other. But this view can be challenged on a number of grounds. Historically, market capitalism has depended on a large degree of state control and intervention without which free markets could not have developed in the first place (Polanyi, 1944); politically and philosophically, there is the Keynesian point that market capit-alism risks imploding without institutional support: a pure, free-market eco-nomy would collapse very quickly.

Fifth, the radical Right concentrate on certain forms of dependency only – that of welfare clients on the state – and wilfully ignore other forms of depen-dency which may be equally pernicious, if not more so, for example of women on men and employees on employers. Similarly, they concentrate on one form of free-riding – benefit recipients on taxpayers – and ignore other forms, for example men on the unpaid work of women. They therefore identify freedom with 'market freedom' and dependency with 'state dependency', but this captures only a very minor dimension of the way in which each person's various freedoms and dependencies interlink with those of other people.

Finally, despite placing an emphasis on social obligations, the radical Right can be accused of *undermining* an ethic of obligations and duties. If free markets undermine the foundations of trust and reciprocity, if they emphasise self-interest and personal gain above all else, the inhabitants of the free-market environment have few reasons to care about or work with others. If free markets exacerbate inequalities, the ethical and cultural links between winners and losers begin to unravel, leading to a reduction in civility, as well as a growing feeling of suspicion and insecurity.

## 7.2  Conservatism

Conservative thought is often left out of accounts of welfare ideology, as it is very easy to treat conservatism as nothing more than an adjunct to the radical Right. In many respects, however, it is the anonymity and slow adaptability of conservative thought which makes it the most resilient welfare ideology of all (Nisbet, 1986). An important distinction to be made is that between philo-sophical and social conservatism.

## 7.2.1 Philosophical conservatism

Philosophical conservatism derives ultimately from Edmund Burke (1968) and his warning that an overreliance on abstract reason, that is, reasoning that is unaware of its limitations because it tries to divorce itself from its own historic and social contexts, can produce the kind of terrifying destabilisation that Burke witnessed in the aftermath of the French Revolution. More recently, Michael Oakeshott (1901–90) has distinguished between two forms of knowledge: rational knowledge is technical and abstract, whereas concrete knowledge is acquired through experience and practice (Oakeshott, 1962). Let us imagine that I want to learn how to drive a car: rational knowledge is the understanding I gain by reading a book entitled *How To Drive*, while concrete knowledge is the understanding I gain by actually getting behind the wheel and learning by making mistakes. For Oakeshott, the latter experience is obviously more valuable than the former.

According to conservatives, all forms of liberal, socialist and Marxist thought are the equivalent of trying to understand society by abstracting ourselves from lived experience; by contrast, conservatives insist that we can learn how to *do* by attending to the ways in which they are *already done*. Reflecting on practice is less important than the practice itself. History and culture should be thought of as stores of implicit knowledge that have been accumulated over many generations and which should be allowed to guide us. Conservatives, in other words, emphasise the historical and cultural continuity of tradition and derived authority. Institutions should be allowed to evolve organically and slowly, for if we start major reforms without being guided by traditional institutions, the social repercussions can be disastrous. Social change is only ever successful when it emerges out of existing social relations; revolutions and transformations that are imposed from the outside, as it were, lead to dictatorship and/or anarchy.

Conservatism, therefore, is a philosophy of limits and restraint. If human nature is inherently flawed and imperfect, so is human society; consequently, avoiding harm must be our first and overwhelming moral and political priority. Instead of asking the question 'what is the best form of society?', we should ask 'what is the least worst form of society?' Conservatives focus on the fragility and vulnerability of human life: hence Oakeshott's depiction of society as resembling a rudderless ship on a harbourless ocean; if this is the case, the most important thing to do is to avoid rocking the boat. Injustice can be corrected only if we are certain that doing so will not upset the established stability and equilibrium of the social order.

There is an immediate problem with conservatism that we must mention: what exactly is to be conserved? Conservatives treat the past's store of knowledge as if there is a single store, a unified past which all can recognise and to which all can appeal; they therefore emphasise the virtues of continuity only by neglecting the realities of conflict and complexity. If, for instance, different social positions generate different forms of knowledge and understanding (so that the understanding of the poor and the rich are radically dissimilar), which type of knowledge should the conservative favour? In short, conservatives cannot disassociate themselves from the imperatives of abstract reasoning to the extent that they imagine.

The dilemma for conservatives is that, on the one hand, they can appear to be passive, content to drift in whichever direction the historical wind is blowing (Hayek, 1960), and, on the other, they often end up hypocritically favouring privileged interests over and above the interests of the disadvantaged. This criticism is especially relevant when we consider the welfare state. Should conservatives denounce the welfare state or not? Those who have denounced it have tended to side with the radical Right desire to recreate the market conditions of the nineteenth century, that is, before the welfare state disrupted society, but it is not too difficult to see why this contradicts the conservative preference for continuity and avoidance of abstract reason. By contrast, *social* conservatives have welcomed the welfare state and have tended to side with a politics of social democracy with its preference for a mixed economy, social consensus and humane capitalism. This is why conservatism is usually overlooked as a welfare ideology: it is often parasitic on the social ideas that lie on either side of it.

## 7.2.2 *Social conservatism*

Social conservatism's support for state welfare systems has a number of origins. Of particular importance is the fact that conservatives tend to be strong nationalists, as the nation is perhaps the most obvious container for the traditions and social order that they hold dear. And although nationalism can assume many negative and violent faces, it can also be an important haven, a source of identity and solidarity. Disraeli (1804–81) famously described nineteenth-century Britain as two nations and so the notion of 'one-nation conservatism', committed to national unity and class consensus, was born. Post-Disraeli conservatism began to make at least some room for working-class interests, attracting a large degree of working-class votes as a result. Family values have also been crucial, with social conservatives often being the most prominent supporters of state education as a means of supporting families and ensuring that children were being properly raised. Social conservatives have always been aware of the extent to which free markets destabilise and disrupt the social order, a lesson that others on the Right have struggled to relearn (Gray, 1993).

Social conservatism really derives from the experiences of the 1930s and 40s. The Liberal Party had declined in importance and social ideas had gained at least some mainstream respectability. Mass unemployment, followed by the

Churchillian sacrifices of war, convinced many conservatives that the state had a substantial role to play in both avoiding a repetition of the 1930's depression and embodying the common interests of the British people. Harold Macmillan (1894–1986) wrote a well-known book that advocated a 'middle way' between free-market liberalism and centralised socialism, and proposed that only conservatives could oversee this middle way effectively (Macmillan, 1938). As prime minister between 1957 and 1963, Macmillan was to preside over the economic and social environment that he had championed decades earlier: full employment, a mixed economy and universal provision for basic social needs. As free-market ideas took a back seat, social conservatism was the ruling philosophy of the British conservatives for at least 30 years. Thatcherism was to eventually purge the Conservative Party of many social conservatives, although some resisted the ideological onslaught (for example Gilmour, 1992) and elements of social conservatism remain.

To some extent, social conservatism survives and continues to offer a buffer against the version of authoritarian conservatism that is especially prevalent in America and which has allied itself closely to Christian fundamentalism.

## 7.2.3 Criticisms

Economic liberals accuse social conservatives of being as confused as the Left about the nature of a good society (Hayek, 1960). Whereas conservatives emphasise the importance of inherited values, liberals argue that individuals' ability and right to choose for themselves is what drives humanity forward; and for the liberal Right this implies the right of consumers to draw their own package of goods and benefits from the marketplace. Social conservatives, therefore, compound this basic error by supporting the anti-consumerist ethic and institutions of the welfare state. Those who favour the regulation of capitalism, whether they be conservatives or socialists, do not understand how and why the invisible hand improves social and individual well-being over the course of time. The conservative suspicion of market capitalism is therefore as misguided as the socialist one.

The Left are also critical of social conservatism. First, although they can be allies in creating and maintaining welfare services, social conservatives are likely to be more contented than the principle of social justice allows with the levels of poverty and inequality that prevail even under welfare state capitalism. Second, the Left also has problems with conservative nationalism. The Left has always preferred a politics of internationalism where workers from different countries should recognise that their common exploitation overrides all considerations of nationality. By contrast, even social conservatism lends itself to the kinds of patriotic feelings of 'blood and belonging' that can easily descend into political extremism. Conservatism is therefore unsuited to an era of multiculturalism and multiethnic hybridity where avoiding racial conflict requires *action* based on *rational principles* rather than a passive acceptance of the values of a racist history.

Finally, feminism has called into question social conservatism's unthinking acceptance of the meaning of 'family'. Feminists have argued that the traditional family has placed women at a disadvantage, locking them into mothering roles and acting as a shelter for violence and sexism. Conservative support for the traditional family has therefore been repeatedly challenged (Barrett and McIntosh, 1982). By family, conservatives generally mean a heterosexual marriage. But in a society where many forms of family now exist what should conservatives do? If they resist developments such as gay and lesbian marriages, they could be accused of undermining family values themselves; if they welcome such developments, they have to recognise the virtues of individual choice and non-conformity in the face of accepted morality, a recognition that hardly corresponds to conservative values.

## 7.3  Social Democracy

If there is any ideology of the welfare state, it has to be social democracy which can be thought of as a blend of two ideological perspectives: social liberalism and democratic socialism. While being theoretically distinct, these ideologies have, in the real world of economic and social policy-making, established a broad Centre-Left unanimity on the desirability of welfare capitalism.

### 7.3.1  Social liberalism

We have already reviewed some of the most important aspects of social liberalism: egalitarian liberalism (Chapter 2), T. H. Green's theory of the common good (Chapter 3), T. H. Marshall's theory of class and citizenship (Chapters 4 and 6) and Keynesian economics (Chapter 5). Social liberalism's starting point is the freedom of the individual to determine the path of his or her own life. Individual autonomy, however, does not exist in a social vacuum: a market economy is a necessary but not sufficient condition of freedom. Some degree of social equality is therefore justified if the worst characteristics of capitalism are to be avoided and an enabling, redistributive, managerial state is required to bring this about. The state's primary task is to create high levels of employment and ensure that national wealth is distributed fairly. Citizenship therefore implies a strong dimension of social rights and entitlements.

Social liberalism identifies a strong connection between political equality and economic equalisation: whereas social conservatives support welfare services in order to *avoid* social disorder, social liberals support them as a means of *strengthening* liberal democratic society. This important distinction means that whereas the former are looking to ameliorate undesirable levels of inequality, the latter are looking to create desirable levels of social equality. Consequently, social liberals are more likely than conservatives to identify a link between extremes of wealth and poverty and so favour policies that assail privileged interests. It is the needs of the individual that count rather than the needs of history, tradition or established authority. Therefore, social liberals can support the formation of collectivist provision where this is shown to enhance individual liberty.

Despite their defence of social rights and equality, however, social liberals are less concerned than the Left with the alleged injustice of capitalism, the nature of inequality per se and the supposed inequities of class. For instance, Rawls regards neither capitalism nor inequality as inherently unjust: what matters is the type of capitalism and the type of inequality and whether these correspond to the demands of just principles. So, whereas socialists believe in the eventual abolition of class, Rawls is, at best, silent on the subject. During the high watermark of social democracy, social liberals were those most likely to defend the notion of the welfare state as a meritocratic society that requires differential rewards for differential effort (see last chapter). Along with a strong ethic of needs, social liberals favour a strong ethic of desert: social rights are mainly rights *within* the market economy, not rights *against* it; equality means equality of opportunity, not outcome; and although the state has a central role to play, pluralistic forms of welfare provision need to be preserved and encouraged.

What are the main criticisms that have been made of social liberalism? From the radical Right comes the by-now familiar criticism that only a *free-market* liberalism can protect the rights and capacities of individuals, for as soon as the state is introduced into the picture, whether on conservative, socialist or spurious liberal grounds, negative freedom begins to be invaded. Social conservatives allege that the equalities and solidarities which social liberals support cannot survive in an individualistic society as individuals can be blindly self-interested and so create a social fragmentation. Equality and solidarity must emanate from, and in turn nourish, the nation's communal way of life; this necessitates an orientation towards the past and a respect for the accumulated wisdom of past generations that individualistic cultures threaten to forget.

Feminists and anti-racists both allege that social liberalism ignores the specificity of female and minority ethnic lives. Social liberalism offers a level playing field without acknowledging that the rules of the game to be played have been written over many centuries by men and by whites. Resisting the extreme inequalities of the free market is only a start, therefore, and it is necessary to engage in a kind of 'cultural redistribution' that simultaneously aims at the equalisation and the differentiation of social groups. For instance, bigoted assumptions about identities and roles must be challenged within the education system if this is to be more than simply a institution for the passing of exams and preparing for the world of work.

For socialists, because social liberals do not recognise the extent to which individuals' fates are determined by their social environment, they neglect the level of social transformation that is necessary for social justice to prevail. Capitalism can be humanised only up to the point where both profits and the interests of rich elites are not threatened; equality of opportunity is meaningless and ineffective unless accompanied by a substantial equalisation of outcomes. Even social rights are merely formal unless the correct economic conditions are in place, and the state has to be viewed as a countervailing force to the inequities of capitalist markets.

### 7.3.2 Democratic socialism

Democratic socialism passed through three stages in the twentieth century, much of which was spanned by Tony Crosland's (1918–77) life and career. Crosland's early years corresponded to the period during which democratic socialism was rising in influence due to intellectuals such as Tawney (1931), G. D. H. Cole (1920) and Harold Laski (1935), and the actions of European labour movements. Whereas social conservatism and social liberalism sought a middle way between free-market capitalism and state collectivism, democratic socialism's version of the middle way was between capitalism per se and communism. Democratic socialists agreed with those to their Right that the constitutional and electoral procedures of liberal democracy ought to be followed, but they also agreed with those to their Left that a long-term transformation of society was possible and desirable. This vision of a socialist democracy therefore offered an alternative both to a market capitalism that failed to realise social justice and to a communistic command economy that embodied neither democracy nor civic freedom. As 'utopian pragmatists', therefore, democratic socialists were willing to accept the imperfections of the present as a stepping stone to the progress of the future.

As the older ideologies became discredited in the 1930s and 40s, democratic socialism had the chance to put its ideas into operation and so entered its second phase. Through the medium of Centre-Left governments, and in the broad alliance that we are here calling social democracy, democratic socialists began to wield a practical influence on Western societies. It was as a rising politician within the British Labour Party that Crosland (1956) gave what remains one of the most important and influential accounts of democratic socialist thought. Socialism, he argued, contains five basic ideas.

First, it objects to the origins, nature and extent of the inequality produced by capitalism. Capitalism tends to generate large pockets of poverty and deprivation because a market economy based on profit and private ownership requires a constant pool of low wage labour. Second, it is concerned with social justice and social welfare, with the fulfilment of universal basic needs and the particular needs of the disadvantaged and underprivileged. Welfare systems of one form or another are therefore indispensable to a socialist society. Third, it protests against a class society and the class exploitation of non-owners by owners. A classless egalitarianism is therefore the goal that democratic socialism tries to achieve by advancing and representing the interests of the working class. Fourth, it prefers cooperation to competition as a means of organising societies and economies. Competition is the driving force of capitalism but not necessarily of civilisation per se and as we cooperatively recreate our social environments so we recreate ourselves and the relations that pertain between us. Finally, it argues that capitalism is inefficient and wasteful: the human waste of unemployment and the material waste of overproduction. Socialist planning can set a more efficient and less anarchic framework for economic activity and so achieve generally higher levels of growth.

In articulating the potentially strong links between the liberal, democratic and socialist traditions, Crosland defines democratic socialism as a middle way that is both practical and radical. At the same time, the Crosland of the 1950s believed that post-war reforms had irreversibly shifted the balance of power away from the capitalist class. By achieving political power, Centre-Left parties could wrestle economic power away from capitalists and hand it to a new class of managers who would organise society for the good of all. The welfare state should not in any way be confused with the free-market capitalism that preceded it: the former represents a victory for the poor and the workers that makes any further major social transformation unnecessary. It is this that makes Crosland the archetypal social democrat: socialist principles, values and ideals allied closely to a 'revisionism' that appealed strongly to those on the social liberal Centre ground.

Unfortunately, like T. H. Marshall, Crosland overestimated the political success and durability of the Keynesian welfare state, interpreting as irrevocable trends that were confined to the 1950s and 60s. By misreading the extent to which there had been a shift in the locus of power, social democracy revealed its underlying weakness. First, it did not prepare for the possibility of major economic crises, and so failed to control the actual economic shocks of the 1970s; second, it left itself theoretically bankrupt and vulnerable to the resurrection of the radical Right in the 1970s and 80s. And as social democracy retreated so democratic socialism entered its third phase, Crosland (1974) being one of those who tried to rethink social democracy's commitment to welfare capitalism. If reforms such as a mixed economy, full employment and a strong public sector could be subverted by capitalist interests after all, if they had not transformed economic and political power to that great an extent, perhaps there was a need for more state ownership and control than had seemed warranted in the 1950s. Crosland's later work therefore tends to be somewhat confused: he wishes to reiterate the essential points that he had made 20 years earlier, while doing so in full knowledge of the subsequent social, economic and ideological developments that had exposed the weakness of that earlier analysis. Yet Crosland's confusion is merely a smaller reflection of the theoretical struggle that both democratic socialism, and social democracy more generally, have undergone over the past 20–30 years.

There are several criticisms of democratic socialism that we should mention (cf. Dell, 2000). First, we can accuse democratic socialism of being too impractical in its hopes for a post-capitalist society. Democratic socialist programmes have only occasionally received more than a minority of votes from Western electorates, indicating that most people are unconvinced that a socialist society would represent a significant improvement on our existing one. Democratic socialists set themselves too ambitious a task, therefore, and have enjoyed their greatest achievements (as in the years immediately after the war) when they have moderated their demands and worked in alliance with non-socialist parties. This might suggest that democratic socialism has little to offer in and of itself, especially when the fall of communism has allegedly discredited socialist thinking in general.

The radical Right regard democratic socialists as naive for believing that cooperation can ever become the principal means of organising an economy. Individuals tend to be more creative and industrious when they are working in their own self-interest. People can be very altruistic, of course, but altruism cannot be an organising principle of society, for experience shows that markets are the best means of distributing the social product due to the price mechanism and competition's tendency to lower the price of goods. Democratic socialists can therefore be accused of being too attached to the state. They complain that capitalism is too centralised and hierarchical but then they advocate handing power over to managers and bureaucrats who are usually unaccountable to those they are supposed to serve. This is the kind of statism that people have consistently come to reject. Democratic socialists may argue then that investing more power in the hands of the state is a means to a longer term end where the state will be decentralised; but history offers few examples of political managers and rulers willingly surrendering the power that has been invested in their hands.

There are also a number of criticisms made by other ideologies that we are reviewing in this book. Conservatives regard socialism as too utopian, too rationalistic and leading to the kind of social engineering that destroys social unity and stability. Social liberals regard the collectivism of socialists as unnecessary and undesirable. Feminists and anti-racists object to the socialist emphasis on class and economic stratification which, they allege, neglects the importance of other forms of social division, exploitation and domination. Finally, Marxists argue that we cannot progress down the road to socialism by means of representative, electoral democracy. Because it is constantly subverted by the actions of wealthy and powerful elites, the democratic process can never deliver more than marginal reforms to a capitalist society, and even these reforms (such as the establishment of a welfare state) are vulnerable to counterattack by ruling elites and their political apologists. Therefore, only non-electoral political mobilisation can be effective in the long term.

# 7.4 Marxism

Although its influence on Western welfare policies has been marginal, Marxists have offered some of the most interesting critiques (see also Chapter 5 and the discussion of class in section 6.2.1). Marx (1977) made a famous distinction between base and superstructure. The base represents the economic foundations of a society: the productive forces (tools, machinery, knowledge) and productive relations (the system of ownership) which are the most important elements of the social order. The superstructure rests on this base and contains things such as the legal, political and cultural systems. The nature of the superstructure therefore reflects the nature of the base: just as a stimulus produces a response, events in the base cause effects in the superstructure.

It is this analysis which led Marx to interpret the state as an organising committee of the ruling class, as we saw in section 5.1.1. At its crudest this implies that the state has no autonomy and is merely an instrument of capitalists; a subtler theory suggests that the state possesses a 'relative autonomy', meaning that it has some freedom of movement but only within the parameters ultimately laid down by the needs of capital to accumulate and generate 'surplus value'. Geras (1989) has likened this to a dog who is chained to a post and can move about within the circumference of the chain but cannot go any further than the distance determined by his owner (cf. Laclau, 1990). It would imply that whereas a welfare state can sometimes alter the rules of capitalism it cannot change the nature of the game itself. This base/superstructure model has undergone many refinements over the years but it seems fair to state that for a theory to be Marxist in the first place a central place must be accorded to the economic relations of class. As such we can identify four important theories of welfare that belong to the Marxist camp.

## 7.4.1 Structures

There are those who concentrate on the base/superstructure model just outlined. For instance, Louis Althusser (1918–90) rejects the suggestion that individuals are in any way prior to the social conditions that form them: we are made by our environments, saturated with the contexts within which we find ourselves and 'interpellated' by institutions and social practices into the roles/positions that we occupy. Althusser (1969; Althusser and Balibar, 1970) regards the systems of the superstructure as possessing a relative autonomy that is determined 'in the last instance' by the economic base. It is wrong, therefore, to assume a mechanical, simplistic, one-way relationship between the base and the superstructure: ideology is not simply an inversion of the economic reality. Instead, the contradictions of capitalism are 'overdetermined' and multicausal, so that only a scientific analysis can reveal the underlying oppression and exploitation of society.

Althusser also distinguishes between a 'repressive state apparatus' (RSA) – police, army and penal system – that helps to maintain capitalism through actual or threatened violence, and the 'ideological state apparatus' (ISA) – church, family and education system – that maintains capitalism by securing support for it by those (the poor, the exploited) who would have most to gain from its abolition. So, the welfare state qualifies largely as an element of the ISA, allowing capitalism to appear more humane than it really is. However, the welfare state dovetails neatly, and occasionally overlaps, with the RSA, for example think of the way that social work is targeted largely on the poor.

Herbert Marcuse (1898–1979) concentrates on what he sees as the unity and homogeneity of capitalist society, arguing that its apparent diversity and plurality are mere surface features that camouflage an underlying sameness and uniformity. Each modern Western society can best be thought of as a totality which contradicts the self-image of these societies as free, open and merito-cratic. According to Marcuse (1964), ours are totalitarian societies that are even more pernicious than those labouring under communist rule precisely because they cloak oppression within the vocabulary of freedom and liberal-ism. For example, we esteem free speech but, because we are taught to identify freedom with capitalist values and habits, free speech allows nothing more than endless proclamations about the virtues of consumption, monetary gain and competition. Marcuse asks us to think of the way in which we are constantly bombarded with advertisements that subtly announce our freedom while actually keeping us in servitude to the needs of capital. Marcuse there-fore concentrates on the one dimensionality of society: the ways in which humanity is flattened out onto the same dimensional plane, organic material that fuels a totally administered and controlled society. On this reading, the welfare state is nothing more than an element of this total administration, a means by which injustice is made to seem just and servitude is made to resemble freedom.

## 7.4.2 Struggles

The problem with Althusser and Marcuse is that they risk eliminating the human element from society and historical development. As noted in the discussion of functionalism (in section 6.2.3), how can injustice be fought if things really are as Althusser and Marcuse interpret them as being?[1] So should we reverse direction and reintroduce agency back into the picture? In an attempt to do so, Ralph Miliband (1924–94) tried to bridge the divide between a structure-centred account of society and an agent-centred one (Miliband, 1969). We can, he believed, acknowledge the centralisation of social power around the capitalist state, while also recognising that opposing interests can mobilise themselves and occasionally change the organisation and distribution of power, even within a capitalist context. The working class, in particular, could take advantage of the relative autonomy of the state to seize some measure of control away from monopoly capital, and the welfare state could be interpreted as one such victory (compare the discussion of conflictualism and the power resources model in section 6.2.3). Of course, the working class faces an uphill battle and any victories short of a socialist transformation are likely to be modest and vulnerable to counterattack, but if we eliminate agency, free will and subjectivity from the picture altogether (for example Poulantzas, 1975), we leave ourselves with nothing to do except wait for history to change according to some kind of deterministic logic.

Similar considerations motivated Ian Gough (1979; cf. Ginsburg, 1979) to interpret the welfare state as an integral feature of a capitalist economy, but one which has emerged partly as a result of the class struggle. So while it is facile to regard the welfare state as a prototype of a socialist society, it does represent a victory of sorts for the working class, albeit a working class that seems to be more or less content with capitalism.

## 7.4.3 Systems

This attempt to unite agency with structure in Marxist explanations of welfare capitalism can also be found within the 'systems theory' school of thought. Jürgen Habermas (1975) and Claus Offe (1984) agree with the radical Right that there is a conflict between the need for capital accumulation and the welfare state's tendency to undermine such accumulation (cf. O'Connor, 1973). But whereas the radical Right have insisted that this conflict can be resolved by either scrapping the welfare state, or else substantially privatising it, Habermas and Offe argue that this can only *displace* the problem of legitimation. Capitalism, they observe, consists of three subsystems: an economic system (capital), a political/administrative system (the state) and a sociocultural system (values and norms). Capital provides the state with finance and, in return, the state ensures that the economic conditions of growth and accumulation are maintained; the state uses that finance to sustain social welfare provision, in return for which it receives mass loyalty back from its citizens. A welfare state, then, is integral to the functioning of 'organised' capitalism. With a welfare state, capitalism always risks a 'crisis of accumulation' (due to rising social expenditure and high taxes) but without it capitalism could not secure the legitimation it requires (because as the state is rolled back people are left to fend for themselves): 'The contradiction is that while capitalism cannot coexist with the welfare state, neither can it exist without the welfare state' (Offe, 1984: 153). It is because they have ignored the importance of legitimation that radical Right reforms have only managed to exacerbate social problems in a new era of 'disorganised capitalism' (Offe, 1985, 1996; Lash and Urry, 1987) and initiate a dictatorial workfare state within a globalised economy (Jessop, 1994).

## 7.4.4 Scarcities

The final Marxist school has received far less attention than the above and can be termed eco-Marxism. Eco-Marxists concentrate not so much on contradictions between the base and superstructure as on a possible contradiction between the base and natural resources. Scholars disagree about the extent to which Marx and Engels were 'environmentally friendly'. On the one hand, they seem to have regarded nature as nothing more than a source of matter that, having been transformed by labour, enables humankind to realise its true potential (Eckersley, 1992). Marx believed that the productive forces would have to develop to the point where scarcity could be overcome so that people would rebel against a class society that kept a large proportion of its population in unnecessary destitution. In this respect Marxists value social affluence as much as capitalists and ecologism is condemned for suggesting that because there are natural limits to growth we will never reach that stage of post-scarcity affluence. On the other hand, there is evidence that Marx and Engels were critical of capitalism due to its destruction of the natural environment and so they can be regarded as potential supporters of ecological reform (Benton, 1996). Eco-Marxists, then, try to combine an ecological critique with a Marxist one (Bookchin, 1980).

James O'Connor (1998), for instance, argues that what is significant is what he calls the 'second contradiction' of capitalism: that between capitalism's propensity for endless economic expansion and the capacity of the environment to (a) supply the necessary resources, and (b) absorb the resulting pollution. Ecological reform, therefore, ultimately implies the formation of a society which is planned, sustainable, restrained and egalitarian, that is, socialist. There *are* natural limits to growth, although these limits are not necessarily fixed as the quantity and quality of natural resources are, in part, socially determined. In these terms, we might also identify a 'second contradiction of the welfare state' where the contradiction between accumulation and legitimation is joined by that between accumulation and the natural environment (Fitzpatrick and Cahill, forthcoming). Ever-higher levels of economic growth have always been the sine qua non of welfare provision: a means by which the poor would accept social inequalities as necessary, and the rich would accept modest forms of state redistribution as acceptable. But if the nature of growth needs to be rethought, and if growth can no longer perform the integrative function that it has to date, eco-Marxism might yet have an important role to play in the future of social policy reform (see section 10.3 on environmentalism).

## 7.4.5 *Criticisms*

There are four major problems with Marxist theory worth mentioning here. First, it has little to offer the practical reformer. Marxists have long debated the extent to which humans can and cannot shape their own destinies, with determinists arguing that individuals have little role to play and humanists insisting that we can collectively shape our own futures. Yet whereas humanist Marxism is able to propose practical suggestions for reform, the extent to which those reforms can retain a Marxist content then becomes debatable. For if we can shape our own futures, the Marxist case has to be made on the basis of moral principle rather than historical determinisms and there is no guarantee that Marxist principles are any superior to non-Marxist ones (Cohen, 1995). And, even if Marxist reform is widely accepted as desirable, the battle against entrenched, worldwide capitalist interests is always likely to be very long term. So, rather than regard the welfare state as a highly qualified victory that falls short of a socialist transformation, it may be the best we can hope for in an imperfect world.

Second, Marxism is vulnerable to NSMT. Marxist explanations of welfare developments have excluded explanations that may be equally relevant and accurate, for example a gender or racial perspective (Williams, 1989). As we saw in Chapter 6, it may be possible to devise a politics that draws flexibly on both the labour movement and new social movements but there is a question mark over whether such a political position can be described as Marxist (Meiksins-Wood, 1985). Over the years, many attempts have been made to make the Marxist interpretation of class consistent with other forms of struggle, and Marxist-feminism is an obvious example of this. Yet these attempts have not resulted in any new theoretical synthesis that has been capable of enduring or attracting a wide consensus.

Third, the supposition that economic power is the most important form of social power has been repeatedly questioned (for example by Weber, see section 6.2.1). Without wishing to go to the opposite extreme of underestimating the role that economic power plays in human affairs, there are many who want to focus on the other forms of power (in addition to the economic) that Marxists tend to lock away within the superstructure, for example political power, cultural power and military power (Mann, 1986). Of course, this kind of theoretical move seems reasonable but, again, there is a limit to which we can make this move and still call ourselves Marxists.

Fourth, just as they may overestimate the unity of 'class' so they may underestimate the divisions and conflicts within the state. Even a definition of the state as relatively autonomous may overlook the extent to which the state is an outcome of pluralistic struggle and political competition. If so, Marxists may be accused of adopting functionalist accounts of the welfare state where everything is interpreted as functional for the reproduction of capital. If we avoid such functionalism, we may come to recognise the welfare state as more progressive than most Marxists allow and possessing a transformative potential that most Marxists ignore.

This chapter demonstrates two points. First, that welfare ideologies have a very long historical genealogy, stretching back several centuries in many cases. Second, that the issues with which they deal are still very much part of the currency of contemporary concerns. Of course, since the 1980s at least there have been those on both the Left and the Right who have been trying to airbrush away the importance of socialist and Marxist ideas. Yet not only would this severely reduce the scope of our political imagination, it might even undermine the basis of welfare theory itself by reducing debates about welfare reform to technical and administrative questions. Welfare theorists must ask two questions: 'what is the best form of society?' and 'what kind of welfare systems facilitate that society?' By contrast, those who insist that we now live in a post-ideological society attempt to close down political debate before it can really get started. What is vital, therefore, is not so much a commitment to any one ideology but a commitment to the breadth of ideas that any open, confident and healthy society must embody. A society that closes down ideological debates about welfare theory, and so reduces the scope of welfare theory itself, is not one that possesses a great deal of self-assurance.

Yet this is certainly not the end of the story. To some extent, welfare ideologies are concerned with class and matters relating to the social distribution of goods. However, there are many other ideas that have emerged over the past few decades which are concerned not only with social distribution but also with social recognition. These ideas relate to the other forms of 'social division' and it is to these that we now turn.

# 'New' Social Divisions

8.1 Feminism
8.2 Anti-racism
8.3 Models of Dis/ability

8.4 Ageism
8.5 Sexuality

Whereas welfare ideologies are characterised largely, although not exclusively, in terms of class and disputes over the distribution of *material* resources, 'new' social divisions are associated more with social movements and disputes over the distribution of material and *cultural* resources.[1] Their relationship to the older streams of political and social thought, therefore, is not always clear. Sometimes they seem to draw on, and contribute to, class-based forms of thought – as is the case especially with feminism and anti-racism; at other times, they seem to eschew such perspectives. So whereas it would be facile to entirely detach the new social divisions from welfare ideologies, we must be sensitive to the extent to which the former are concerned with cultural cleavages as well as material ones.

In other respects, of course, these 'new' social divisions are nothing of the sort. We have always had divisions based on gender (section 8.1), race and ethnicity (section 8.2), mental and physical abilities (section 8.3), age (section 8.4) and sexuality (section 8.5). What is *new* is the acknowledgement that we now give to the importance of these divisions in terms both of personal identity and social relations. If our task was to review each and every facet of these divisions, this would become a book-length chapter; we will therefore therefore limit ourselves to (1) outlining the essential ideas and critiques pertaining to each of these social divisions, and (2) explaining the relevance of each to Social Policy.

## 8.1 Feminism

As already noted, feminism could have been included in the previous chapter (and see the debate about feminism and citizenship in section 4.9). However, it is precisely because many anti-feminists wish to regard feminism as worn out and old fashioned that I have included it in this chapter. Feminist ideas have made enormous strides, especially since the 1960s, but it is fatuous to believe that such ideas have thereby become redundant.

Of central importance to feminist thought is the category of gender. Gender relations refer us to cultural distinctions between 'masculinity', and 'femininity', with feminists claiming that the economic, political and social dominance of men means that it is the masculine value that dominates. In other words, these distinctions describe a series of hierarchical divisions whereby men dominate, exploit and oppress women within a patriarchal society. Even this basic description of feminism has already raised some contentious issues that we shall return to below, but, for now, it is worth pointing out that we can immediately identify three schools of thought.

First, there are those for whom gender is the sole point of reference, meaning that society simply is a 'gender division' and that all societies at all times are characterisable in terms of a fundamental conflict between the sexes (Daly, 1979). Here, gender performs the same function that class performs in some aspects of Marxist thought. However, this school has never achieved much prominence (except in the imaginations of anti-feminists) due to its essentialism, that is, the way in which it ignores other, equally important, social divisions. The second school of thought relates gender to class, race and ethnicity and so on, in order to encompass a broad spectrum of identity and experience (Davis, 1982). For instance, a women is describable not only in terms of gender, but also in terms of her class position, racial and ethnic background, mental and physical abilities, age and sexuality. The final school of thought might be called 'post-feminism'. Post-feminists argue that the battle has largely been won, older schools of feminism are themselves now part of the problem and it is time for individual women to shape their own destinies rather than having a collective whinge about being the victims of men.

It is within the second of the above schools that most feminists have located themselves, giving rise to a number of important variants. Liberal feminists from Wollstonecraft (1759–97) to Friedan (1983) have sought to promote gender-related issues within the context of the liberal principles of liberty and citizenship (Wollstonecraft, 1975). Liberal institutions and existing democratic systems are sufficiently flexible to allow women to gain equality with men. This brand of feminism is often regarded as simplistic and naive in that it underestimates the extent to which those institutions and systems are both dominated by men and embody masculine values. In short, critics allege that because these are the *sites* of power and conflict they cannot also constitute a means of resolving the latter. Nevertheless, liberal feminism has wielded a certain amount of practical influence since its moderate and reformist prescriptions are those most in tune with the status quo.

By contrast, socialist and Marxist feminists (Rowbotham, 1973) have sought to confront existing society with its hypocrisies and contradictions. Deploying both class- and gender-based analyses (although to differing degrees among differing authors), the argument here is that a real equality between the sexes is ultimately dependent on achieving a classless society.

For instance, if capitalism requires a reserve army of labour, a class of the underemployed and the low paid, as well as the domestic and generational reproduction of labour, the subordination of women can be explained. Capitalism reduces women to the biological role of child-bearers, mothers and homemakers, and a reserve army who can be drafted in and out of the periphery of the labour market depending on the needs of the economy. Some critics allege that this analysis misreads the extent to which women have made, and are capable of making, real strides within capitalist society and renders gender equality dependent on the utopian dream of a socialist revolution. Others have argued that this emphasis on class neglects other social divisions.

As such, postmodernist and post-structuralist feminists are those who have adopted a non-reductive and non-essentialist approach to gender, regarding it as just one of a series of important relations (Butler, 1990). This is to argue that there is no such thing as *feminism* but a set of *feminisms*, all with differing emphases and points of view that ought to be respected. Rather than reduce male and female, and masculinity and femininity, to simplistic common denominators, we ought to recognise and celebrate the complex spectrum of differences that both unify and distinguish the infinite diversity of men and women. For only by valuing difference can we overcome the patriarchal and economic inequalities of existing society. The problem with postmodern feminism, however, is that it risks overlooking the specificity of women's experiences and of reducing real-life struggles to the status of a philosophical debate.

Therefore, some prefer to emphasise particular aspects of women's lives. First, there are anti-racist and 'Third World' feminisms that examine gender in terms of race, ethnicity and colonialism (Rodgers, 1989; Shiva, 1994; Lewis, 2000). There are several critiques in this respect: about the racism and ethnic oppressiveness of whites (including white feminists), about the sexism of men (including black men) and about the bigoted construction of women in developing countries as unenlightened and passive. Second, there is a lesbian feminism (Rich, 1983) that examines the extent to which heterosexuality is an effect of patriarchy and male domination rather than a 'natural' relation between the sexes. Third, there are feminist analyses of disability (Morris, 1991) and the way in which women are often the main care receivers and caregivers. Fourth, there are feminist analyses of age (Greer, 2000) and the way in which the older female body is undervalued due to the valorisation of youth and beauty. Finally, there is eco-feminism (Collard, 1988) that relates the domination of women to the domination of nature.

This brief but comprehensive survey of feminist thought now allows us to introduce Social Policy into the discussion. The following account tries to identify the basic feminist analysis of Social Policy but the reader is warned that what follows is a simplified account that neglects the depth and variety of feminist thought.

The feminist critique of social policies involves an examination of three areas that overlap considerably: state, family and labour market (Sainsbury, 1999; Daly, 2000). The essential point made by this critique is that most social policies embody the economic, political and cultural power of a patriarchal society and they reinforce such dominance by making women dependent on men and by giving priority to masculine values and aspirations (Charles, 2000). In terms of the welfare state, women can be said to occupy three roles: they are reformers, providers and clients. Here we concentrate on the roles of provider and client.

As providers, women contribute to social welfare in two ways: as public sector employees and as domestic carers. Women's employment patterns in the public sector have been concentrated within 'feminine' areas such as nursing and primary school teaching but they remain underrepresented within managerial positions (Pascall, 1997); outside the labour market women contribute the bulk of domestic and familial care work. In short, a 'breadwinner' model persists with women being assigned the roles of homemaker and child-raiser that are supposedly consistent with their essential 'nature', so that their workplace activities are limited to, and are a reflection of, this underlying distinction between the male worker and the female carer (Fox Harding, 1996). Given the close association between citizenship and employment, therefore, women's status as rights-bearing citizens has not equalled that of men (Lister, 1997). Instead, female citizenship consists more of obligations, or an 'enforced altruism', towards significant others: gendered duties that are constructed to appear natural and which remain economically under-valued.

As clients, women draw on state welfare services to a greater extent than men and this is partly due to the fact that, on average, they live longer and are more reliant over the long term on state pensions, health services and social services. Therefore, most feminist commentators express a considerable amount of support for the *idea* of collectively organised state welfare services but this support translates into a broad criticism both of existing provisions and the socioeconomic context within which the welfare state is to be found.

For instance, about half of the British labour force is now female but there are dramatic differences in the employment patterns of the sexes: in the mid-1990s, 88 per cent of all part-time jobs were occupied by women compared to only 35 per cent of full-time ones, women with children being twice as likely to take part-time jobs as women without (Callender, 1996), and 47 per cent of women worked part time compared to just 11 per cent of men (Walby, 1997: 32). Part-time employment is usually inferior to full-time employment, that is, lower pay, poorer conditions, worse entitlements and fewer opportunities for training and promotion. Women still tend to be occupationally segregated both 'horizontally', in that they are largely concentrated in clerical, secretarial, sales and service sector jobs, and 'vertically', in that they are more likely than men to be on the bottom rung of the career ladder (Walby, 1997: 34–7). Overall, and as a percentage of average hourly earnings, women's pay stands at 80 per cent of men's (compared to 64 per cent in 1970), but this drops to 60 per cent for women working part time.

Despite certain improvements, why have these patterns of disadvantage persisted over time? Because everyone knows that men currently have the greater earning power, both sexes may adopt attitudes and behaviour patterns that perpetuate this disparity and prevent the equalisation of wages no matter how strong the legislation on equal pay. In addition, women are also more likely to be excluded from the labour market altogether, although this is not necessarily reflected in unemployment counts, most of which are wedded to male employment patterns. Therefore, women have a greater incidence, a higher risk and longer durations of poverty compared with men (Millar, 1996: 52). Of those experiencing poverty in the early 1990s, 56 per cent were women, with lone mothers being especially vulnerable: 58 per cent of lone parents (90 per cent of whom are women) were in poverty in 1992/93 (Oppenheim and Harker, 1996: 36, 93).

So, a vicious circle is set in motion (Pascall, 1997: 30–72). Disadvantage in the labour market implies low pay and few entitlements so that many women are thrown back onto the least generous and most means-tested aspects of the welfare state which, in turn, fails to relieve their poverty and so contributes to the continuance of labour market disadvantage. In short, women's status as the dependent clients of welfare services is a construction: a consequence of their assumed dependency on the wage-earning status of men (Arber and Ginn, 1995a). Women have traditionally been defined as spouse and/or as mother whose job opportunities and welfare entitlements are effectively conditional on assuming and performing these types of role. It is difficult to decide whether, and to what extent, the situation is improving, for example more women are now economically active in the formal economy than at any time over the last 150 years (Walby, 1997: 28), but is this a victory for sexual equality or a consequence of economic changes where, although more men now perform 'women's work' and more women succeed in the job market, the underlying gendered distinctions remain intact?

The feminist critique of social policy is ultimately a critique of the sexual division of labour that structures the relations between men and women across all parts of society. Disadvantages in the welfare state, the family and the labour market all feed into one another. Of those women working part time, 80 per cent say that it is because they do not want a full-time job as working full time would make it harder for them to fulfil their domestic commitments. This is a choice which many women make, as post-feminists observe, but it is a choice heavily influenced by the structural constraints of gendered assumptions and patriarchal behaviour patterns. Those assumptions were made explicit in Beveridge's Report and his infamous remark that married women have less need of the earned entitlements of social insurance because they have 'other duties'.

In other words, a single (male) breadwinner is to act as a conduit between the household and market in order to ensure both the internal stability of the family and its external mobility within the labour market.

So despite a broad support for the general principles of state welfare, most feminist commentators have been heavily critical of its current form. Of course, we also need to allow for the fact that some welfare states are better than others (Sainsbury, 1999). The American system comes in for particular criticism with some arguing that it controls women both directly, by limiting claimants' reproductive rights, or indirectly, by trapping women in low-wage jobs. The Scandinavian welfare states tend to be regarded more favourably in their commitment to a form of gender equity linked to high levels of employment. However, some have alleged that even the Scandinavian approach merely replaces one form of patriarchy with another. Overall, then, and despite these important differences of emphases, feminist commentators adopt a critical stance towards existing state welfare systems.

What are the potential weaknesses of these critiques? Many on the radical Right (Friedman, 1962) allege that a commitment to state welfare services implies an ignorance of the beneficial effects that the free market could have on sexual equality: patriarchy has thrived because the state is a male-dominated institution resistant to change, whereas in an economy of free competition those employers who ignored the talents and abilities of female workers would be punished by those who did not. Sexual equality would therefore improve over the course of time and most feminists are consequently misguided in supporting the welfare state. Conservatives, by contrast, argue that a women's place really *is* in the home because men are essentially hunter-gatherers and women are essentially care-providers. Another possible criticism is that feminist prescriptions for welfare reform are either too utopian or too dependent on the traditional ideologies that we reviewed in the last chapter. Feminists may make valuable *contributions* to social liberal or democratic socialist thought and so on, but very little else.

A final and more recent criticism comes from post-feminists who believe that the important collective battles have been won and the job now is for women to make changes to their lives and society *as individuals* struggling and working with, and alongside, men. Second-wave feminism is portrayed as outdated and divisive, meaning that a third-wave 'power feminism' is now required that adopts a can-do attitude rather than an endless whinge about the injustices and awfulness of men that encourages women to define themselves as victims (Wolf, 1991). The debate surrounding post-feminism is ongoing and currently unresolved, but seems to hinge on the age-old dispute as to whether, and the extent to which, social problems are collective problems requiring collective solutions. In its individualism and demand that second-wave feminism disarm itself, post-feminism has found many friends on the Right who seem content to continue fighting the 'sex war' while pretending otherwise (Faludi, 1992). Like any progressive ideology, feminism can only become redundant once its goals have been achieved, which would not, as yet, seem to be the case.

## 8.2 Anti-racism

Anti-racist thought is less an ideology and more a political and social movement that challenges all forms of overt and covert racism within society. Therefore, we cannot imagine that the category of 'race' performs for anti-racism the same role that 'gender' performs for feminism because the very existence of the category is called into question by anti-racists themselves. On one level, this questioning seems to offend common sense. Surely we can see different races around us all the time: white, black, Asian, oriental and so on? If called on to do so, most people would probably nominate skin colour as that which clearly differentiates one race from another. Yet is this any less arbitrary than differentiating humans into other types, for example those based on eye colour, height, weight and so on? Why do we not assign equal importance to those divisions? Perhaps we do not because there is a widely held assumption that race has a biological foundation that is more important to our notion of humanity than these other types of division, and the scientific attempt to discern this foundation stretches back well into the nineteenth century (Banton, 1987). Are there any grounds for this belief? Well, yes and no. On the one hand, there are genetic differences between humans that might be categorisable as racial differences, but, these differences are insignificant; there is far greater genetic variation between individuals of the *same* 'race' than there is between individuals belonging to *different* races (Jones, 1996). This means that we assign such importance to race due to social reasons rather than biological ones: race is a social construction (Rex, 1970) in that it is people's *belief* in the importance of biological difference which is significant and deserving of analysis. From where do those beliefs stem?

One possibility is that such beliefs can be explained in terms of social psychology: to identify themselves with one group individuals need to differentiate themselves from other groups and skin colour represents an easy and dramatic means of doing so. Racial prejudice is therefore a more violent and extreme manifestation of this: the clinging to a narrow and simplistic form of identity, where 'race' and 'nation' are usually confused. Another possibility is that racism is an economic effect (Cox, 1970). Marxists, for instance, argue that racism is a means by which the working class is kept divided from itself, for if workers attribute their poverty and exploitation to 'the blacks', they are distracted from the real causes of their problems, as well as from the collective solutions that require the unity of all workers. The problem with this analysis is that it explains racism solely in terms of capitalism. A more sophisticated account (for example Gilroy, 1987) introduces cultural and political factors into the explanation and regards the struggles over racial identity as central to our notions of nationality and sense of belonging. Beyond this lie 'institutional' explanations which examine the perpetuation of racist sentiments across time by reference to social structures and political systems. In Britain, for instance, racism is bound up with our imperial past, for example Kipling's reference to the 'lesser breeds without the law' expresses an equation between 'the blacks' and 'the colonised'. With the passing of the British Empire in the middle of the twentieth century, British identity experienced a sense of loss that many attempted to mitigate by focusing on 'the other' who was, all of a sudden, apparently, in their midst. Moral panics about immigration, asylum seekers and 'black muggers' originate from this point (Hall et al., 1978). The restrictive immigration laws and the various race relations acts that were passed from the 1960s to the 1990s are two sides of the same coin: the attempt to exclude those who could not be assimilated and assimilate those who could not be excluded. Only gradually and with much reluctance has Britain grown into some semblance of a multiethnic, multicultural and multireligious society.

The key concept at work here has been 'ethnicity'. Once race is defined as a social construction rather than a biological fact we can make room for a host of other factors: language, customs and traditions, art forms, fashions and aesthetic values, religion.[2] In short, ethnicity is a form of cultural identification and affiliation that articulates the importance of difference. This emphasis may still be limited, however, if ethnic differences are regarded as fixed and rigid, and if ethnicities are interpreted as homogeneous groups. The concept of ethnicity is most valuable if it regards differences as complex, fluid and inclusive, and if we utilise it as a means of cultural and political emancipation (Donald and Rattansi, 1992).[3]

As we might expect, social policies play an important role in all of this in three ways (Lewis, 2000). First, social policies across English-speaking nations were developed against the background of Western colonialism and so may continue to embody notions of racial superiority and inferiority. Second, welfare systems and institutions may have discriminatory and prejudicial effects, whether directly or indirectly. Third, appropriate welfare reforms *may* offer a means of rectifying the injustices of racial discrimination and oppression. Let us review each of these in turn.

The 'other duty' that Beveridge ascribed to women was the rearing of the children who would maintain the British Empire in a post-war world. The founding of the British welfare state, both before and after the Second World War, therefore occurred at a time prior to the emergence of the anti-racist movement, so the idea that poverty may bear a racial dimension was not taken into account at that time. John Rex (1986) notes how the importation of immigrant workers into the labour market was shaped by colonial relations, with far more attention being paid to black immigrants (the colonised) than to white ones, for example Australian immigrants in the 1950s and 60s usually had a British heritage and so were thought to be unproblematic. So, the black working class was not only economically disadvantaged but also culturally excluded. This means that post-war social reforms took place in a context where black immigrants were perceived as an alien presence, as a threat that had to be neutralised and assimilated. Racial harmony implied that the 'blacks' should change to become British (with British identity being defined in terms of *white* ethnicity) with the white population required to do nothing more than, at best, tolerate their new neighbours or, at worst, prepare for a race war, for example Enoch Powell's 1968 'rivers of blood' speech.

Given this imperial background to its development, what effects have social policies had on racial inequalities (Modood et al., 1997)? Essentially, indirect discrimination is at least as important as direct discrimination in explaining the persistence of racial inequality. Indirect discrimination results not from the intentions of any one person, or group of people, but from a series of 'structural' interactions. As a hypothetical illustration of this, suppose that Gurch applies for a job that he fails to get. The employer is genuinely committed to racial equality, but Gurch's qualifications are simply too inadequate compared to those of the other (white) applicants. Why is this? After all, he attended a school that was also genuinely committed to racial equality, yet the school could do very little to compensate for the fact that Gurch grew up in a poor household. And why was his household poor? Because of the direct and indirect discrimination that his parents had experienced all their lives. In short, Gurch fails to get the job not because of any identifiable bigotry, but because of a vicious circle of circumstances. Direct and indirect discrimination are both present in what is referred to as 'institutional racism'.

The labour market provides evidence of such racism. The unemployment figures consistently demonstrate that the economic inactivity of ethnic minority men and women is double that of white men and women, a pattern that is replicated regardless of whether the economy is booming or receding (Oppenheim and Harker, 1996). Within this general headline, however, there are important variations with black African, black Caribbean, Pakistani and Bangladeshi groups being particularly disadvantaged, whereas employers seem less likely to discriminate against Asian and Chinese groups. Black migrants tended to have been channelled either into the public sector or into the low-waged, low-skilled parts of the private sector, and so have suffered disproportionately from the economic restructuring of the past 20 years. Those who find themselves in the 'secondary' labour market are often trapped there over the long term and those who do penetrate the 'core' of well-paid, highly skilled, desirable and secure jobs still tend to occupy the lower rungs of the occupational ladder.

Similar patterns are discernable in the education sector. Here, the influences of race and class are often difficult to disentangle, but surveys from the 1980s onwards indicate that black African and Caribbean pupils are particularly disadvantaged, although the qualifications achieved by Asian pupils are comparable to white ones. This may explain why a significant proportion of ethnic minority students go onto further and higher education, although they tend to be grouped within the 'new universities' and are less visible within the 'elite' institutions (Modood et al., 1997). Local educational policies were altered in the 1970s and 80s in many areas in order to reflect more of an anti-racist and multicultural approach, one where cultural differences are recognised and where racial inequalities are addressed. But whereas educational inequalities between ethnic groups have narrowed over the past two decades, it is social background that continues to disadvantage within the education sector those who are disadvantaged within wider society.

When we introduce the social security system into the picture we find that ethnic minority communities are three or four times more likely to be poor than those belonging to the white majority (Craig, 1999). The former groups are less likely to be eligible for contributory benefits, as entitlement to these requires uninterrupted periods of well-paid employment, and so are more likely to claim means-tested benefits, although their 'take-up' of these benefits is usually low. There is also considerable evidence of both direct and indirect discrimination. Further disparities exist in the housing sector, with ethnic communities more likely to be living in local authority housing, often on the poorest estates and less likely to be owner-occupiers (Skellington, 1992). The decline in social housing since the early 1980s seems to have contributed to the vicious circle of discrimination and disadvantage, with ethnic groups being four or five times more likely to be homeless.

The record to date of social policy, therefore, appears to be less than admirable. However, anti-racist prescriptions rarely disregard the need for a welfare state of some form or another (Solomos and Back, 1995, 1996). Indeed, defeating racial inequality would seem to require *more* welfare provision rather than less. This means several things. First, that Social Policy academics must continue to highlight such inequalities and, indeed, give more attention to areas that have been strangely neglected, including the benefits system. Second, it is obvious that reductions in overall social inequality would benefit ethnic minorities considerably. Third, further steps must be taken to eliminate discrimination which means paying more attention to subtle and discreet forms of bigotry, that is, institutional racism, and making employers more financially accountable for their actions and inactions. Finally, positive steps must be taken and racially sensitive policies devised, although there is a question mark over whether this means positive discrimination and quotas (see the relevant discussion in Chapter 2), consciousness raising, or just a recommitment to equal opportunities.

The main criticisms of such prescriptions come from both the libertarian and the conservative Right. Such criticisms often derive from black commentators who, like post-feminists, object to what they see as an outdated collectivism (D'Souza, 1996). In short, libertarians allege that the free market is the best means of promoting racial equality, on the same grounds as it is alleged to promote gender equality (see previous section). Conservatives argue that it is the welfare state that has trapped ethnic groups in long-term, intergenerational poverty by portraying them (and having them portray themselves) as victims of injustice rather than as autonomous agents who are capable of changing their circumstances without having to rely on government and bureaucrats. The anti-racist policies advocated by the Left are therefore likely to exacerbate the underclass status of black men and women, especially in the USA, rather than offering any practical solution (cf. Wilson, 1987). To a large extent, the 'culture war' of the 1990s has been fought between those who interpret the anti-racist movement as a form of political correctness and those within the movement who regard the discourse of political correctness as a fictitious invention of the Right in its attempt to defend the existing inequalities of power (Donald and Rattansi, 1992). Although not often associated with culture, the future of welfare reform vis-à-vis racism will be partly dependent on which side emerges victorious from this ongoing conflict over language and representation.

## 8.3 Models of Dis/ability

A similar, although certainly less virulent, version of this culture war has taken place in the debate over dis/ability. If we have not given much thought to the subject, we might be tempted to say that a disability is equivalent to a handicap of some kind. The image of disabled people that many able-bodied people have is of someone who is wheelchair bound or else walking with a white stick and/or a guide dog. A rather patronising sympathy for 'the disabled' then falls into place, perhaps accompanied with a feeling of 'Thank God that's not me' which can cause the able-bodied to experience discomfort in the presence of disabled people. While they may not be able to put a name to it, these perceptions and attitudes derive from a 'medical model' of disability.

The medical model treats disability simply as a physical or mental impairment of the individual concerned. This model implicitly treats able-bodied as the norm and disabled people therefore lack one or more characteristics of so-called normality. So, if a person's mobility is reduced, this is due to physiological or psychological conditions which mean that they cannot take full control of their lives and require outside assistance from medical experts and social services. The medical model began to be challenged in the 1970s. For instance, the World Health Organization made a useful distinction between impairment (a physical or mental loss), a handicap (a limitation due to the impairment) and disability (the social restrictions that result).

The 'social model' goes still further and focuses not so much on the individual as on the inadequacies of the 'disablist' society within which he or she lives (Swain et al., 1992; Oliver, 1996): it is not that the individual *is* disabled but that he or she is *made* disabled by a society that does not accommodate varying levels of ability. If someone in a wheelchair cannot gain access to a building, this is due not to any inadequacy on his or her part but on the part of those who designed and administer the building. The problem that disabled people have is not their disability but the perception which able-bodied people have of it. Accordingly, a disability movement has emerged that challenges the perception of disabled people as 'charity cases' and has campaigned for the rights of the disabled, sometimes engaging in direct action and civil disobedience when reform has been slow in coming. 'Independent living', where disabled people have access to the resources and means which give them the greatest possible control over their own lives, has been a widespread objective (Kestenbaum, 1996). Effective legislation, however, is barely in evidence and the movement became far more direct in the 1990s when campaigning for something better than the Conservative's Disability Discrimination Act of 1995 and against New Labour's cuts to certain disability benefits in 1999.

The debate has taken several interesting turns in recent years. First, it has become bound up with that concerning political correctness. If there are varying levels of ability, how do we appreciate and value each one without reimposing an insulting distinction between normality and abnormality? What descriptions should we use? The term 'the disabled' is now as outdated as 'the crippled' or 'the handicapped', but should we ditch 'disabled people' in favour of something like 'people with disabilities'? Does the former term impose a debilitating label that the latter avoids? It is such questions as these which attract the ire of the Right. Second, there has been a slight counter-reaction against the social model (Shakespeare, 1998). Although disability is undoubtedly a social construction, does the social model distract too much attention away from the lived experience of impairment? Critics do not argue for a return to the medical model but for a model that is more sensitive than its predecessors to the interaction of environmental factors with certain mental and physical conditions. Finally, disability has been examined in relation to other social divisions. For instance, Morris (1991) has alleged that feminism has traditionally ignored the interests and identities of disabled women and disvalued their abilities by appealing automatically to statist solutions. Instead, disabled and non-disabled feminists should support forms of living and care assistance that avoid the two extremes of institutional care, on the one hand, and simplistic family care on the other (where women do all of the caring).

As in the previous section, social policies have played three roles (Campbell and Oliver, 1996). First, they have responded only slowly and often reluctantly to the social model as this makes far greater demands on economic and political resources than a medical model that concentrates on the individual's impairments. By the mid-1990s, there was an obvious gap between the demands of the disability movement and the fiscal conservatism of the government.

Second, social policies have not, generally, met the needs of disabled people. Helen Barnes and Sally Baldwin (1999) estimate that 45 per cent of disabled people are in poverty, a figure corresponding to that given by Oppenheim and

Harker (1996: 57). The unemployment rate for disabled people is two to three times higher than that for the rest of the population. As in the previous section, we can attribute much of this either to direct discrimination and inflexible working practices on the part of employers or to the vicious circle of indirect discrimination: poor social background, few qualifications, low skill levels, infrequent work experience and so on. And those disabled people who are in employment are twice as likely to be in the periphery of the labour market than their non-disabled counterparts, earning about three quarters of the average weekly wage, and half as likely to be found in professional and managerial positions. All in all, about two-thirds of households with a disabled person receive no income from employment and almost one-third of those households are totally dependent on benefits.

The benefit system, however, hardly meets the additional costs of disability. These costs relate to nutrition and diet, heating and transport, special equipment and furniture, and home services. Disabled people have always been less entitled to claim social insurance benefits due to its contribution rules and so have been reliant upon means-tested benefits. The research suggests that disabled people spend approximately 25 per cent of their income meeting the costs that relate to their disability. The benefits available for disabled people constitute what is widely held to be the most complex and confusing element of the social security system, but it is clear that disabled people have lost out due to the benefit reforms that were introduced both in the late 1980s and late 1990s. Nor do many people consider the benefits available for carers to be anywhere near sufficient.

Social policies, then, do not appear to have served disabled people particularly well. As before, however, this failure leads to demands for more welfare provision rather than less (Barnes et al., 1998). If future welfare reforms are to be effective, they must be underpinned by strong and comprehensive legislation that emphasises the social rights of disabled people. One implication is that disabled people must no longer be defined as the passive recipients of taxpayers' largesse, but as agents in control of their own welfare provision. Furthermore, the additional costs of disability must guide increases in income replacement benefits, in-work benefits and legislative reforms to the pay, entitlements and working conditions of disabled people.

There are potential criticisms that can be made here of these critiques and prescriptions. First, perhaps the changes to social and public policies demanded by the disability movement are simply too expensive for society to provide all at once, so that compromises are unavoidable. Second, it can be argued that the recent militancy of certain wings of the movement are likely to alienate public opinion if carried too far: public opinion may exhibit a patronising attitude towards disabled people yet this also means that they are perceived as more deserving than most other claimant groups. Third, it could be argued that disability is a matter of brute luck, a regrettable but inevitable part of life's lottery that can affect any of us and for which no society will ever be able to compensate fully. Finally, disability is associated with age and so is an inexorable consequence of increased longevity: ultimately, it is better for us to live longer and risk disability than to live the shorter lives experienced by our ancestors.

# 8.4 Ageism[4]

Demography has become an increasingly important aspect of Social Policy as greater numbers of people live beyond retirement age than ever before (Bytheway, 1995; Arber and Ginn, 1995b). In one respect, an increased longevity can be interpreted as a partial success for modern social policies, yet it also generates certain economic and cultural dilemmas. The welfare state was founded at a time when the temporal distance between cradle and grave was a lot shorter than it is today. At the turn of the twentieth century, many people in the lower socioeconomic classes did well if they lived into their fifties or sixties; at the turn of the twenty-first century the average life expectancy is in the late seventies for men and the early eighties for women. Many people can expect to live for 20 or 30 years beyond the current retirement age. Such longevity places a strain on pensions and health care systems, in particular, as the proportion of working age individuals in employment declines relative to the proportion of those who have retired (Walker and Naegele, 1998).

This creates both a political and an intergenerational conflict. The Right insist that tax-based universal services are outdated (because a significant percentage of elderly people are well off) and unaffordable, whereas the Left argue that only the state can underwrite the costs of an ageing population and that the 'burdens' of an ageing population have been exaggerated by those carrying an anti-welfare state agenda. Older generations point out that they have paid for their entitlements through years of taxes and contributions, whereas younger people observe that, as individuals are required to take a greater role in insuring themselves against future contingencies, they are being asked to pay twice: once for today's pensioners and again for tomorrow's pensioners, that is, themselves. Faced with such political and demographic pressures, governments may be tempted to let the retirement age creep upwards so that we are able to spend *fewer* years in non-employment retirement.

Despite the emergence of a pensioners' rights movement (or the 'grey panthers' in the USA), social policies have failed to correct the 'generational inequalities' that have grown in recent years. On the one hand, we have an affluent strata of retirees who have substantial savings, who own their homes and who have access to generous private or occupational pensions; on the other, we have those who are reliant on means-tested benefits and supplements, the declining state pension and council housing. This division also bears a gender dimension, with women being far more likely to belong to the latter group than the former. Yet just as people have been living longer so the economic activities of the elderly have been decreasing: in a post-full employment economy there are subtle pressures for older workers to retire and make way for younger ones. This indirect form of discrimination accompanies a more direct form whereby older workers are assumed, without any real evidence, to be less trainable and less flexible than their younger counterparts. Yet despite lip service being paid to such ageism in the workplace, little seems to have been done to counter it. The generational inequality has been compounded by welfare reforms that have made a significant number of pensioners among the poorest in society (Evason, 1999). In the UK, the basic state pension declines in value with almost every year that passes.

Yet elderly people are also confronted with a number of cultural difficulties. Age is as much a social construct as it is a physiological fact about our lives, yet as society's members have become older so we have become more oriented around the needs, wants and interests of youth. While more of us can expect to live longer and longer lives, so the cultural representation of elderly people has become cruder and more simplistic: youth is identified with a forward-looking independence and old age with a nostalgic dependency. On television and in films elderly people are either portrayed as senile, cantankerous and old fashioned, or else as wannabe youngsters who take up anything from aerobics to bungee jumping. In both cases we are faced with a negative stereotype, as if we are unable to deal with the ageing process without constant references to the unquestionable benefits of youth, and a happy medium between the two extremes is rarely in evidence. The traffic is not all one way, however. The status of elderly people remains high and, as in the case of disabled people, images of dependency can generate a general sympathy that other disadvantaged group fail to receive, for example the public underestimate the costs of pensions and overestimate those of unemployment benefits, probably because pensioners are thought of as deserving and the unemployed as undeserving. However, these images of dependencies have a downside. The elderly are far less housebound and far less at risk of street crime than they are represented as being in both television programmes and newspapers.

The social division of age therefore presents us with a puzzling paradox: it is the one division that most of us in Western societies can reasonably expect to experience (and think of the alternative!) and yet we have made relatively minor attempts to combat the economic and/or cultural disadvantages that are associated with growing old. As ever, social policies may have a role to play in improving a situation for which they are partly responsible (Joseph Rowntree Foundation, 1996). Systems of social insurance are unlikely to disappear despite the wishes of the Right – indeed, in the USA social insurance benefits are that part of the nation's minimal welfare state which have proved to be the most popular – yet the reliance on private and occupational systems of welfare provision looks like being here to stay. The pension reforms of Britain's New Labour government seem to suggest that many people in the future will draw on both the public and private sectors for their post-retirement incomes. As with other forms of discrimination, legislation to outlaw age-related discrimination is required, yet, as always, governments have a preference for voluntary codes of practice rather than for laws that enhance the social rights of those being discriminated against.

## 8.5 Sexuality

Greater attention is now being paid by Social Policy researchers to the relevance of sexuality and the discrimination which same-sex couples experience (Carabine 1996; Donovan et al., 1999; Richardson, 2000). In one respect, sexual discrimination is the one form of discrimination that, unlike the others we have reviewed above, has relatively little to do with class and socioeconomic inequalities and it is this which perhaps explains why the Social Policy literature dealing with homophobia and heterosexism is fairly thin on the ground.

Homophobia, the hatred of same-sex relationships of gays and lesbians, is the one bigotry that still dares to speak its name, as was revealed in 2000 in the comments that several politicians and religious figures made when responding to the New Labour government's proposal to repeal Section 28 of the Local Government Act 1988, which prevents local authorities from 'promoting' homosexuality. Yet although the debate was characterised by the usual homophobia and moral panic, it was also noticeable that British public opinion had become more liberal towards differing sexualities in the years since Section 28 was passed. To some extent, this is due to the gay rights movement that emerged from the late 1960s onwards as a response to the oppression of non-heterosexual relationships and lifestyles that continued to characterise a decade otherwise informed by cultural and social revolutions across the Western world. However, such tolerance is often still of the don't-frighten-the-horses kind: one which says 'I don't care what people get up to in their own homes, as long as they don't flaunt it in public'. (That this halfway tolerance is still a prejudice can be illustrated if the same logic were applied to race and ethnicity: 'I don't mind black people being black in their own homes, but do they have to black in public as well?') There is therefore a world of difference between a grudging tolerance of alternative sexualities and an active acceptance and celebration.

This implies that heterosexism constitutes the long-term obstacle to sexuality equality. Heterosexism is that which constructs heterosexuality as a norm from which male and female homosexuality 'deviates', the underlying assumption being that, because biological reproduction is normal, any relationship that cannot bear children is not normal (Weeks, 1986). This also has the effect of reducing homosexuality (and heterosexuality as well?) to the status of sexual behaviour. The most extreme form of heterosexism proposes that gays and lesbians have been converted, cajoled or even forced into being sexually immoral (no doubt by those who promote homosexuality) so that they can also be converted back. Butler (1990) and Rich (1983) argue that in a 'heterosexist' society it is heterosexuality that is virtually compulsory: a narrowly repressive form of love and sexual attraction between humans into which we are socialised so that most people are given a sexuality rather than being free to explore their sexuality for themselves. If heterosexuality is such a social construct (Foucault, 1979), the 'sexuality movement', consisting not only of gays and lesbians but also bisexuals, transsexuals, transgendered individuals and, arguably, transvestites, is that which tries to deconstruct heterosexuality by 'normalising' a range of alternative sexualities.

Donovan et al. (1999) have traced the social exclusions that can result from heterosexism. In terms of civil rights, gays and lesbians are generally able to be less expressive and open about their emotions and desires, at risk from public ridicule and even violence if their appearance and actions deviate too far from the heterosexual norm. Homosexual men and women have fewer legal rights when it comes to inheritance, adoption and fostering, and equality at work (employers are not required to grant the same entitlements to same-sex partnerships as they are to heterosexual ones). Politically, the sexuality movement has raised the profile of gay and lesbians issues in recent years, both through behind-the-scenes lobbying and direct action. More politicians than ever before are open about their non-heterosexuality, although very few become figureheads for the movement.

In terms of social rights, the welfare state offers little recognition of same-sex partnerships. Local authorities are not required to design their housing policies to accommodate the particular needs and interests of same-sex couples. Schools take relatively little action against homophobic bullying, while the emphasis which schools give to religious instruction and moral persuasion will still allow considerable amounts of heterosexism to linger, for example if 'marriage is good' and gays and lesbians cannot marry, the implicit message is that 'homosexuality is bad'. The benefit system is also blind to the importance of same-sex partnerships, for example if a gay or lesbian person dies, their partner does not inherit their pension; although, for the purposes of calculating benefit entitlements, a same-sex couple may not be interpreted as cohabiting, whereas suspicion does fall on heterosexual couples whether or not they are actually partners. Finally, the health system denies infertility treatment to same-sex couples and both medical research and health care systems around the world were initially slow to respond to the HIV/Aids crisis due to the lower priority that policy-makers afforded to this so-called 'gay disease'.

Social policies undoubtedly have a significant role to play in the formation of sexuality equality, but because heterosexism is non-class specific this role may be less effective than that to be played in tackling the forms of discrimination outlined in previous sections. The welfare state can be culturally reformed and institutionally reorganised in order to weed out heterosexism and homophobia, yet the subject's traditional emphasis on poverty and material inequality means that the theoretical resources needed to make this happen are barely visible. This is one respect in which Social Policy, often the handmaiden of economics, may have to become the handmaiden of socio-cultural studies if large-scale progressive reform is ever to be initiated.

By taking a look at feminism, anti-racism, disablism, ageism and homophobia, we have concluded our review of the ideological aspects of Social Policy. Chapters 7 and 8 have hopefully communicated the point that ideological ideas continue to vibrate with innovation and controversy. Some of these ideas may lie at a distance from the Left–Right spectrum, yet they all contribute to a theoretical debate about welfare and state provision that, despite its historical foundations, sometimes appears to be in the early stages of development. Indeed, this is the theme that I would like to carry us forward to the end of the book. Welfare theory has roots that stretch far into history and yet new ideas and debates are being added all the time. Chapters 9 and 10 provide an introduction to those ideas and debates, a snapshot of where we are now, although, like all snapshots, the picture is likely to be blurred and dependent on the interests of the photographer. Rather than this being a problem, however, it is more of an invitation for you to step forward and begin to sharpen the focus of welfare theory as we move further into the twenty-first century.

# 9
# Recent Economic Developments

Having spent the last two chapters outlining the ideologies at work within Social Policy, we now need to understand what some of the main contemporary debates are. The final two chapters give a flavour of those debates and we begin, below, by reviewing some of the key theories that have been proposed in recent years regarding changes to the political economy.

It has often been noted that Keynesian economics provided the background to the classic welfare state: full employment, high levels of demand, corporatism, regulation, macro-economic stability. But since the early to mid-1970s Keynesian economics has been undermined by successive economic crises and the ideological onslaught of neoclassical economics that has emphasised the importance of low inflation, supply-side reforms, capital mobility, deregulation and market flexibility. Had this book been written in the 1980s it would have been appropriate to contrast these two economic philosophies at some length. By the mid-1990s, however, such arguments had been incorporated into the debate about globalisation with, at the risk of oversimplification, neoclassical economists arguing that the emergence of global free markets has fatally undermined any Keynesian-type settlement and Keynesians arguing either that globalising processes have been overexaggerated or that such processes do not constitute a barrier to a regulatory economics. We consider such ideas at length in section 9.3. Before discussing globalisation, however, we need to understand something about the debates that prefigured it. As such, we review the post-industrial thesis in section 9.1 and post-Fordism in section 9.2.

## 9.1 Post-industrialism

The welfare state is a product of the industrial era. The growth of industrialism in the nineteenth century gave rise to various social problems that demanded collective remedies and a labour movement that demanded substantial changes to the institutions and practices of industrial capitalism. The consolidation of industrialism in the first half of the twentieth century would eventually give rise to an extended period of growth and development that allowed social expenditure to rise alongside personal expenditure. However, social and economic changes over the past 30 years have magnified to a point where few now describe Western nations as industrial societies per se. In retrospect, we can see that the impetus for these changes was industrialism itself. In the 1960s, for instance, many anticipated that leisure rather than work would become the main activity and source of identity in the future as the affluence and mechanisation of industrial development would make labour both less desirable and less necessary: industrialism would make itself redundant. This 'leisure society' never arrived, or at least not in the form that many expected, but events in the 1970s fuelled the suspicion that industrialism was transforming into something else. The post-war era of full employment came to an end and the economy began to 'deindustrialise' as the large 'smokestack' industries either disappeared, declined or substantially reorganised.

Initially, this process was described as 'post-industrial' (Bell, 1973; cf. Toffler, 1980): just as agricultural society had given way to industrial society in the first half of the nineteenth century so, now, industrial society was giving way to a post-industrial one. The key feature of this post-industrial society is held to be service sector employment rather than employment in manufacturing and production. This does not mean that manufacturing is absent from post-industrial society (any more than agriculture vanished during the industrial era), but it does mean that the production of physical commodities becomes less socially and economically important than the creation, exchange and reception of knowledge and information. For instance, mining, shipbuilding and engineering have been outstripped by the growth of education, tourism, banking and financial services. And as information becomes the 'axial principle' of society, so those unskilled in the use of information would find themselves locked into the periphery of the labour market, for example cleaning, delivery and catering services. Indeed, those such as Touraine (as we saw in section 6.3 when discussing social movements) went so far as to announce the imminent demise of the industrial classes: the working class would be replaced by new social movements dedicated to alternative forms of critique, organisation, rebellion and change, while the industrial ruling class (exemplified by Gatsby-like tycoons such as Carnegie and Morgan) would be replaced by the 'symbolic analysts' of the managerial middle class (exemplified by Bill Gates).

For the welfare state, post-industrialism was thought to represent both a threat and an opportunity: it was a threat in so far as the class structure on which state welfare had been founded looked set to dissolve, implying that welfare states would have to accommodate themselves to a more individualistic and market-orientated society (Esping-Andersen, 1999); yet it was an opportunity in so far as welfare institutions, albeit to differing degrees, already embodied the service ethic that post-industrialism seemed to require.

The thesis of post-industrialism was immediately subjected to a range of criticisms (Kumar, 1978). First, it can be criticised for overestimating the degree of change that Western societies have undergone. Postulating a great socioeconomic revolution allows the theorist to represent him or herself as the interpreter and legislator of the future, as someone who has their fingers on the social pulse. The post-industrial literature is therefore replete with an awful lot of starry-eyed futurism, wishful thinking, hyperbolic claims and non-verifiable hypotheses (Toffler, 1980). Second, therefore, the service sector is too flimsy a peg on which to hang such a social revolution. Services have long been an essential part of industrial capitalism and employment in the manufacturing sector has always been relatively modest anyway. Third, post-industrialists are also too quick to herald the death of the class system. The knowledge industries of information processing are undoubtedly more important than formerly, yet it could be argued that this has reinforced the old class divisions (as we argued in sections 6.2.2 and 6.2.3). Finally, work practices for the poorest have not altered greatly: Taylorist scientific management (see below) is more than evident in call centres and fast-food restaurants (Ritzer, 1993). If such criticisms hold, the implications for the welfare state of socioeconomic change are not as significant as the post-industrialists assume.

Neverthless, much of the post-industrial critique has been widely accepted and more recently incorporated into theories of the 'information society', which we will review in the next chapter, and post-Fordism.

## 9.2 Post-Fordism

In the 1980s the thesis of post-Fordism became as popular and controversial as that of post-industrialism. Here, the contrast was with the Fordist era, named after the car maker Henry Ford and described very early on by the Italian Marxist Gramsci (1891–1937) (Gramsci, 1971). Fordism refers to the mass production of large economies of scale and hierarchical workplace structures. For instance, the Chaplinesque assembly line captures this notion of mass production, where the worker is little more than a cog in a machine, an appendage of repetitive processes who is alienated from himself, his colleagues and his work, taking his orders from distant managers and overseen by aggressive supervisors. At the heart of Fordism is the scientific management of F. W. Taylor. Taylor took a typical job, such as the assembly of a car, split it into its component parts and worked out how long it would take to complete each part at an efficient rate of production. The productivity of a plant could therefore be measured according to this rate and workplace practices altered accordingly. However, this assembly line process is inflexible in terms of what is produced: the commodities tend to be identical to one another.

Consequently, consumers must alter their tastes to suit the nature of the supply (or as Ford put it himself: 'you can have any colour car you want, as long as it's black'). Therefore, Fordism also implies mass consumption where demands are standardised and easily manipulable through the fashion and entertainment industries (think of the 1950s-style holiday camp), and where sustaining the level of demand requires high social expenditure, full employment and a state-maintained compromise between employers and organised labour: corporatism.

According to post-Fordists (Hall and Jacques, 1989; Amin, 1994), Fordism began to break down in the 1970s. Fordist practices could no longer guarantee increases in productivity: as technology became more sophisticated so the inflexible assembly line became a counterproductive obstacle to workers' creativity and job satisfaction. At the same time, consumers also became more sophisticated and were less willing to suppress their individualistic and non-standardised wants and desires. Post-Fordism therefore refers to flexibility in production, or 'flexible specialisation' (Piore and Sabel, 1984), and diversification in consumption. Single-function machinery has been replaced by computerised systems that can be reprogrammed; vertical hierarchies have been replaced by horizontal networks as economies of scale (centralised factories) become economies of 'scope' (decentralised sub-units to which work is contracted out); assembly line practices have been replaced by team working, with workers being treated less as supervisees to be ordered around and more as autonomous experts that management itself can learn from; a 9-to-5 culture has been replaced by flexitime; mass marketing has been replaced by niche marketing, where supply is tailored to specialised demand; mass warehousing has been replaced by 'just-in-time' forms of storage and delivery. Furthermore, consumption becomes an even more vital part of society. Since people are less likely than before to follow single trends and fashions, shops and showrooms grow in number and diversity. Consumerism is less about 'keeping up with the Joneses' and more about being distinct from the Joneses, and following a crowd is less important than exploring one's own tastes and interests.

The post-Fordists welcomed these changes yet also worried that the Right had taken advantage of them much more quickly and effectively than had the Left. Indeed, the term 'Thatcherism' was invented by Marxists to express the conjunction of radical Right ideas with post-Fordist developments, one that inspired a politics of cutting social expenditure, preferring low inflation to high employment levels and giving capital more power over labour. If the Left was to revive, therefore, it would need to find new ways of harnessing post-Fordism that avoided both the crude capitalism of the Right and the statist egalitarianism of the traditional Left.

However, some have denied the relevance of these ideas (Kumar, 1995). Post-Fordism can be criticised as being too deterministic, that is, too concerned with technology and political economy, and not enough with social forms of resistance to these developments, and too ready to identify radical discontinuities with the past that overestimate the degree of change that has actually occurred. Post-Fordists can also be accused of adopting a 'gee-whiz' attitude and incorporating the ideology of managerialism into its theoretical accounts, for example flexibility is often given a positive spin when it usually involves little more than a 'hire and fire' culture.

If there is disagreement over the extent to which we do now live in a post-Fordist society, there is a corresponding disagreement over what the implications of this might be for social policy (Burrows and Loader, 1994). The most influential application of post-Fordist ideas has been developed by Bob Jessop (1994, 1999). Strictly speaking, Jessop derives his critique from 'regulation theory' (Aglietta, 1979) which focuses not merely on the workplace but on the wider socioeconomic environment. Regulation theorists prefer to identify as many continuities with the past as discontinuities and so speak of neo-Fordism, that is, the socioeconomic restructuring initiated in the 1970s has been a crisis *within* Fordism rather than *of* Fordism. This, too, is a Marxist analysis, but one that focuses on the 'regime of accumulation' (the macroeconomic system that maintains capitalist production and consumption) and the 'mode of regulation' (the institutions, organisational forms, practices and networks that protect and steer the accumulation regime). Nevertheless, regulation theory and post-Fordism are closely related and Jessop frequently interchanges the concepts.

Jessop argues that the Keynesian Welfare National State (KWNS) has gradually been replaced by a Schumpeterian Workfare Postnational Regime (SWPR). The KWNS prevailed for at least 30 years after the war and incorporated four dimensions. First, it was Keynesian in so far as it secured the conditions for full employment through a demand-side management of the economy. Second, it was concerned with welfare by generalising the norms of mass consumption as well as the specific forms of collective consumption that perpetuated Fordist growth patterns. Economic and social policies were therefore closely attached to citizenship rights. Third, the KWNS was predominantly national in that even local, regional and international states were subordinated to national economic and social priorities. Finally, the KWNS was statist in so far as the mixed economy was shaped and guided by state institutions. Jessop is at pains to acknowledge that the KWNS came in the diversity of shapes and sizes that comparative analysis (Esping-Andersen, 1990) has categorised as social democratic, conservative and liberal. Therefore, the transformation of the KWNS has taken a variety of paths towards a variety of destinations. Nevertheless, Jessop claims that the destinations all share some basic features which are so similar that they can be grouped under the heading of the SWPR.

As with its predecessor the SWPR incorporates four dimensions. First, it is Schumpeterian rather than Keynesian. Schumpeter (1883–1946) was an economist who famously described the capitalist economy as consisting of gales of 'creative destruction' (Schumpeter, 1992). In a Keynesian economy, the aim is long-term macro-economic stability whereas a Schumpeterian economy is characterised by a permanent revolution of innovation and flexibility in the name of competitiveness. Economic and labour market instability therefore becomes the organising principle. Second, the SWPR is concerned with workfare rather than welfare in that social policy is subordinated to the demands of competitive flexibility. The needs and rights of individuals take second place to the needs and interests of business, as paid employment is widely assumed to be the main source of well-being. Social policies become less concerned with demand-side interventions and more with improving the supply of labour by equating 'citizens' with 'workers' and remaking the latter into dynamic, risk-taking entrepreneurs who embrace market insecurity. Those at the bottom of the income ladder can then be assisted with workfare policies (where claiming benefits becomes a highly conditional exercise) (King, 1995, 1999). Third, policies become post-national as the nation-state is 'hollowed out' in three directions (see next section): upwards towards international agencies and inter-state forums, downwards towards regional and local levels and sideways towards cross-border forms of governance. Finally, the state plays less of a role in the SWPR. Or, rather, the state must enter into a variety of partnerships with the private and voluntary sectors in a 'mixed economy' of social welfare provision.

The virtue of Jessop's analysis is that it recognises the plurality of welfare systems that can be found around the world yet is also willing to identify a common denominator that allows us to give a meta-descriptive shape and form to the analysis of the comparativists (Esping-Andersen, 1996). The potential problem, however, is that his neat contrast between the KWNS and the SWPR misses the extent to which the latter is a neo-liberal version of the former. According to Jessop (1999: 357):

> ... the neo-liberal form of SWPR is hegemonic on the international level, but important counter-currents exist in specific national and regional contexts.

Yet if neo-liberalism is hegemonic on the international level and if many social policies now consist of supply-side interventions into the discourses, belief systems and habits of citizen-employees, this hegemony cannot be confined to the international level. Precisely because it has lost its grip at the international level, the state must tighten its grip on the inward spaces of the national socio-economy in order to establish regular flows of inward investment and conformity to the gaze of the IMF and so on. Therefore, drawing on Foucault's analysis, the state *extends* its reach through the formation of public–private and public–voluntary partnerships (Fitzpatrick, 2001). So the divergence of the SWPR is much less pluralistic than that of the KWNS and represents a 'relative reconvergence' around the neo-liberal pole of its predecessor.

Others have trouble with the whole attempt to apply post-Fordist analysis to social policy. Taylor-Gooby (1997) reacts against what he calls the 'new sociology' in its focus on post-Fordism, globalisation, market flexibility, family/household complexity and non-class forms of social division. This new sociology engenders a 'new welfarism' that abandons goals such as full employment, redistribution, universalism and generous amounts of public expenditure. So although the new sociology professes to value diversity, by ignoring the recent intensification of class inequalities it surrenders to a globalised, radical Right agenda that enforces a substantial *convergence* of policy regimes around the destructive logic of free markets. According to Taylor-Gooby, global constraints should therefore be interpreted primarily through the lens of the old sociology's concern with class, capital and the nation-state, implying a wholesale rejection of post-Fordist analysis.

As with post-industrialism, however, much of the sound and fury concerning post-Fordism has subsided as new ideas, theories and concepts have arisen that often assimilate the old, yet set off into territory that was previously unexplored. Since the early 1990s the key debate has revolved around globalisation and generated a body of literature which has dwarfed that of post-industrialism and post-Fordism put together.

## 9.3 Globalisation

Globalisation swiftly became *the* buzzword of the 1990s, constantly invoked by academics, politicians, policy-makers and journalists. However, following the law of diminishing returns, the more the term was used the more its meaning and implications seemed to shift and transform. And the literature dealing either directly or indirectly with globalisation is now voluminous, filling more shelves than could be read in a single lifetime (Lechner and Boli, 2000). Fortunately for us, we do not have to review every facet of the debate, merely those that relate to Social Policy and the welfare state. However, this still gives us a lot of ground to cover.

Our definition of globalisation alters depending on whether we think of it as a verb or a noun. As a verb, globalisation refers to a set of economic, political and cultural processes of increasing spatial and temporal interdependency. As a noun, globalisation might be thought of as the outcome of such processes. However, the trouble with defining globalisation as an outcome is that it reifies contemporary developments and risks ignoring the dynamic nature of global changes, therefore many theorists have preferred to define globalisation as a series of processes.

Giddens (1991) and Harvey (1989) both draw attention to the ways in which space and time shrink and compress, distances become annihilated as globalisation takes hold, meaning that events in one part of the world can have immediate and far-reaching effects on other parts. Events in one stock exchange can spread like wildfire throughout all others; a virus in one computer can quickly infect millions of others; and it becomes as easy for me to

communicate with a colleague in Australia, via email, as it is to communicate
with another who is working in the next office. Indeed, globalisation does not
simply imply that everything becomes global, it also implies that localities
become globally significant. Therefore, the 'global' and the 'local' have,
according to many, succeeded the 'social' and the 'national' as the main
reference points of theoretical commentary and analysis. This intermingling
of the global and the local is referred to by Robertson (1992) as 'glocalisa-
tion': everywhere becomes both local and global, both centre and periphery.

At the risk of oversimplifying, there are four basic positions that we can take
vis-à-vis globalisation (see section 4.10.1). The first position is held, broadly
speaking, by those who are in favour of globalisation: the sponsors. Sponsors
regard globalisation as a reality, as that which defines the age in which we live,
and they also welcome the changes that globalisation implies as both necessary
and desirable. Ohmae (1995), for instance, believes that the nation-state is
dead or dying as there are no longer any national boundaries for the state to
police and defend. By and large, the sponsors are those on the political Right
who interpret globalisation as the first stage of the post-Communist era where
the world is no longer divided into two military and ideological blocs and
liberal democratic capitalism becomes the norm (Fukuyama, 1992). Sponsors,
therefore, are the kind of supply-side economists who reject the post-war
Keynesian settlement.

The second position is held by those who also identify global processes as
real but who are more ambivalent about this than the sponsors: the sceptics.
The sceptics welcome some aspects of globalisation but not others. For
instance, environmentalists are happy to witness Green ideas spread around
the world as people become more conscious that they are all common inhabitants of a single, and rather finite, planet; but they criticise the economic
forms of globalisation that allow multinationals to undermine regulation
designed to protect the environment. Castells (1996, 1997, 1998) insists
that globalisation is now a fact of life due to the proliferation of information
networks, but he warns against right-wing versions of globalisation that allow
the mobility of financial capital to dominate all other forms of social interaction. He and Bauman (1998) argue that an unrestrained global capitalism is at
risk of imploding and creating instabilities and inequalities that could attract a
backlash from the excluded. For Giddens (1999), the unchartered turmoils
and uncertainties of globalisation might encourage a resurgence of fundamentalism as some try to reconstruct the walls of certainty and security that
have been abruptly torn down.

The third position is held by those who deny that 'globalisation' is an
appropriate description of what is happening in the world today: the doubters.
Doubters introduce an historical perspective into the discussion, pointing out
that any analysis of contemporary changes must involve a comparison between
the present and the past. Hirst and Thompson (1996), for instance, identify
more continuities with the past than discontinuities. There is nothing unique

about our time, we have been here before: between the 1870s and the First World War we also experienced a series of economic, political and technological leaps. The danger posed by the sponsors, in particular, is that they undermine our confidence in our ability to change things through collective and cooperative action. By overemphasising the extent to which we have broken with the past they divert attention away from previous, successful attempts to tame global capital: namely, the Keynesian welfare state. There are certainly important changes occurring in the world today, but this might, with less hyperbole, be termed 'internationalisation'.

(Sceptics and doubters can often be identified as latter-day Keynesians, opposing the neoclassical certainties of the sponsors. Sceptics tend to believe that Keynesianism can be reinvented at the global level, whereas doubters insist that there is no reason to believe that national Keynesianism has been fatally undermined.)

Finally, there are some who insist that globalisation is a myth promoted by those who have most to gain from the worldwide adoption of unrestrained capitalism (Piven 1995): the hecklers. For the hecklers, globalisation is an ideological sleight of hand, a concept that was disseminated through right-wing think tanks and research institutes at the very time (the early 1990s) when the radical Right seemed to have lost its economic momentum. Bourdieu (1998) interprets globalisation not as a process, first and foremost, but as the intellectual colonisation of social consciousness, a hegemonic war waged by those who want to sweep away the few gains made by the poor and dispossessed in the middle decades of the twentieth century: it is the latest stage of a counter-reaction to the humane capitalism of the post-war era. Capital is certainly becoming more powerful and mobile but this is due to the actions of Western governments (principally America) and multinationals who then invoke globalisation as a means of neutralising criticism and resistance. Therefore, globalisation is a reification: a means by which we interpret the consequences of our actions as processes over which we can have no control.

Of course, the debate is not as clear cut as these distinctions suggest: Giddens, for instance, can appear both as a sponsor and a sceptic (Hutton and Giddens, 2000); however, this at least gives us some purchase on a subject that shows few signs of dying down. The disagreements taking place between sponsors, sceptics, doubters and hecklers rages mainly across four interrelated disciplines: economics, politics, cultural studies and Social Policy. Let us review each of these in turn.

## 9.3.1 Economics

It is economic globalisation that has occupied the foreground of the debate and this is thought to encompass five areas: financial markets, trade, multi-nationals, investment and labour markets.

The sponsors are on their firmest ground when they point to the apparent globalisation of finance (Held et al., 1999: 189–235). In the late 1990s approximately $1.5 trillion was flowing through the foreign exchanges every day – about $1 billion every minute – driven by Nobel prize-winning mathematical models and advanced computer systems. To put this in context, a figure slightly higher than the UK's *annual* national wealth was being exchanged within a 24-hour period. Yet by the time you read these words even this figure will probably have been exceeded because the financial markets have been inflating at an ever-accelerating rate since the early 1980s due to the growth of mutual and pension funds (worth $20 trillion in the USA alone in 1995), the computer revolution that allows real-time transactions and the instantaneous flow of capital, and the proliferation of international bonds, portfolio investments and financial instruments called derivatives. London, Tokyo and New York effectively merge into a single financial sector, dispersed across a number of geographical regions (Sassen, 1991), which virtually constitutes a global capital market, a frictionless economy.

Financial globalisation can easily induce the kind of gee-whiz response that the sponsors urge on us, but even successful investors such as Soros (1998) observe that capital markets are not fully autonomous and depend on an institutional framework set principally by the IMF and the American Federal Reserve. Nor are we helpless in the face of global finance. The economist James Tobin has long recommended the imposition of a small tax on all foreign exchange transactions, a tax that could raise billions of dollars each year and be operated through the electronic technology on which the financial markets now depend. The regulation of global finance is not yet a reality due to a lack of political will rather than a lack of technical means.

Trade has also expanded rapidly, especially during the 1990s (Held et al., 1999: 149–88). Global free trade was overseen in the post-war decades by the General Agreement on Tariffs and Trade, but this was superseded in 1995 by the World Trade Organization (WTO), a much more powerful institution that can enforce the deregulation of protectionist measures. According to some, then, we are well on the way to a global trading system with exports and production for foreign markets, rather than domestic markets, on the increase. Critics observe, however, that this system is not an inherent tendency of markets but is the agenda of powerful governments exercised through the WTO. Since free trade threatens to undermine domestic legislation concerning social and environmental protection, the WTO has recently experienced a backlash of environmentalists and trade unions that oppose market liberalisation. Furthermore, some argue that, when compared to GDP ratios, trade is no more voluminous now than it was in the half century before the First World War and is mainly concentrated within developed nations (Hirst and Thompson, 1996).

When people think of globalisation they often think of multinational corporations (MNCs) and transnational corporations (TNCs). MNCs have bases in a number of countries, whereas TNCs are 'baseless', that is, geographically rootless and perfectly mobile. Both types of firm have an internationalised management, an internationalised labour force, internationalised consumer markets and no specific national identification. MNCs and TNCs are treated as the powerbrokers of globality because of their wealth (they are often richer than many medium-sized countries) and their ability to play countries off against one another: 'lower your taxes and your wage costs or we'll invest somewhere else'. The largest 300 MNCs account for a quarter of the world's capital and three-quarters of its foreign direct investment (FDI). However, critics argue that the power of these firms has been repeatedly overstated. Weiss (1998) comments that most are *national* firms which operate internationally for three reasons: by emphasising fixed costs, new technologies reduce the cost savings which result from migrating to low-wage countries; new production methods favour a close physical proximity between producer and supplier; and a competitive advantage arises from maintaining domestic linkages and networks.

FDI occurs when an investor owns and/or invests in an enterprise located in a country other than that of the investor. FDI has grown throughout the post-war period and, by the mid-1990s, FDI stocks had reached $2.5 trillion (Held et al., 1999: 242–5). However, Hirst and Thompson (1996) establish that, despite being huge and of global reach, FDI tends to be concentrated on three regions: North America, Europe and Japan. It is these three regions which act as the originators and destinations for most international investment, a clustering of investment flows suggesting that globalisation is not yet a fact of life. Castells (1996, 1998), by contrast, acknowledges that these regional clusters exist, but rather than this disproving the global economy thesis, it merely points to a 'regionalisation' of the global. This is not a contradiction in terms, he believes: an investment triangle between USA, Europe and Japan certainly exists, yet it is precisely this clustering which enables the global economy to emerge.

Finally, what of the labour market? Nobody can claim that there is a global labour market as the number of migrant workers is only a small percentage of the total global workforce: about 2%, in fact, concentrated mainly in Africa and the Middle East. However, many have claimed that there is an international division of labour with industrial capital relocating to low-wage countries in the developing world and so contributing to the hollowing out of domestic labour markets. Developed nations then have to 'sell' the highly skilled, competitive flexibility of their workforces, through supply-side measures emphasising education, training, multiskilling and various wage/tax subsidies, in order to attract investment capital back. Again, critics insist that this is an overstatement with such firms being far less mobile than financial capital, so that globalisation does not extend to labour in the way that it arguably extends to trade and finance. However, Castells (1996) insists that there is a historical tendency towards the increasing interdependence of job markets on a global scale, because labour has to act *as if* capital were perfectly mobile, even if the reality falls short of perfect mobility.

There are, therefore, compelling arguments both for and against the thesis of economic globalisation. The sponsors are those most likely to treat economic forces as somehow detached from their institutional settings, whereas sceptics, doubters and hecklers all point to the importance of political decision-making.

## 9.3.2 Politics

There are three questions that we need to address here (Held et al., 1999: 49–86). To what extent has the nation-state driven forward the processes of globalisation? Is the nation-state becoming redundant? Can we envisage the globalisation of politics?

The post-war decades were characterised by a relative stability on the currency markets. The Bretton Woods System (BWS) fixed the exchange rates of all currencies to that of the dollar which, in turn, was fixed to the price of gold. Controls on capital ensured that financial flows were regulated and the IMF policed the system, offering conditional loans to those countries who ran into balance of payments difficulties in order to avoid the uncontrolled and competitive devaluations of the interwar period. The BWS was the backbone of the post-war welfare state. By giving domestic objectives priority over global finance it helped nations to maintain high levels of employment and growth, thereby pleasing both the pro-market Right and social democrats. Why then did the BWS break down in the early 1970s?

Those such as Gowan (1999) draw attention to the deliberate actions of the USA. The Nixon administration felt that the BWS gave too much control to debtor nations at the expense of America. Therefore, it was better to deregulate the international system, so that currencies would 'float' against one another, and allow American institutions to regain control both directly (through lending institutions) and indirectly (through the IMF). An alternative explanation suggests that it was the growth of eurocurrency markets in the 1960s, markets that could evade capital controls, that placed a fatal strain on the BWS: the US dollar came under pressure and Nixon had little choice but to end its convertibility into gold. The coffin lid of the BWS was then firmly nailed down by (1) the quadrupling of oil prices in the 1970s, thus giving international banks huge surpluses with which to fuel the money markets, and (2) the explosion in the financial markets in the 1980s.

So, to what extent has the nation-state driven forward the processes of globalisation? Sponsors insist that the nation-state has been the ailing victim of globalisation, able to do very little to stem the tide of its own demise. Critics of this position, however, insist that globalisation is, in large part, a consequence (partly intended and partly unintended) of the most powerful nation-states attempting to consolidate their power through financial liberalisation.

Such arguments also determine the main responses to the next question: is the nation-state becoming redundant? Sponsors believe that national sovereignty is in terminal decline due to the advent of a borderless world (Ohmae, 1995). For instance, at the beginning of the twentieth century there were only a few dozen intergovernmental organisations (IGOs) and less than 200 international non-governmental organisations (INGOs), whereas by the end of the century there were almost 300 IGOs and 5500 INGOs. This means that political decision-making is now far more decentralised than at any time in the past so that the nation-state is becoming just another political actor on an increasingly crowded global stage. By contrast, critics allege that political sovereignty may have *changed* but change is not the same as *decline*. Decision-making is now mediated across a range of interested parties but, if anything, financial globalisation has *enhanced* the power of nation-states, for example the WTO was the product of several years of careful negotiation between governments eager to reap the benefits of the very globalisation that they were encouraging.

Therefore, the 'globalisation of politics' can imply different things to different commentators. For sponsors it can mean nothing more than the regulation of global markets by the financial police of the IMF and the WTO, while for others it can imply the necessity of constructing a new BWS system in order to regain control of global capital. In between these two positions there are those who call for a new cosmopolitan political order.

For Held (1995), such an order would replace (a) the Westphalian model which governed international relations from the seventeenth century until the Second World War, and which guaranteed the sovereignty of states from external interference, and (b) the UN model which subsumed the Westphalian model and which guarantees both national sovereignty and human rights. Held argues that the UN model has failed to respond adequately to the crises of global economics and politics (often because the UN is a mask for US interests) so that a cosmopolitan model is called for. This would embody the global diversity of power, would be underpinned by a robust legal order with strong international courts and means of enforcement, and would reflect principles of social justice, the common good and global citizenship. Held believes that it should be easier for people to sue national governments for violating international law and recommends the establishment of regional parliaments (similar to the EU), transnational referenda and a democratically elected global legislature to either supplement or replace the existing UN.

## 9.3.3 *Culture*

Yet the globalisation debate is not only concerned with economics and politics, since globalisation is also taken to imply important cultural changes. Here we face two main questions. Is there a single global culture? Do all cultures now have the opportunity to appear on a global stage?[1] There are basically four answers that have been given to these questions.

Some postmodernists have observed how heterogeneous and diverse cultures have become (Featherstone, 1991). Whereas the modern period was dominated by cultural stability and immobility, the cosmopolitan hybridisation that now surrounds us indicates that we have passed into a postmodern society. Younger generations, for instance, are far more open to international and multiethnic influences than their parents and grandparents. One consequence of this is that social identities are now far more fluid and constructed than they used to be: we assemble our biographies and life trajectories for ourselves, through experimentation and bricolage, rather than having them handed to us in religious and/or social and/or national packages of meaning. Many postmodernists therefore welcome cultural globalisation as a liberating force that overturns the homogeneity of modernity. They are, in this context, sponsors who identity a multiplicity of overlapping cultural logics.[2] So, there is no single global culture but there is a global stage on which all cultures are able to walk.

At the opposite end of the spectrum we find hecklers who state that this heterogeneity is only a surface feature of global culture and that, beneath the surface, we can identify a single cultural logic at work: that of market consumerism centred on America. Everywhere we look we find basically the same symbols advertising themselves to us, the symbols of individualistic affluence, profit, greed and selfish comfort. The apparent diversities of the global supermarket conceals a monopolisation of power by a few dominant MNCs, for example Rupert Murdoch's News Corporation. We may be free as consumers but consumerism represents only a restricted form of freedom by which we are seduced into the capitalist game of competition and commodification. Ritzer (1993) has identified the 'McDonaldization of society' where we are easily deceived by the standardisation and subtle controls of our 'fast-food' culture. And for Marxist postmodernists such as Jameson (1991) cultural globalisation is little more than the logic of advanced capitalism where the exploited fetishise the commodities that they themselves produced. Therefore, the hecklers perceive a single Americanised global culture at work. Tomlinson (1991), however, argues that this thesis of cultural imperialism ignores the extent to which local cultures adapt and transform the media products that US companies transmit around the globe.

Cultural sceptics and doubters mark out a position between these two extremes. Rather than propose either the heterogeneity of multiple logics or the homogeneity of a single logic, they claim that we need to map the dominant logics that confront each other in the global age. For instance, Barber (1995) acknowledges that Americanised popular culture (the 'McWorld') has tried economically and culturally to saturate the globe, undermining local traditions, languages and customs, but proposes that this has generated a counterreaction of nationalisms and religious faith (Jihad). McWorld and Jihad are often antagonistic but also interdependent: two sides of the same coin of cultural globalisation. Huntington (1997) takes this analysis further and thinks that the world is now divided into several civilisations, each incommensurable with the others and all locked in a struggle that reduces the power of America and may threaten world peace.

Finally, it is worth mentioning Baudrillard (1988) who subverts the distinctions drawn here between sponsors, sceptics, doubters and hecklers. Baudrillard seems to identity *both* an homogeneity *and* an heterogeneity at work. Reality has been occluded by the 'hyperreal', a stream of signs, images, simulation and facsimile beyond which no original master copy can be detected. Global culture(s) implode(s) as a self-referential code that loops infinitely into itself and from which we cannot escape because there is no 'we' to do the escaping and nothing to escape from. Because everything is a media event there is nothing to mediate; because there is so much to choose, choice becomes meaningless. Economics and politics become branches of aesthetics and aesthetics denotes an 'open enclosure' of endless seduction.

## 9.3.4 Social policy

If these are the main coordinates of the globalisation debate, where does this leave Social Policy? There is a certain amount of consensus within the discipline regarding what has been happening to developed welfare states in recent years, so the main disagreements revolve around why these developments have occurred and what may be done in response.

Globalisation seems to imply something like the following for welfare systems (Mishra, 1999: 94–109; Bonoli et al., 2000: 70–1):

1. The continuing integration of economies makes it much harder for countries to initiate Keynesianism within one country, that is, full employment, demand management, reflation and deficit spending.
2. Unemployment and underemployment undermine comprehensive, redistributive and universal welfare services. The labour market becomes post-Fordist and characterised by core–periphery polarisation, insecurity, flexibility and, at the bottom end of the market, by low-skilled, part-time service jobs.
3. Welfare reforms usually, with a few exceptions, resemble a 'race to the bottom'. Due to lower growth rates than in the post-war period, the

possibility of taxpayer revolts and demographic pressures and deficit reductions, social expenditure is on a downward trend. (As a percentage of GDP social expenditure has remained constant over time but this is due to rising demand, for example because of mass unemployment, rather than any rising quality in welfare provision.)

4. Private forms of welfare grow in importance as ideological commitments to egalitarian and expanding welfare services weaken.
5. Power shifts away from labour movements, trade unions and the corporatist state and towards capital, management, shareholders and employers' organisations.
6. Welfare reforms involve either a rush towards deregulation, retrenchment, recommodification, marketisation and privatisation, or the attempt to consolidate and preserve existing structures and expenditure levels through restructuring. Traditional left-wing reforms (public sector expansion, egalitarianism, universalism) become harder to implement and less electorally popular.
7. Across the developed world, the trend, even with Centre-Left governments in power, is towards the Right (private sector expansion, social inequality, selectivism). However, within this 'reconvergence' of welfare regimes there are still significant differences based on political priorities, historical and cultural traditions, and institutional structures.

Yet, if there is a consensus regarding the diagnosis of existing developments, there is a dissensus regarding the prognosis and recommended courses of action. Basically, there are four positions worth outlining, from those who think that the welfare state is effectively dead to those who believe that it can be reinvented (Rhodes, 1996). Let us conclude this chapter by outlining each of these in turn.

Sponsors are those who are most willing to identify or anticipate the demise of state welfare (OECD, 1994; Graham 1994). The premise at work here is that the welfare state has reduced economic growth, efficiency and national competitiveness. Globalisation requires that levels of social expenditure and taxation be cut and labour market regulations be dismantled. If a nation refuses to do so, it will find capital refusing to invest, for why should a firm build a plant in country (a) where it will have to pay higher tax and payroll contributions, when country (b) offers tax breaks and little bureaucracy? Consequently, country (a) will experience rising unemployment and declining growth rates. Nations are now integrated into the world economy as 'inward investment sites' and the job of governments is to implement supply-side measures that will increase the competitiveness of its workforce and attract international capital (Reich, 1992). Governments should regulate the private welfare market and maintain means-tested safety nets but should divest themselves of the role of welfare providers. As proof of these arguments, sponsors draw attention to the USA and UK which now have higher rates of job growth than the over-regulated European continent, and the fact that the Scandinavian social democracies have also scaled back on state welfare in the 1990s is also taken as proof.

It is this interpretation which has been most persuasive among senior politicians and policy advisors, despite the fact that it rests on shaky empirical foundations.

Gough (1996, 2000; cf. P. Pierson, 1996), for instance, cites a wealth of evidence suggesting that the above analysis is misplaced. For instance, during the 1980s the UK implemented many of the reforms that the sponsors now urge on all welfare systems in a global era, yet UK unemployment went up and growth rates decreased. The USA and Germany have long experienced similar rates of growth despite the fact that the latter has much higher levels of social expenditure than the former. So there is no strong correlation between generosity in welfare expenditure and declining rates of growth. Sceptics, therefore, assert that global competitiveness need not necessarily undermine social democratic welfare systems. Goodin et al. (1999) suggest that, even if what is now important is economic efficiency and growth, it is social democratic welfare systems which are best able to achieve such goals, in addition to their beneficial effects on poverty reduction and social equality.

What might be called 'strong scepticism' asserts that globalisation and state welfare are perfectly compatible, indeed, that the former requires the latter in a non-zero-sum game (Bonoli et al., 2000: 65–7). Global competitiveness requires high levels of education and training that only the state can provide. State provision is also required to compensate workers for the effects of flexibility and the demise of jobs-for-life: both to forestall the possibility of social unease and to help workers become re-employed through active benefit and employment policies. Finally, the state is also needed if new technologies are to be developed and introduced effectively, because only the state can underpin an appropriate culture of research and development.

Unfortunately, many governments (such as Britain's New Labour) seem torn between the position of the sponsors and that of the strong sceptics. On the one hand, they recognise the value of state welfare yet, on the other, they are afraid of middle-class revolts and a right-wing backlash.

What might be called 'weak scepticism' asserts not that globalisation and state welfare are automatically compatible but that they can be made so through appropriate compromises (Bonoli et al., 2000: 68–9). Globalisation does not signal the end of the welfare state but it does require far-reaching reforms if the latter is to survive. For instance, as well as pursuing active benefit and employment policies, it is thought necessary by some to coerce the unemployed into training and job subsidy schemes through workfare requirements: a competitive workforce cannot afford to carry free-riders. Similarly, while state provision can remain as the bedrock of well-being, people are going to have to take a greater responsibility for their own future welfare, for example through private and occupational pensions, and be required to do so by the state. Therefore, weak scepticism seems to be the preferred position of many Western European governments.

There are also those who believe that welfare can be globalised in order to counterbalance the threats to social well-being posed by extreme forms of economic globalisation. Minimum welfare standards can be protected through the construction of political institutions and regulations at the global level.

At present, the main global agencies and institutions demonstrate varying degrees of fervour for economic liberalism (Deacon et al., 1997). This is certainly the case with the IMF, the World Bank, the OECD, the WTO and the G7 group of nations, but less so with the EU and the International Labour Organisation. However, there are also, at the global level, other organisations which establish that a commitment to collective well-being is not necessarily a national affair, for example Greenpeace, Amnesty International and Unicef. Therefore, we can envisage the formation of a new global regime that institutionalises a concern for social welfare at the transnational level.

Those such as Mishra (1999) insist that while globalisation has despatched socialism and even stronger forms of social democracy, we can still defend the welfare state by supporting the 'Rhine' model of capitalism in preference to the Anglo-American model (Hutton, 1995). The superiority of the former is that it subjects economic forces to social standards of well-being whereas the latter allows the economic logic of free-market forces to subdue social welfare. So, it is still possible to imagine social standards being formulated through some form of communal consensus, standards that would be relative to that national community's level of economic development. It is these standards, rather than the traditional focus on social rights, that could then establish the rules according to which global capitalism would be regulated (cf. Fitzpatrick, 2001).

Others go further and believe that Keynesianism can be reinvented at the post-national level. Keynesianism within one country may no longer be possible, since investors can now shift capital from one country to another with relative ease, as was shown in France in 1982–83. However, if a group of countries reflate simultaneously, the scope for 'capital flight' may be more restricted. Such Euro-Keynesianism was popular on the Left in the 1980s. However, sponsors argue that globalisation renders 'Keynesianism within one region' equally redundant since capital can also fly between Europe, the USA and East Asia with relative ease. If so, might we conceive of a global Keynesianism where all developed nations reflate, taking many developing nations with them, and leaving capital with nowhere to escape to? It is currently difficult to imagine such cross-national economic strategies being agreed on let alone implemented and successfully maintained. However, if it is feasible to anticipate the introduction of global standards, the subsequent introduction of global Keynesianism may not be so utopian after all.

Finally, we have the hecklers who believe that, because globalisation is an ideological rather than an economic force, even pro-welfare discussions of global social policy represent a surrender to the radical Right agenda (McQuaig, 1998). By distracting attention away from the ongoing war between capitalism and socialism, the globalisation debate encourages a welfare politics that has already given ground to the enemy. Retrenchment is not, as governments represent it, a regrettable but unavoidable response to external constraints but an approach that those governments have chosen to make rather than pursue the longer term objectives of socialist transition. Therefore, a radical politics demands that the political will which is sapped by the globalisation debate be re-engaged through struggle and resistance.

Section 9.3 has not touched on each and every aspect of the globalisation debate but it has established that this debate embodies so many of the discussions and arguments that preceded it and that we examined in sections 9.1 and 9.2. Globalisation is often taken to represent the death of the Left–Right spectrum and yet so many of the relevant arguments are *between* Left and Right, each side constantly seeking to reinvent and renew itself in contrast to its opponent.

The debate concerning globalisation is possibly the most important debate taking place at the moment, the outcome of which will shape the societies of the twenty-first century. However, it is by no means the only important such debate. Indeed, as we turn away from economics to review, in Chapter 10, some of the more abstract theoretical innovations of recent years, we can see the extent to which Social Policy is at the forefront of some of the most interesting ideas of recent years. Social Policy may have been born in the twentieth century but the twenty-first century looks like being its coming of age.

# 10

# Recent Theoretical Developments

Inevitably, the contents of this final chapter are shaped not only by what is being debated by social theorists (Drover and Kerans, 1993; Lewis et al., 2000) but also by my own views as to what is most important and my own level of expertise (which explains my own appearance in a number of the following sections!). There is, for instance, no extended discussion of culture and cultural policy, an absence motivated by my sense that such ideas have yet to be fully addressed by the Social Policy community so that their inclusion in a textbook would be premature (Chamberlayne et al., 1999), although see below. Since the task here is to begin to think about the future, it is certain that one or more of the following subjects will not turn out to possess any long-term significance after all. Yet that is part of the game and it is a delicious irony that attempts to describe or anticipate the future are almost always foiled by the future itself. If Social Policy is coming of age, the last thing I would wish to do is to suggest that its future evolution can already be chartered in any detail.

Since telling the story of the future is a lot harder than telling the story about the past, this chapter also lacks a strong, internal narrative. The following subjects could have been arranged in any order. Yet since the point is no longer to present the reader with a neat package of ideas and theories, but to encourage you to join a conversation that is very loud and wide ranging, this hardly matters. We cannot hear everything that is going on in that conversation at any one time. All we can do is jump in and start talking ourselves. This chapter invites you to do so.

## 10.1 Postmodernism and Post-structuralism

We have touched on both postmodernism and post-structuralism throughout this book and it is now time to summarise each. However, it must be remembered that a summary can only *over*simplify a wide variety of debates and ideas.

Postmodernism condemns any attempt to devise a single, all-encompassing explanation and description of the human condition (Lyotard, 1984).[1] Such 'grand-narratives' search for a universal Truth which is, at best, a futile quest since centuries of philosophising have failed to reveal it and, at worst, have motivated the periodic cleansing of those heretics who do not believe in the Truth that many have claimed to have found (Bauman, 1993). All Enlightenment ideologies and belief systems may be defined as grand-narratives that have the potential to mutate into fundamentalism and autocracy, and the ideal of progress is nothing more than the latest attempt to find epistemic, ontological and moral certainties that are as secure as the certainties once provided by God and the Church.

In the work of Jean-François Lyotard (1925–98), postmodernism is the insistence that we abandon all grand-narratives and nurture the local narratives of particular truths and perspectives; however, according to Baudrillard (1988) such normative assumptions are themselves outdated and postmodernism is a convenient heading for an age of 'simulacra' and 'hyperreality' where it is no longer possible to distinguish between reality and representation, leaving us with the task of playing among the fragmented wreckage of the real. Somewhere in between Lyotard and Baudrillard lies the claim either that the postmodern age of pluralism, disintegration, cultural democratisation, irrationalism and eclecticism has superseded that of the modern, or, which is more likely, that what we now call the modern and the postmodern have been intertwined throughout the last three or four centuries. Postmodern theory, therefore, may celebrate relativism and the passing of all moral and political absolutes, or it may argue that since it was *absolutist* philosophies that generated relativism, postmodernism's abandonment of absolutism represents a victory *against* and not *for* relativism (Rorty, 1989).

What has all of this to do with Social Policy? A number of theorists have given several different answers to these questions (Leonard, 1997; Carter, 1998) but the following two points would seem to be most relevant. First, Social Policy has always been highly universalist, for whether the subject is concerned with how society changes or why we should change society, there has been an underlying belief in the existence of a universal human nature and universal human goals. This means that the subject may have overlooked the extent to which humanness has particularistic dimensions that cannot be compressed into a universal account without doing damage to those dimensions. Consequently, Social Policy may have been working with a distorted conception of social identity and welfare provision. Williams (1992) argues that policy debates have privileged already-dominant groups and that the kind of 'new' social divisions we reviewed in Chapter 8 have been excluded and silenced for too long. Thompson and Hoggett (1998) identify a bias in the delivery of welfare which has neglected the particular needs of groups and clients that do not conform to universal ideals. They argue for policies that are both universal and particular in their orientation.

Second, Social Policy has recently acquired more of an interest in culture and identity. As indicated in Chapter 9, cultural postmodernists often insist that our cultural contexts are much less collectivist and more consumerist than ever before (Featherstone, 1991). This means that traditional sources of identity such as class, the extended and nuclear family, religion and community are less important than they once were, so that our cultural likes and dislikes, our social bonds and affiliations, and our sense of ontological security are all far more fragile, differential and heterogeneous. Therefore, a postmodern culture is a curious blend of novelty (New Age spiritualism, experiments with identity and appearance) and nostalgia (kitsch, recycling and repackaging) as we simultaneously yearn for and reject the certainties of old. For some, the emphasis on culture means that Social Policy has to accommodate itself to the ethos of consumerism (Cahill, 1994), for others it means emphasising the importance of cultural difference, for example multiculturalism, while others are investigating the ways in which culture and structure form elements of 'the social' (Clarke, 1999). In terms of identity, some have argued in favour of communitarian accounts, some in favour of 'reflexive modernisation' (we shall review both of these below) and some argue that postmodern theory is necessary if we are to 'resocialise the individual' by recognising that identity is both differential and unified (Taylor, 1998).

Many, however, argue either that postmodernism is a distraction from the bread-and-butter issues of Social Policy or that such theories are the philosophical equivalents of free-market economics (Taylor-Gooby, 1994). The argument that postmodernists are dupes of the Right is one that has often been made (Habermas, 1987b), for, if grand-narratives ought to be abandoned, as Lyotard insists, what happens to the dreams of human emancipation and liberation? Might postmodernism be no more than an elaborate justification for the status quo? Such criticisms are suspiciously accurate, given the intellectual cartwheels that Lyotard turned in arguing that while socialism is a grand-narrative, capitalism is not. Similarly, stressing particularism may be reasonable, but, if this is allowed to supersede or, even worse, replace universalism, postmodern theory would have us abandon a humanistic vocabulary at the very time when we need it the most.

Post-structuralism is related to postmodernism but the two should not be confused as the former began its life as a specific reaction to the structuralism that grew to prominence in the humanities and social sciences in the 1960s. Structuralism can be traced back to the linguistic theories of Saussure (1857–1913) and the discipline of semiotics (the science of signs) that he inspired. Having lain dormant for several decades, semiotics was revived in the 1950s as a reaction to the dominance of humanistic theories (existentialism, liberalism) and to the dogmas of Stalinism. Structuralism attributed social phenomena not to individual action and psyche but to 'structural factors'. This meant different things to different people but the core of structuralism is a focus on the sign, that is, the linguistic unit through which meaning is produced and circulated. The sign consists of a signifier (a word, image or sound) and a signified (the concept to which the signifier is 'internally' related), both of which are 'externally' related to a referent (an object, event or relation in the non-linguistic world). Structuralists contend that all forms of understanding are dependent on understanding the total system of signs and relations between signs, with the referent being of minor importance.

The post-structuralists, however, were to go still further. They argued that structuralism had not fully escaped from humanist subjectivism and Western metaphysics, and that a concentration on the signifier would dispel the illusions of the coherent self and reveal the textual nature of the world, a text that only a post-structuralist emphasis on difference and non-identity could reveal. If the world is a text, and if there is nothing outside the text, we (I who am writing and you who are reading) are simply the textual constructions of a differential signification: we do not speak, we are spoken in and through the text; the 'self' is not unified and stable but a dispersed and fragmented flow that constantly confronts that which is 'other' to itself. This means that understanding is not about the search for origins because the text has nothing outside itself to refer to; instead, it is about tracing the fragments and flows of the text. The work of Foucault, Derrida, Bataille and Deleuze was to exert a considerable influence throughout the 1970s and 80s, although it is to Foucault that the social sciences have most often turned.

As we have seen in previous chapters, Foucault subverts our normal categories of understanding. He focuses not on knowledge and ideas but the conditions through which knowledge and ideas are generated, that is, discourses; he does not make truth-claims, nor does he assess the truth-claims of others, but examines the practices of truth-claiming. Order is not something essential to society and history but is imposed in retrospect through discursive practices and Foucault sets himself the task of unpicking those practices through a genealogical approach that dispenses with Truth and systematic explanations: it is the syntax of society that is important, not its content. Much of his work therefore consists of genealogical analyses of the institutions (the means by which knowledge/power operates) through which discursive practices are woven: the prison, the asylum, the clinic, as well as the 'institutions' of sexual conduct.

For instance, Foucault (1967) traces the historical conduits of reason and madness. During the Renaissance 'the mad' were regarded as potential sources of truth and profundity but by the seventeenth and eighteenth centuries they were equated with the antisocial forces of the criminal and the pauper, and so silenced through incarceration. The Age of Reason needed the 'unreasonable' against which to define itself. In the nineteenth and twentieth centuries madness was medicalised, that is, redefined as mental illnesses that require specialised treatment rather than punishment. So while we may like to regard the psychiatric treatment of mental illness as a sign of our enlightenment, Foucault underscores the extent to which it is another form of confinement and incarceration, albeit one that is done in terms of the rights and welfare of the individuals concerned ('rights' and 'welfare' also being discursive constructions). The modern fear of 'madness', for example schizophrenia, is a fear of the unreason which we carry within us always.

Foucault identifies the 'panopticon' as the essential metaphor for all modern institutions. The panopticon was Bentham's design for a prison and accorded to utilitarian principles. The underlying rationale was the need for as few prison officers as possible to survey as many prisoners as possible at any one time. Therefore, the officers would need to work within a central tower around which would be built many tiers of cells. The cells would be perfectly exposed, so that the prisoners would always be visible to those within the tower, but the officers would be effectively invisible. As such, the prisoners would not know when they were being observed and so would need to act as if they were under constant surveillance. Bentham's design was never actually built, but Foucault treats it as a metaphor for modern forms of discipline and normalisation. Therefore a Foucauldian reading of social policy involves the application of this metaphor as a devise for interpreting welfare institutions and administrative practices.

So, post-structuralism potentially enables us to rewrite the history of social policy and to understand welfare systems as regimes of knowledge/power that do not necessarily follow a steady incline of progress, liberation and empowerment (Dean, 1999; Rose, 1999a; Petersen et al., 1999; cf. Dean, 1991). For instance, Fraser (1989) analyses needs not as units of human nature but as constructions that emerge through a long series of discursive and social struggles. Needs do not precede politics, they are politicised through and through: sites on which experts try to turn the body into objects of administrative knowledge, where oppositional movements challenge these disciplinary strategies and where 'privatisers' try to separate the sphere of private responsibility from that of public action. Therefore, post-structuralism does not offer prescriptions for welfare reform because it insists that all truth-claims are manifestions of, and articulated by, particular (non-universal) 'power interests'. Instead, it is an exercise in 'clearing the ground', in undermining accepted narrative accounts so that the disadvantaged are able to make new claims against those with whom they are in perpetual struggle.

As with postmodernism, however, many have argued that this is all an unwelcome diversion from real-world issues: a need still has to be fulfilled whether or not it is a discursive construction. Furthermore, if post-structuralism rejects universal accounts of the good, what reason do we have to prefer one truth-claim over another, for example why should the Right's discourse be rejected in favour of the Left's? What is the point of clearing the ground unless we are trying to build the universal foundations of human liberation? Political post-structuralists (Laclau and Mouffe, 1985) observe that social struggle is never ending and that a final resting place, a post-political utopia, can never arrive; yet, even if this were true, are not some struggles more just and less cataclysmic than others, and do we not need a universal reference point if we are to identify them? In short, post-structuralism contributes some interesting insights to Social Policy, ones that the subject cannot afford to neglect, but, like postmodernism, perhaps cannot *by itself* form the basis of a 'new Social Policy' for the twenty-first century.

## 10.2 Communitarianism

According to communitarianism (as we noted in Chapter 4), postmodern and post-structuralist theories are understandable reactions to the contentless abstractions of liberalism, yet they only compound the liberal error of neglecting the extent to which we are *communal* beings. For communitarians, it makes no sense to regard ourselves as separable from the communal and associative contexts which give us meaning and purpose: we understand and communicate with the world through interrelational networks and spend our lives within a web-like series of kinships and alliances from which we derive our sense of self and of right and wrong. Ferdinand Tonnies (1855–1936) identified two forms of social relationship: *Gemeinschaft*, which refers to the spontaneous and affective relationships that resemble familial groupings, and *Gessellschaft*, which refers to more calculative and impersonal associations (Tonnies, 1955). On the basis of this distinction communitarianism makes two claims: first, that *Gemeinschaft* is the superior form of relationship and, second, that *Gessellschaft* has come to dominate developed societies with detrimental effects for social welfare. The welfare state has failed because it has welded superficial forms of equality onto a hollow caricature of the individual self. Communitarianism is therefore not only an explanatory but also a prescriptive theory of human society which says that social reforms must always create and maintain strong communal bonds.

Conservative, liberal and radical versions of communitarianism have all been proposed. Communitarianism fits neatly into the conservative emphasis on family values, patriotism and social obligations; it also ties into those versions of liberalism that eschew the universalist abstractions of traditional liberal thought (Dagger, 1997); and it also bears comparison to the fraternal and solidaristic values that have been proposed by socialists (Walzer, 1983). Those such as Etzioni (1994; cf. Sandel, 1996) therefore argue that communitarianism is ideologically neutral and can reappear under any number of political guises. The key to understanding many social policy developments in the 1990s is understanding why Etzioni is both right and wrong: he is right in the sense that communitarianism can stand above the ideological fray but wrong if he imagines that it can do so for any length of time.

Feminists have argued, for instance, that communitarianism is a masculinist theory that resurrects 'golden age' versions of community that were often less than ideal for women and so ignores the disadvantages experienced by women both then and now (Frazer and Lacey, 1993). Communitarians can be condemned for lauding the injustices of patriarchal marriage, of communities and families that depended on the unacknowledged and unpaid care work of women defined as nothing more than wives and mothers. Furthermore, socialists charge communitarians with concentrating on culture and ignoring economics (Miller, 1990). Although society should be built around a strong communal ethos, this cannot happen unless the injustices of capitalism are overcome. By painting itself as ideologically neutral, and by ignoring the primary importance of economic reform, communitarianism only associates itself with right-wing versions of community that stress social inequality, cultural homogeneity and anti-welfare politics.

These criticisms surfaced as communitarianism began to wield a certain amount of political influence in the 1990s, especially in the USA and UK. Both Clinton and Blair utilised the communitarian vocabulary as a means of distinguishing themselves from the Right's laissez-faire individualism and the Left's egalitarianism that they each claimed to have rejected. However, communitarianism's influence became intermingled with the continuing influence of the radical Right that had already adopted an emphasis on obligations and duties (see section 4.2.2). Therefore, any radical implications of communitarianism were quickly drowned out by a moral authoritarianism that stressed the duties of the poor (although usually not of the rich), which tied rights into responsibilities (so that what had formally been defined as social rights became redefined as acts of taxpayer largesse for which recipients should be humbly grateful), which focused on the 'undeserving' poor (and never the undeserving rich) and that repudiated the ideology of the free market (although usually not the practice). Many have therefore suspected that the 'Third Way' is nothing new, being little more than an expression of the most recent accommodation which social democracy has made with free-market capitalism (Levitas, 1998).

Welfare reform in the 1990s, therefore, was based much more on right-wing than left-wing versions of communitarianism (cf. Driver and Martell, 1998) (see Table 10.1). In some respects, therefore, welfare reform in the 1990s was a continuation of the 1980s with an emphasis on self-help rather than dependency, benefit sanctions rather than benefit entitlements, market-type competition rather than government-directed cooperation, supply-side skills rather than demand-side management, an emphasis on standards rather than institutional structures, reforms driven by political prescriptions rather than the opinions of independent experts, league tables and consumerism rather than a bottom-up consensus between service providers and users, managerialism rather than professional autonomy, bean-counting rather than service quality. Yet in other respects residual traces of an older social democracy can be

**Table 10.1** Two versions of communitarian welfare

|  | *Left* | *Right* |
|---|---|---|
| Citizenship | Fundamental civil, political and social rights precede duties | Social duties are fundamental. Rejects category of social rights |
| Justice | Equality of opportunities and equalisation of outcomes | Equality of opportunities only |
| Social order | Economic justice and common ownership | Moral prescription and restrictive codes of behaviour |
| Morality | Democratic, progressive, plural and multicultural | Elitist, traditional and homogeneous |
| Market | Obligations of employers and corporations | Obligations of employees and benefit claimants |
| State | Sets framework for egalitarian justice through redistributive policies | Minimal welfare provision and emphasis on security, social control, law and order |
| Individual | Altruistic and cooperative | Self-interested and competitive |

detected. Some measure of redistribution was effected through fiscal measures, minimum wages and in-work benefits.

If it is the right-wing version of communitarianism which has been most influential, there are theoretical innovations which tend more towards the Left. Although he eschews communitarian thought, Paul Hirst (1994) has been at the forefront of a theory of 'associational democracy' (cf. Cohen and Rogers, 1995) that bears certain similarities. The state may have become a remote, impersonal and alien force in modern society but the solution is not to privatise society and collectivise morality, as the Right seem to wish, but to 'pluralise' the public sphere and democratise civil society. Hirst argues that large parts of government can and should be devolved to self-governing, voluntary, publicly funded and publicly accountable associations whose members would have varying degrees of control over public systems of provision. Sometimes that control would be direct, at other times it would be more indirect. This would combine the traditional socialist emphasis on the social control of the economy, while empowering people as citizens rather than consumers.

An associational welfare system would maintain an emphasis on distributive justice but would be less collectivist than the classic welfare state. Self-governing associations would deliver and/or purchase many of the services that are currently provided either by the state or the market, yet play a more systematic role in the welfare of society than the traditional independent sector. Hirst envisages that we would all become members of these associations, with rights to vote and exit if we choose, and that the associations will have to meet

certain criteria if they are to receive public funds. Therefore, around a bureau-
cratised 'core' of state services there would be an associational periphery,
bolstered by a basic income (Fitzpatrick, 1999a), within which there is a far
closer relationship between the providers and recipients of welfare than at
present.

Associational democracy, therefore, stresses the importance of communal
interaction but in a far more liberal and open fashion than moral communitarians such as Etzioni et al.

## 10.3 Environmentalism

Ecological thought represents an attempt to broaden our conception of community beyond the present generation of humans and encompass all ethically
significant beings – both humans and non-humans of both present and future
generations – as well as the ecosystem of which we are all an interdependent
part.

Although environmentalism has deep historical roots (Pepper, 1996), its
political import really dates from the 1960s. The Green movement arose
partly as a reaction to the self-destructive practices of Western societies
and partly as a response to a growing environmental consciousness. Environmentalism basically says that we cannot make infinite demands of a planet that
only has a finite store of resources. The political case is made by pointing out
that demand has been exceeding supply for some generations now due to the
practices of (mainly) Western societies: namely, unsustainable rates of growth,
production and consumption. The effects of these practices are alleged to
manifest themselves in a number of ways: an accelerating rate of species
extinction, the disappearance of rain forests and arable land, the thinning of
the ozone layer, global warming and the growing incidence of environmental
disasters. Therefore, we ought to develop new ways of living and working that
are both ecologically and socially sustainable.

It is from this point on that ecological thought fragments into a number of
competing ideas as to how this could be achieved. Initially, the Green movement was ill served by the alarmism of those who created social (and arguably
racist) panics about the 'population explosion' and those who predicted
worldwide ecological collapse in the near future (Meadows et al., 1972). In
the long term this was to have two consequences. First, it gave rise to a
survivalist discourse where some Greens and many anti-Greens regarded
environmentalism as an anti-modern philosophy of austerity and crisis management. Some went so far as to insist that averting crises meant that democracy would have to be abandoned in favour of rule by an ecological elite of
scientists and technocrats (Ophuls, 1977). Second, once the alarmist predic-
tions did not manifest themselves a Green backlash set in, often driven by the
radical Right, which portrayed environmentalists as anti-capitalist misfits who

overlooked the ingenuity of humans and our ability to adapt technologically and economically to changing ecological conditions.

Within these parameters at least three versions of environmentalism can be identified (cf. Dryzek, 1997).[2] First, there is a free-market environmentalism which identifies only modest ecological problems that can be addressed through market mechanisms (Anderson and Leal, 1991). For instance, as a resource becomes scarce the cost of extracting it becomes higher, the price of purchasing it will therefore rise, so demand for it will fall and the resource will be preserved as a result. And if government action is necessary, this can take the form of regulatory frameworks that help the market to work better, for example through carbon emissions trading.

Second, there is an environmental pragmatism (Brundtland Commission, 1987) which envisages the necessity of some changes to our socioeconomic systems, if 'sustainable development' is to be realised, through any number of instruments depending on the nature of the problem being addressed: market, state, or both, at local, national and international levels. Growth can be made environmentally benign so that Third World deprivation can be solved without damaging living standards in the developed world. Of importance here is an 'ecological modernisation' (Hajer, 1995) which refers to the adaptation of existing policy-making processes to new environmental goals by the construction of a broad consensus between governments, corporations, environmental lobbyists and scientists.

Third, there are several schools of eco-radicalism: socialist, feminist and anarchist. All of these agree that wide-ranging institutional reforms are necessary and that tweaking existing political and economic structures is unlikely to be sufficient. Eco-socialists (Pepper, 1993; Benton, 1996; Little, 1998) maintain that environmental destruction is linked to class exploitation and social inequalities: the privileged consume resources in trying to maintain their advantages and the underprivileged consume them by trying to improve their position relative to the privileged. Therefore, a system of common ownership, social equality and global, macro-social planning would rationalise our use of resources by abandoning the waste-producing competitiveness of market capitalism. Eco-feminists (Merchant, 1992) claim that the domination of nature is tied into the domination of women by men. In other words, the urge to dominate, subdue, exploit and oppress is essentially a patriarchal impulse that has to be socially and morally overturned by the values of caring, nurturing, cooperation, empathy and sharing. Shiva (1994) relates this critique to the particular position of Third World women. Eco-anarchists (Bookchin, 1980) contend that relying on either the state or the market is likely to be futile and only the cooperative actions of egalitarian, autonomous collectives can produce the decentralised, 'horizontal' systems of social and economic organisation that we need for sustainability. Whatever their differences, however, each of the above seems to support a 'Green democracy' (Doherty and de Geus, 1996) on the basis that a long-term sustainability can only be built from the bottom up and cannot be imposed by scientific and political elites without incurring some kind of popular backlash that will divert us away from environmental objectives.

Environmentalism did not begin to exert more than a marginal impact on Social Policy until the 1980s, although at least two important precursors can be identified. Ivan Illich (1990) offers numerous critiques of productivism (the idea that economic growth is an end in itself) and contrasts this with the 'conviviality' of creative autonomy and the interrelations of the social and natural environments (cf. Schumacher, 1973). Modern society may be incredibly affluent in material terms but not in its quality of life since it is science and technology that controls us rather than we who control science and technology. A convivial society would reverse its priorities, methods of organisation and means of reform. James Robertson (1983) calls for a SHE (sane, humane and ecological) society which observes the limits to growth and where human activity is more concerned with 'being' than with 'getting'. 'Ownwork' rather than paid employment would become the source of wealth. Ownwork refers to self-organised, meaningful work, whether performed in the formal or informal economy, that is valued for reasons other than those of financial remuneration.

In the 1980s it was Andre Gorz (1982, 1989) who carried these ideas forward. Gorz bade farewell to the working class as a potential agent of social transformation and began to elaborate an eco-socialism that, he believed, would be supported by a 'non-class of non-workers', that is, those who exposed the failings of both capitalism and welfare statism. Rather than regard paid work as the means to prosperity, Gorz has consistently regarded liberation *from* paid work as the true goal of radical politics. He therefore distinguishes between two spheres: that of heteronomous activity (the realm of necessity) and that of autonomous activity (the realm of freedom). An eco-socialist society would minimise the amount of time which we have to spend in the former and maximise the amount of time we can spend in the latter. The policy instruments supported by Gorz are working-time reductions and basic income. Working-time reductions would correct the maldistribution of paid employment which currently exists (with some having too much and others not enough). The working life of each able-bodied individual could thereby be equalised out at 20,000 hours during their lives: the equivalent of 10 years' full-time work. The basic income would be a 'second cheque' that would compensate for the reduction in wages as a source of income and would demonstrate that one's citizenship duties had been performed (cf. Gorz, 1999: 85–93).

Environmentalism began to influence Social Policy in the 1990s (Pierson, 1998; George and Wilding, 1999) and it is now rare to find either a general or a theoretical introductory textbook that does not mention it. A number of different approaches have been taken. Ferris (1993) has affiliated ecologism to postmodern ideas, Cahill (1994) dealt with it as part of the 'new consumerism', Huby (1998) adopted a social administration approach that focuses on the use of resources and Fitzpatrick (1998) sketches an 'ecological model of welfare'. At the very least, Green social policies require an ethical rethinking, so that material growth and consumerism are no longer regarded as the yard-sticks of well-being and 'welfare sustainability' becomes an organising principle of welfare reform, and an institutional reorganisation that recognises the value of the informal economy and takes the emphasis away from paid employment.

However, the implications of these general principles are not necessarily clear. A 'conservative' approach to the design and implementation of Green social policies takes existing policy-making procedures and political priorities, for example low taxation and market flexibility, as its starting point and so resembles ecological modernisation. More radical approaches seek the reform of those procedures and priorities by reaching back to some older ideas, such as common ownership of both the social and natural commons, and by making the Green social movement a key actor of social and welfare reform. This opens up a space for a radical version of ecological modernisation that tries to combine both pragmatism and idealism. There is no reason why, at least in the short term, these two approaches cannot both be elaborated upon and pursued by theorists of different ideological persuasions who are willing to learn from each other. Nevertheless, an ideological tension between the two undoubtedly exists and, if the specifics of Green social policies are to be developed, a lot depends on whether this tension can be transcended into something new. If not, contrasting theorists may have to plough their own contrasting furrows as best they can and contend against each other for influence within the social arena (Fitzpatrick and Cahill, forthcoming). The best conclusion for us to reach here is that solid conclusions are going to take another few years to be worked out.

## 10.4 Risk Society

However, some insist that one such conclusion is already in place: namely that we live in a 'risk society' and that Green social policies must aim at the management and prevention of risks. The literature dealing with risks and risk society is vast but the most important figure within the debate is that of Ulrich Beck (1992, 1995; Beck et al., 1994).

Beck's basic thesis is disarmingly simple. It is not the end of modernity and the beginning of postmodernity that we have reached, but the end of *first* modernity and the beginning of *second* modernity. The first modernity was an age of industrial progress and all political and social institutions were designed to generate 'goods' (welfare, growth) in a world that was taken to be stable, knowable and scientifically calculable. By contrast, the second modernity that emerged in the latter period of the twentieth century is a risk society characterised by the attempt to limit, manage and negotiate a way through a series of 'bads' and hazards. Beck had been struck by the worldwide consequences of the Chernobyl and Bhopal disasters, and the way in which invisible but deadly contagion had crossed spatial borders (national boundaries) and temporal borders (since the effects will be felt for generations) without any respect for the tidy assumptions of industrial modernity. For instance, nuclear and industrial pollution undermines the simple class hierarchies of the industrial order, affecting the ghettoes of the rich as well as those of the poor. Generalising, he proposed that these were simply the most extreme examples of the riskiness of second modernity. It is not that the world has become a more dangerous place: it is that hazards are the unintended consequences of our centuries-old attempt to pacify and control the world. The second modernity is therefore the first modernity turned in on itself in a process of reflexive modernisation and coping with riskiness necessitates the democratisation of science and policy-making: decisions can no longer be left to technocratic elites but must be subjected to the discursive visibility of public space.

In the English-speaking world Beck's ideas were initially popularised by Tony Giddens. Giddens (1994) drew a distinction between traditions and communities that are open and self-reflexive and those that are closed and dogmatic. In a globalised world in which the pace of change accelerates, making it seem ever-more volatile and unknowable, the battle is on between those who wish to construct new forms of social democracy that can encompass the reflexivity of open communities and those fundamentalists who wish to invoke a new golden age of simple, certain and unquestionable authority (Giddens, 1999).

Of what relevance is all of this to Social Policy (Taylor-Gooby, 2000)? The welfare state was a direct descendant of industrialism, urbanisation and collectivism, that has been concerned both with the production of goods through economic wealth generation and with the just distribution of those goods through social institutions. If this type of industrial society has been superseded, the welfare state's traditional roles of economic intervention and social management can be identified as one of the main sources of risks. Through the principle and systems of social insurance and universal provision, the welfare state has always been concerned with the calculation and amelioration of collective risks. Today, not only are those 'safety systems' less effective but they are, themselves, the origins of risk and insecurity: insurance against old age, unemployment and sickness is aimed at the predictable and collective events of the life course and not at the individualised contingencies of a risk society.

Beck seems to suggest that social policy reform is now characterised by something of an 'insurance panic' where we each rush to the private market to insure as much of our lives and circumstances as possible. Yet whereas social insurance was meant to decrease our sense of fear and anxiety, the new forms of state and private insurance increase insecurity by reminding us of the ever-present possibility of bankruptcy and deterioration. To put it simply: the poor are insecure because they are conscious of their *actual* vulnerability and the rich are insecure because they are conscious of their *potential* vulnerability. For Giddens (1998) the solution is not a tax-and-spend redistribution of material resources but an ethic of 'positive welfare' where people are armed with the emotional and moral tools, and the equal opportunities, they need to construct their own social biographies without reliance on either the dirigiste state or the economic liberal market. Giddens has repeatedly welcomed the Blairite Third Way as such a solution.

The UK Social Policy literature is now replete with discussions of risk, anxiety, insecurity and a host of similar concepts (Manning and Shaw, 2000). For instance, Culpitt's (1999) contention is that it is the economic liberalism of the radical Right which has exploited and, to a large extent, generated the risk society in order to consolidate its own ideological hegemony by defeating the concepts and values of the classic welfare era. The vocabulary of individualism (choice, preference, consumption) has replaced that of collectivism (altruism, needs, the public sphere) and the emphasis in policy-making is now on minimising risks and fears rather than on maximising social justice. However, economic liberalism's success depends on the constant manufacture of the risks that only the free market is supposedly able to subdue. Therefore, those who are victimised and excluded by right-wing economics, that is, the dependent underclass, are those who are identified by economic liberals as representing a danger to the well-earned prosperity of the suburban taxpayer. Engaging with risk theory, therefore, means turning the debate back on the radical Right discourse that neither Beck nor Giddens deal with adequately.

## 10.5 Information and Communication Technologies

Some social policy theorists have recently been taking an increasing interest in the information society thesis and information and communication technologies (ICTs) (Loader, 1997, 1998). ICTs include all forms of computer-based information systems (informatics), Internet-related technologies and virtual reality (machine–body interface) technologies. In developed societies it is now virtually impossible to live and work without encountering one or all of these, and, as we experience the convergence of televisions, personal computers and mobile/video phones over the next few years, the new technologies will become even harder to avoid. We can analyse ICTs from a social administration perspective which focuses, for instance, on the delivery of welfare, or from a theoretical and interdisciplinary perspective that requires us to re-examine the fundamental meaning of welfare and the welfare state. Lying somewhere in between can be found a discussion of poverty and whether new forms of information inequality and digital injustice are being created.

*Welfare Theory*

The social and public administration approach is concerned with several overlapping areas. First, there is the issue of computer availability and literacy: the extent to which schools and universities are online; the quality of the skills being taught; the implications of home computers for the learning process; the implications for distance learning. Second, government publications can be increasingly accessed with relative ease: the web pages of government departments can now provide at least some information for researchers, welfare rights advisers and campaigners. Third, there are those who allege that ICTs make it easier for those with the will and resources to evade national tax authorities, placing a question mark over the future funding of generous welfare services. Fourth, these technologies bear consequences for employment levels, research and development, and supply-side interventions into the labour market. Finally, cyberspace is the realm of financial globalisation which supposedly flows over and around the immobilities of welfare states.

To date, it is the subjects of sociology, politics, law and cultural studies that have set the terms of the wider, theoretical debate. To a large extent, this debate assumes that we now live in a post-industrial network society, although one whose basic characteristics have been carried over from the industrial hierarchies of the post-Enlightenment. This means that although the debate is highly contemporary it is built around some familiar themes. First, to what extent do ICTs empower or disempower individuals and under what circumstances should the state have the power to monitor ICT-related messages or determine what is posted on the web? Second, do ICTs bring people together in new 'cyber-communities' or help to fragment society? Third, can ICTs enhance democracy, civic association, the public sphere, citizenship and the political process, or might they perpetuate a widespread alienation and estrangement from public affairs? Finally, are ICTs the means by which a surveillance society of social control is enhanced or the means by which the holders of power can be made visible and brought to account? Running throughout these debates is a contest between the technophiles for whom ICTs can do no wrong and the technophobes who concentrate on the negative effects of ICTs.

Yet Social Policy has also helped to set the terms of this debate. After all, it was the welfare state that constructed the original databases that ICTs have merely modernised and integrated. Welfare citizens have always had their employment, contributory, educational, marital and medical histories catalogued and monitored from cradle to grave. By and large, therefore, it is the technophiles who have dominated the 'digital welfare' debate, often allied to an ideology of market globalisation: for in a global knowledge economy, where perpetual competition is assumed to rule out egalitarian redistribution, it is easy to interpret ICTs as representing the inevitable individualisation of post-state welfarism (Lawson, 1998). If this view prevails, policy reforms are likely to create a 'self-service' welfare system where individuals are given the basic tools to access the information network and so, supposedly, have no excuses for failure. In this hands-off 'remote control' system, bureaucratic paternalism is replaced with cybernetic perfectionism ('use the technology to help yourself, or else!'), a digitally updated version of Victorian self-help with penalties for the undeserving. This vision is most likely to be realised in the social security system. The electronic submission of benefit applications and inquiries (teleclaiming) is becoming more widespread and most benefits are soon likely to be paid via smart cards, and while these innovations may cut down on administrative costs and bureaucracy, reduce the number of errors and increase the flow of information to the claimant, they also make it easier for authorities to control and survey the habits and movements of claimants. Data matching (the computerised integration of databases) makes it easier to target fraud and so easier to distract attention away from the social origins of behaviour which may not be fraudulent at all.

Fitzpatrick (2000) tries to develop a critical response to this market-based technophilia. The concept of 'virtual rights' is intended to supplement and strengthen Marshall's distinction between civil, political and social rights. At the simplest level, it means centring the information society on embodied and interrelated individuals rather than on the atomised 'data-selves' that once shadowed us but whose shadows *we* are starting to resemble. It also means appreciating the complex interactions of the offline and online worlds and ensuring that individuals have control of, and access to, the information which is circulating about them through the informatic networks. Finally, as citizenship becomes more digitalised, the concept is meant to reinvigorate the social rights of citizenship so that the latter become enshrined in the constitutional and legislative acts of the information age and are no longer the 'charitable entitlements' that they have become during the laissez-faire era. Ultimately, then, the lesson for Social Policy is that 'cyberpolicies' are only as good as the socioeconomic policies that they accompany.

## 10.6 Social Control and Surveillance

As noted in the previous section, it is possible that ICTs are enhancing systems of social control and surveillance. For instance, Bauman (1998) observes how, in a world of cultural and economic globalisation, the wealthy become more mobile whereas the poorest become less mobile, both physically and symbolically. This distinction manifests itself in a number of ways. Geographically, the poor are segregated into ghettoes of deprivation while the rich *segregate themselves* into gated communities of security, exclusivity and privilege (Davis, 1990). This spatial polarisation is maintained through the construction of material walls, for example security patrols and zero-tolerance policing, and 'virtual walls', for example the low credit ratings and high insurance premiums which poverty attracts. Social control is therefore directed by the cosmopolitan elites against the hire-and-fire underclass: the former wage war on the latter by replacing social policy with penal policy, the welfare state with a strict law and

order regime, the commonality of fate with communities of exclusion. Globalised capital needs the underclass of cheap, flexible labour to be invisible when
*inside* the labour market, with few rights and little collective voice, and visible
when *outside* the labour market as a criminalised, demonised and controlled
subclass of scroungers and fraudsters. The 'criminalisation of poverty' is therefore the means by which the privileged justify their good fortunes to themselves
and construct a moral consensus with the less affluent middle classes against the
poorest. Bauman notes the extent to which the costs of prison-building, impri-
sonment, policing and private security are immune from the kind of taxpayer
revolts that inhibit the proper funding of welfare services. As a consequence, the
prison populations of America and Britain have shot up since the 1980s (Christie, 1994; Jones-Finer and Nellis, 1998; Taylor, 1999; Young, 1999).

This analysis implies that a politics of welfare is being replaced with a politics
of enforcement (Jordan, 1998) and that it is basic fears rather than basic needs
that increasingly drive social policy-making. Fitzpatrick (2001) characterises
these changes as a shift towards a 'post-social security state': 'post-social'
because 'globality' and 'community' have largely replaced 'society' as the
main reference points for Western governments, and 'security' because the
need for individual security is more prominent than the need to join collectiv-
ities of mutual well-being. However, the security nets of the state capture all,
even if the consequences of this ensnarement are much more severe for the
poorest. On the one hand, then, we have a polarisation and ghettoisation of
society, and yet, on the other, we also have a certain reconvergence of experience. As society is subjected to the permanent revolutions of market modernisation, as the worker becomes no more than a unit of profit and loss (Sennett,
1998) and as retraining and multiskilling replace job security, so all employees
are exposed to the 'creative anxieties' of the new managerialism. For the
poorest this leads to a constant revolving door between unemployment and
cheap, unsatisfying jobs, for the affluent it implies overwork, 'presenteeism'
and endless career moves (Schorr, 1992). ICTs now militarise the skyline in
the form of CCTVs and infiltrate every component of the informational web
net: for instance, the indiscriminate surveillance of employees through their
computer terminals is now a common practice of corporate employers on the
lookout for theft, disloyalty and malingering.

All of this implies that the paternalism of the classic welfare state has fused
with the disciplinary and correctional systems that had lain more or less
dormant since the time of the Victorian Poor Law. Social control, social
surveillance and social welfare are becoming increasingly harder to distinguish.

## 10.7 The Body

The body is of increasing interest within the Social Policy literature (Ellis and
Dean, 1999). When we talk of 'the body' we may be referring to the actual,

physical body of individuals, or to the way in which bodies affect (and are affected by) the spatial and temporal environments through which they move, or to the body as a metaphor, or to social bodies such as populations. We may also be investigating how bodies are represented and/or controlled.

This concern with the body is another that can be traced back to Foucault (1979; cf. Turner, 1996). Foucault draws attention to the extent to which bodies are medicalised and managed within modern societies so that there is a range of 'normality', a range out of which each of us must not stray if we wish to avoid the label of deviant. The contemporary obsessions with fitness, dieting and healthy lifestyles reflect the ways in which bodies may be disciplined, with so much social interaction hinging on judgements concerning bodily appearance: how we appear to others and how others appear to us relates to this assumed deviation from some cultural norm. Indeed, disability theorists have long drawn attention to the means by which 'disabled bodies' are represented as less than, rather than different to, 'abled' bodies. In short, when we look at bodies we are looking not just at the corporeality of the physical body but at the way in which it is commodified, fetishised and managed by a complexity of expert discourses. The body is a site of social struggle.

This focus on disciplinary embodiment offers a new way of looking at Social Policy. Ellis (1999) identifies several stages in the development of capitalism. In the first phase of industrial capitalism bodies were defined in terms of their physical efficiency as extensions of factory machines that had to be regulated into the public and private spaces of the urban environment. With the first signs of welfare capitalism bodies became collectivised and subjected to the techniques of statistical quantification. The 'labouring bodies' of the late nineteenth and early twentieth centuries were the bodies that had to be made physically and morally fit for the good of the empire. The classic welfare state demanded the 'socially efficient' bodies of a full employment economy. Finally, the period since the 1970s has seen the emergence of 'independent bodies' that define themselves as market consumers, detaching themselves from relations of social interdependence and absorbing the risks endemic to a flexible economy. Fitzpatrick (1999b) has extended this analysis and identified 'cyborg bodies' as being significant to Social Policy. Cyborgs are bodies whose boundaries become indistinct, with the organic and the machine-like permeating one another. Think, for instance, of the way in which fibreoptic technology allows us to visualise the interior of bodies and the implications of this for the battle over abortion and women's reproductive rights.

## 10.8 New Genetics

Perhaps the most contentious area of 'biopolicy' concerns that of genetics. Social Policy and genetics have a common history (King, 1999), with many of

the architects of the welfare state professing a belief in the eugenic programmes that were popular in the first third of the twentieth century and
which were applied in an extreme form in Nazi Germany.[3] In fact, the welfare
state can be interpreted either as a reflection of eugenic presumptions, that is,
the institutionalisation of social superiority and inferiority, or as an attempt to
create an egalitarian society that would reveal genetic inferiority to be as much
a characteristic of the upper as of the lower classes. The 'new genetics',
however, emphasises humanitarian goals that were anathema to many eugeni-
cists. For instance, through somatic cell therapy we can address debilitating
conditions such as Alzheimer's and Parkinson's diseases, with genetically
modified (GM) foods, it is alleged, we can cure world hunger and through
the creation of transgenic species we can solve medical conditions such as
haemophilia. However, critics allege that the new genetics has worrying
implications: if people are able to breed designer babies, this might create a
'genetic underclass'; GM foods undermine biodiversity and are possibly dangerous; genetic engineering might discriminate against disabled people (Rifkin, 1998; Shakespeare and Kerr, 1999).

There are five main areas where genetics and Social Policy interact. First,
there are implications for health care and health costs. Will genetic innovations
make us less dependent on medical biotechnology or more dependent? Will
they lower health care costs in the long term or raise them? Second, there are
implications for insurance systems. The genetically disadvantaged may have to
pay higher premiums than others and may not even receive any coverage at all.
Also, people may be less reluctant to be genetically screened for life-threatening
conditions if the resulting information is to be released to insurance companies. Third, there are implications for workplace discrimination. Workers and
job applicants may be judged not on proven ability but on their genetic
endowments. Fourth, the patenting of genes and of gene-related techniques
may hand excessive amounts of power over to biotechnology companies.
Fifth, the combination of genetics and ICTs, known as bioinformatics, has
implications for individual privacy.

In short, biopolicies may shift the emphasis away from social explanations
of, and social solutions to, inequality, injustice and oppression and towards
pathological explanations which concentrate on the failings of individuals
rather than the institutional contexts within which they live together. That
such social policies may take us further towards the pathological utopia
described at the beginning of this book is a possibility that we are all going
to have to think about in the not-too-distant future.

The conversation that I mentioned at the beginning of this chapter should be
slightly more audible now and you should have a better idea as to which parts
of it you wish to join first. Be aware, however, that once you join there is a
sense in which you can never leave. This is because theoretical debates are not
just academic exercises but resources which forever change our view of the

world. For some, this involves knowing more about where they already are; for others, it involves sighting alternative forms of society and ways of life. If the first nine chapters of this book established that welfare theory has roots which stretch back for many centuries, this chapter makes clear that we are still only at the very beginning of the journey that welfare theorists have to make. As such, this book is both an introductory text and an attempt to make sense of that journey. But this cannot be done in isolation. Those of you who choose to do nothing more than eavesdrop on the conversations of welfare theorists are actually accumulating very little: theory has to be *done* in order to be learned, and listening to others is a fairly pointless exercise unless you are also prepared to *talk*. Theory is a collective discourse, a dialogue between those who share similar concerns and those who are not afraid of returning to first principles whenever necessary. Welfare theory gives an order to the social world, and to our attempts to improve the well-being of interdependent individuals, but, paradoxically perhaps, we can only maintain that order if we are prepared to subvert our cosy assumptions and favourite ideas from time to time. In short, the conversation never ends.

# Concluding Remarks

If nothing else, this book should have provided evidence for the following three claims. First, it is possible and necessary to take welfare-related themes and issues into account when discussing social and political theory. Indeed, we might go as far as to insist that there is a school of welfare theory in addition to the schools of social and political theory that textbooks normally focus on. The boundaries between these schools are certainly porous and subject to constant negotiation, yet to narrate the histories of social and political thought without substantial reference to welfare and welfare policies is to miss a key feature in the development of modern societies.

Second, welfare theory has roots that extend far into history. Some of these roots are theoretical, so that 'well-being' was an important although, in many cases, unarticulated aspect of a theorist's work; some are institutional, in that welfare institutions helped to shape the social background against which theorists laboured, influencing their outlook on society and social problems. In short, we need to be aware of the extent to which present debates evolved out of those which occupied our predecessors. Yet welfare theory is by no means limited to the history of ideas, for, as the last chapter should have demonstrated, the subject is forever renewing itself, adding imaginative and innovative issues to its panorama of concerns. The roots of history carry us far into the future.

Finally, any cogent account of welfare theory must aim to balance its ideological and non-ideological dimensions. The former is organised largely, although not exclusively, around the Left–Right spectrum, the epitaph for which should not yet be written; the latter denotes the less political and more philosophical elements of the subject, that is, those which make political theorising possible in the first place. Any account of welfare theory which veers too closely towards the ideological will reduce itself to little more than a political party manifesto, yet any account that ignores the ideological will miss the most exciting question which Social Policy asks: how can we improve our social environments? Hopefully, this book has balanced the ideological and non-ideological in such a way that readers are now better equipped to address this question than they were before.

Yes, Social Policy can be an incredibly boring subject, and quite right too. It is not the primary job of Social Policy to be sexy but to critique welfare systems and the effect that those systems have on the well-being of the population.

Such critiques are needed now more than ever, for although it would be misguided to idolise the post-war welfare state, the shift away from that kind of system (albeit a shift that has occurred at different speeds and for different reasons in different countries) has yet to find an alternative that is both as humane *and* efficient as its predecessor. Therefore, if academics and policy-makers adopt a stripped-down approach to language and debate, this is an entirely appropriate response to the demands of the subject. None of which is to claim that Social Policy is never sexy and inspiring. Indeed, the best texts are those that combine rigorous analysis of policy and welfare with a passion and commitment that puts the rest of us to shame.

And yet, I cannot help feeling that something has been lost in recent years. As I have just reiterated, the theoretical roots of Social Policy reach deep into history and, time and again, that history demonstrates how the utopian impulse has been a major source of inspiration. It is this impulse which has become more muted in recent years, perhaps because there has been something of a double movement occurring within the subject of late – certainly evident in the UK where the ideology of welfare has altered quite profoundly.

The first movement is a process of retreat. Initially, the Right expected that social expenditure could be cut and welfare institutions could be dismantled quite easily, demonstrating an almost Maoist faith in the power of political will. Since state welfare services have proved to be more robust than their detractors anticipated – although not to the extent that the classic welfare state (with its ideology of redistributive universalism) can be said to have survived intact – those expectations have either had to be revised downwards or else, as with those who constantly predict the end of the world, pushed further into the future. Consequently, those on the Right who have not convinced them-selves that we already live in a capitalist paradise spent much of the 1990s becoming obsessed (or re-obsessed, it might be said) with culture, ethics and behaviour. 'If the capitalist paradise has failed to arrive', they reasoned, 'this cannot be because our ideas were wrong but because the feckless poor, spurred on by their apologists in the public sector, have not altered their attitudes and habits sufficiently.' Therefore, the retreat I am describing is not so much a retreat from state welfare institutions, even though the contemporary emphasis on markets, quasi-markets, voluntarism and charity is undoubtedly important, as a retreat from the view that collective action on the social environment, motivated by liberal and egalitarian principles, will facilitate communal and altruistic forms of social citizenship. By contrast, at the heart of the radical Right can be found a dystopian image of the human self as that which requires the disciplines of the market and the authority of social order if anarchy and lawlessness are to be avoided (Fukuyama, 1999). Therefore, when critics contend that the Third Way lies on a continuum with the radical Right, this is not because the former is as mean and penny-pinching as the latter, but because the ideology of welfare has barely changed, even as both social expenditure and the status of the public sector begin to rise.

The second movement is a reaction to this counterreaction: an attempt to recolonise some of the ground that has been lost. For the most part, these forays are conducted by those academics and policy-makers who wish to revitalise and re-embody the previous ideology of welfare in a variety of institutions, some of which would be familiar (state universalism) and some of which would be new (watch this space). Often, what is being conducted here is the construction of 'micro-utopias': oases of progressive radicalism in a seemingly endless desert of market forces and authoritarian centralism. Yet it is more rare now than it once was to find these micro-utopias being joined up into a grand-narrative, a macro-utopia that represents a vision of general social emancipation. Of course, various anti-capitalist 'isms' still exist and may have an important role to play if we can ever leave behind the manic depressiveness of the present age. This manic depressiveness exists because while the global 'victory' of capitalism breeds triumphalism it has also deprived capitalism of an 'other', that is, something with which it can be contrasted. Hence, triumphalism and anxiety now alternate with one another at an ever-increasing speed and ferocity. This partly explains the current crisis of the welfare state, for if the latter was a means by which capitalism could assert its economic and moral superiority to communism, the disappearance of capitalism's traditional enemy leaves state welfare without its former rationale. Yet, given that the welfare state helped to stabilise post-war capitalism, this crisis is also a crisis of capitalism, one that the process of globalisation has yet to resolve because that process is itself a manifestation of crisis.

So what we arguably lack is, first, a convincing macro-utopian account of social change and, second, the willingness to translate the macro-utopias we do possess into practical schemes of reform. Social Policy cannot be blamed if such schemes have been thin on the ground in recent years. If you are retreating from the enemy, you don't stop to paint the landscape. Yet Social Policy might be blameworthy if it allows itself to become trapped within that landscape, focused forever on what is immediate to it and ignoring what is potentially beyond the horizon. This is where welfare theory has a role to play. For the job of welfare theory is not only to provide the theoretical resources by which critiques of the immediate can be carried out; it is also to stoke the flame of the utopianism that can light the way towards that imaginary horizon, if and when we decide we want to make the journey. It is not possible for any single text to perform this task alone, but a book such as this can help to keep the tradition of welfare theory alive. Indeed, my influence is far less considerable than yours: since welfare theory is ultimately something that has to be *done*, rather than merely written about, it can only be done collectively by those, yourselves, who decide to step out of the path of the onrushing storm. Pragmatic Social Policy can win individual conflicts but only utopian Social Policy can end the war.

None of which is to forget the caveat noted at the beginning of the book: it is as dangerous to arrive at utopia as it is to avoid its call. Utopianism is a journey without a destination, a target that we must aim to miss, and progressive social policies are most effective when this contradiction is admitted – just as radial Right policies are most damaging when it is ignored. If we fail to dream of utopia, we may sleepwalk forever through the infinitely replicated aisles of global capitalism, but if we forget that these are just dreams then we might never wake up from the nightmares that utopianism can also conjure. The war will never end after all. The utopian needs the pragmatist as much as the pragmatist needs the utopian. The war may never end but some wars are more just than others, some horizons are wider than others, and the battles that are fought within them more capable of improving social welfare than those we seem to be engaged in at the moment.

# Notes

## Chapter 1

1. In more modern terminology, the mathematical means by which individual welfares are aggregated together into social welfare is called the 'social welfare function'. That debate, however, takes us too far into the realm of economics to be worth pursuing here.
2. The question of whether someone is better or worse off is based on the value judgements and preferences of the individual concerned.
3. Although Hirsch (1977) argues that many goods are 'positional': the value and efficacy of a positional good to me depends on how many others possess it, for example a degree is worth more when only 10 per cent of the population have degrees than when 50 per cent of the population possess them.

## Chapter 2

1. Against this argument, the philosopher David Hume (1711–76) would point out that this is to perform an illegitimate move from an 'is' (a fact) to an 'ought' (a value). The fact that we all have basic needs does not, in and of itself, require that public funds be made available to fulfil those needs. A further argument concerning why we should value basic needs in the first place is required, but this cannot be derived from the existence of those needs themselves (Hume, 1969).
2. Although Arneson (1989) believes that people cannot be held entirely responsible for their tastes due to the effects of social circumstances, for example people are heavily influenced in their tastes by their parents (cf. Roemer, 1993).
3. This is an admittedly generous reading, since a utilitarian society has the potential to be profoundly unequal if that is what the maximisation of utility was interpreted as requiring!
4. It can be objected that Rawls is justifying *inequalities* rather than social equality as such (Temkin, 1993). If it could be shown that massive inequalities were to the benefit of the least well off (something approximating to Blue society) then, according to Rawlsian justice, so be it. In one sense this is true. Yet given that natural talents and social resources tend to generate vast inequalities and given that these talents and resources are undeserved, according to Rawls (see below), the translation of Rawlsian principles into real-world settings would seem to require a politics of equalisation. So although he is not primarily a social egalitarian, his liberalism does imply a distinct egalitarian dimension.

5. This definition of equal outcomes refers to the effects that a particular service has for its users and is therefore slightly different to the definition discussed above which referred to the overall consequences that social policies could be said to have for society.
6. The strongest commitment to equal outcomes has been found in Scandinavia (Esping-Andersen, 1990).
7. Or we might prefer a kind of 'affirmative action', whereby preferential treatment is given that falls short of a 'quota system'.

# Chapter 3

1. A distinction is sometimes made between liberty and freedom, but here we shall treat the two as synonymous for reasons of simplicity.
2. Although the Nazis, who were inspired by both Nietzsche and Spencer, went even further than social Darwinism in believing that the state did have a significant role to play in weeding out the so-called biologically inferior.
3. See the Wilt Chamberlain argument (Nozick, 1974: 160–4).
4. Although Thomas Paine (1737–1809) had also rebelled against a crude individualism at the end of the eighteenth century, arguing for state-run welfare services and benefits to be made available to all (Paine, 1969).
5. Additionally, very few of the earth's regions could be properly self-sufficient (cf. Sale, 1985).
6. Anarchism shares many ideas and assumptions with the environmentalism that we examine in Chapter 10.

# Chapter 4

1. The principle defined by J. S. Mill (1989) which says that you can morally do whatever you wish as long as you do not harm others in the process.
2. Although see the argument of Kymlicka in section 4.10.3; also, some argue that animals have rights, see section 4.10.2.
3. This is known as 'moral hazard'.
4. In addition to the following three categories, it is also possible to conceive of a 'virtual citizenship' that relates to information and communication technologies (ICTs) (Fitzpatrick, 2000). However, we will omit this heading here as it would unnecessarily replicate section 10.5.
5. We will examine ecologism at greater length in Chapter 10.

# Chapter 5

1. On the surface, this resembles an organic state that binds the disparate elements of society together, yet Hobbes is ultimately a materialist philosopher who works squarely in the empirical tradition, for whereas he firmly rejects the idea of limited government, his absolutism originates in an idea of the state as the outcome of a social contract and elements of individualism would survive in a Hobbesian society.

2. Weber also famously defined the state as that which holds a monopoly on the use of legitimate violence within a given territory.
3. The other forms of authority are traditional or historical authority and charismatic authority.
4. Horizontal redistribution implies redistribution within a lifetime, that is from the wealthier times of your life to the poorer, and from low-risk occupations to high-risk ones. Vertical redistribution implies redistribution between classes, especially from rich to poor.
5. It should also be noted that whereas pluralists welcome the idea of a pluralist state, elitists are split between those who dislike the idea of elitist power and those who regard it as natural and inevitable.
6. Now, don't you feel just a little bit manipulated?

# Chapter 6

1. Compare this with the organic/individualistic distinction we applied to the state (section 5.1).
2. For the main critiques of pluralism and elitism, readers are referred back to the previous chapter.

# Chapter 7

1. Marcuse (1969) tried repeatedly to identify a potential agent of social transformation by looking to the new social movements.

# Chapter 8

1. Ecologism can also be fitted under this heading but is discussed in Chapter 10.
2. This enables us to focus more effectively on things such as anti-Islamic, anti-Irish and anti-semitic prejudices.
3. However, use of the term 'black' is still widespread in academia as an umbrella term, an inadequate yet inescapable shorthand for the diversity of non-white ethnic groups.
4. Ageism can be perpetrated against both young and old, but we are here concerned with the latter.

# Chapter 9

1. By 'culture' I mean social value systems.
2. Note, however, that 'cultural sponsors' often reject the free-market zeal of 'economic sponsors'.

# Chapter 10

1. Here, I shall make no distinction between 'postmodern', 'postmodernity' and 'postmodernism'.
2. These follow an ideological spectrum even though many Greens have claimed to be 'beyond Left and Right' in their opposition to all forms of industrialism. Note that I am leaving 'deep ecology' to one side as the social implications of this kind of romantic spiritualism are far from clear.
3. The subject of eugenics is concerned with heritability and can lead to the promotion of policies based on sterilisation and selective breeding.

# Bibliography

Ackerman, B. and Alstott, A. (1999) *The Stakeholder Society*, New Haven, CT: Yale University Press.

Abel-Smith, B. and Townsend, P. (1965) *The Poor and the Poorest*, London: G. Bell & Sons.

Ackroyd, P. (1999) *Thomas More*, London: Vintage.

Aglietta, M. (1979) *A Theory of Capitalist Regulation*, London: New Left Books.

Alcock, P. (1997) *Understanding Poverty*, 2nd edn, Basingstoke: Macmillan – now Palgrave.

Althusser, L. (1969) *For Marx*, London: Allen Lane.

Althusser, L. and Balibar, E. (1970) *Reading Capital*, London: New Left Books.

Amin, A. (ed.) (1994) *Post-Fordism*, Oxford: Blackwell.

Anderson, T. and Leal, D. (1991) *Free Market Environmentalism*, Boulder, CO: Westview Press.

Arber, S. and Ginn, J. (1995a) 'The Mirage of Gender Equality: Occupational Success Within the Labour Market and Within Marriage', *British Journal of Sociology*, 46(1): 21–43.

Arber, S. and Ginn, J. (eds) (1995b) *Connecting Gender and Ageing*, Milton Keynes: Open University Press.

Aristotle (1988) *Politics*, Cambridge: Cambridge University Press.

Arneson, R. (1989) 'Equality and Equal Opportunity for Welfare', *Philosophical Studies*, (56): 77–93.

Arneson, R. (1997) 'Egalitarianism and the Undeserving Poor', *Journal of Political Philosophy*, 5(4): 327–50.

Aron, R. (1970) *Main Currents in Sociological Thought*: Vol. 2, Harmondsworth: Penguin.

Askonas, P. and Stewart, A. (eds) (2000) *Social Inclusion*, Basingstoke: Macmillan – now Palgrave.

Axelrod, R. (1984) *The Evolution of Cooperation*, New York: Basic Books.

Baker, J. (1987) *Arguing for Equality*, London: Verso.

Baldwin, P. (1990) *The Politics of Social Solidarity*, Cambridge: Cambridge University Press.

Banton, M. (1987) *Racial Theories*, Cambridge: Cambridge University Press.

Barbalet, J. (1988) *Citizenship*, Milton Keynes: Open University Press.

Barber, B. (1995) *Jihad vs. McWorld*, London: Ballantine Books.

Barnes, H. and Baldwin, S. (1999) 'Social Security, Poverty and Disability', in Ditch, J. (ed.) *Introduction to Social Security*, London: Routledge.

Barnes, H., Thornton, P. and Campbell, S. (1998) *Disabled People and Employment*, Bristol: Policy Press.

Barnett, C. (1986) *The Audit of War*, Basingstoke: Macmillan – now Palgrave.

Barrett, M. and McIntosh, M. (1982) *The Anti-social Family*, London: Verso.

Barry, B. (1995) *Justice as Impartiality*, Oxford: Oxford University Press.

Barry, N. (1987) *The New Right*, London: Croom Helm.

Barry, N. (1999) *Welfare*, 2nd edn, Milton Keynes: Open University Press.

Baudrillard, J. (1988) *Selected Writings*, edited by M. Poster, Cambridge: Polity.

Bauman, Z. (1987) *Freedom*, Milton Keynes: Open University Press.

Bauman, Z. (1993) *Postmodern Ethics*, Oxford: Blackwell.

Bauman, Z. (1998) *Globalization*, Cambridge: Polity.

Beck, U. (1992) *Risk Society*, London: Sage.

Beck, U. (1995) *Ecological Politics in an Age of Risk*, Cambridge: Polity.

Beck, U., Giddens, T. and Lash, S. (1994) *Reflexive Modernisation*, Cambridge: Polity.

Bell, D. (1973) *The Coming of Post-industrial Society*, New York: Basic Books.

Bentham, J. (1984) *Chrestomateia: The Collected Works of Jeremy Bentham*, Oxford: Clarendon.

Benton, T. (ed.) (1996) *The Greening of Marxism*, New York: Guilford Press.

Berlin, I. (1969) *Four Essays on Liberty*, Oxford: Oxford University Press.

Bonoli, G., George, V. and Taylor-Gooby, P. (2000) *European Welfare Futures*, Cambridge: Polity.

Bookchin. M. (1980) *Towards an Ecological Society*, Montreal: Black Rose Books.

Bourdieu, P. (1977) *An Outline of a Theory of Practice*, Cambridge: Cambridge University Press.

Bourdieu, P. (1998) *Acts of Resistance*, Cambridge: Polity.

Bourdieu, P. and Passeron, J. (1977) *Reproduction in Education, Society and Culture*, London: Sage.

Bradshaw, J. (1972) 'A Taxonomy of Social Need', *New Society*, (496): 640–3.

Brundtland Commission (1987) *Our Common Future*, Oxford: Oxford University Press.

Buchanan, J. (1986) *Liberty, Market and the State*, Hemel Hempstead: Harvester Wheatsheaf.

Bulmer, M. and Rees, A. (eds) (1996) *Citizenship Today*, London: UCL Press.

Burke, E. (1968) *Reflections on the Revolution in France*, Harmondsworth: Penguin.

Burrows, R. and Loader, B. (eds) (1994) *Towards a Post-Fordist Welfare State?*, London: Routledge.

Bussemaker, J. and Voet, R. (1999) 'Citizenship and Gender: Theoretical Approaches and Historical Legacies', *Critical Social Policy*, 18(3): 277–307.

Butler, J. (1990) *Gender Trouble*, London: Routledge.

Bytheway, B. (1995) *Ageism*, Milton Keynes, Open University Press.

Cahill, M. (1994) *New Social Policy*, Oxford: Blackwell.

Callender, C. (1996) 'Women and Employment', in Hallett, C. (ed.) *Women and Social Policy*, Hemel Hempstead: Harvester Wheatsheaf.

Callinicos, A. (2000) *Equality*, Cambridge: Polity.

Campbell, J. and Oliver, M. (1996) *Disability Politics*, London: Routledge.

Carabine, J. (1996) ' "Constructing Women": Women's Sexuality and Social Policy', in Taylor, D. (ed.) *Critical Social Policy: A Reader*, London: Sage.

Carter, J. (ed.) (1998) *Postmodernity and the Fragmentation of Welfare*, London: Routledge.

Castells, M. (1996) *The Rise of the Network Society*, Oxford: Blackwell.

Castells, M. (1997) *The Power of Identity*, Oxford: Blackwell.

Castells, M. (1998) *The End of Millennium*, Oxford: Blackwell.

Cavalieri, P. and Singer, P. (eds) (1995) *The Great Ape Project*, New York: St. Martin's Press – now Palgrave.

Chamberlayne, P., Cooper, A., Freeman, R. and Rustin, M. (eds) (1999) *Welfare and Culture in Europe*, London: Jessica Kingsley Publishers.

Charles, N. (2000) *Feminism, the State and Social Policy*, Basingstoke: Macmillan – now Palgrave.

Christie, N. (1994) *Crime Control as Industry*, London: Routledge.

Clark, T. and Lipset, S. (2000) *The Breakdown of Class Politics*, Washington DC: Woodrow Wilson Centre Press.

Clarke, J. (1999) 'Coming to Terms with Culture', in Dean, H. and Woods, R. (eds) *Social Policy Review 11*, London: Social Policy Association.

Cohen, G. A. (1990) 'On the Currency of Egalitarian Justice', *Ethics*, (99): 906–44.

Cohen, G. A. (1995) *Self-ownership, Freedom and Equality*, Cambridge: Cambridge University Press.

Cohen, J. and Rogers, J. (1995) *Associations and Democracy*, London: Verso.

Cole, G. D. H. (1920) *Guild Socialism Re-stated*, London: Leonard Parsons.

Coleman, J. and Fararo, T. (1993) *Rational Choice Theory*, London: Sage.

Collard, A. (1988) *The Rape of the Wild*, London: The Women's Press.

Commission on Social Justice (1994) *Social Justice*, London: Vintage.

Cox, O. C. (1970) *Caste, Class and Race*, New York: Monthly Review.

Craig, G. (1999) ' "Race", Social Security and Poverty', in Ditch, J. (ed.) *Introduction to Social Security*, London: Routledge.

Crosland, T. (1956) *The Future of Socialism*, London: Jonathan Cape.

Crosland, T. (1974) *Socialism Now and Other Essays*, London: Jonathan Cape.

Culpitt, I. (1999) *Social Policy and Risk*, London: Sage.

D'Souza, D. (1996) *The End of Racism*, New York: Free Press.

Dagger, R. (1997) *Civic Virtues*, Oxford: Oxford University Press.

Dahl, R. (1961) *Who Governs?*, New Haven, CT: Yale University Press.

Dahl, R. (1985) *Polyarchy*, New Haven, CT: Yale University Press.

Daly, M. (1979) *Gyn/Ecology*, London: The Women's Press.

Daly, M. (2000) *The Gender Division of Welfare*, Cambridge: Cambridge University Press.

Davis, M. (1990) *City of Quartz*, London: Verso.

de Jasay, A. (1989) *Social Contract, Free Ride*, Oxford: Clarendon.

de Tocqueville, A. (1990) *Democracy in America*, New York: Vintage Books.

Deacon, B. with Hulse, M. and Stubbs, P. (1997) *Global Social Policy*, London: Sage.

Deakin, N. (1987) *The Politics of Welfare*, London: Methuen.

Dean, H. (1991) *Social Security and Social Control*, London: Routledge.

Dean, H. and Taylor-Gooby, P. (1992) *Dependency Culture*, Hemel Hempstead: Harvester Wheatsheaf.

Dean, H. with Melrose, M. (1999) *Poverty, Riches and Social Citizenship*, Basingstoke: Macmillan – now Palgrave.

Dean, M. (1999) *Governmentality*, London: Sage.

Dell, E. (2000) *A Strange Eventful History*, London: HarperCollins.

Della Porta, D. and Diani, M. (1999) *Social Movements*, Oxford: Blackwell.

Doherty, B. and de Geus, M. (eds) (1996) *Democracy and Green Political Thought*, London: Routledge.

Donald, J. and Rattansi, A. (eds) (1992) *Race, Culture and Difference*, London: Sage.

Donovan, C., Heaphy, B. and Weeks, J. (1999) 'Citizenship and Same Sex Relationships', *Journal of Social Policy*, **28**(4): 689–709.

Donzelot, J. (1979) *The Policing of Families*, Baltimore, MD: John Hopkins University Press.

Doyal, L. and Gough, I. (1991) *A Theory of Human Needs*, Basingstoke: Macmillan – now Palgrave.

Driver, S. and Martell, L. (1998) *New Labour*, Cambridge: Polity.

Drover, G. and Kerans, P. (eds) (1993) *New Approaches to Welfare Theory*, Aldershot: Edward Elgar.

Dryzek, J. (1997) *The Politics of the Earth*, Oxford: Oxford University Press.

Dubos, R. (1998) *So Human an Animal*, New Brunswick, NJ: Transaction Publishers.

Durkheim, E. (1984) *The Division of Labour in Society*, Basingstoke: Macmillan – now Palgrave.

Dworkin, R. (1977) *Taking Rights Seriously*, London: Duckworth.

Dworkin, R. (1981a) 'What is Equality? Part 1: Equality of Welfare', *Philosophy & Public Affairs*, (10): 283–345.

Dworkin, R. (1981b) 'What is Equality? Part 2: Equality of Resources', *Philosophy & Public Affairs*, (10): 655–69.

Eckersley, R. (1992) *Environmentalism and Political Theory*, London: UCL Press.

Eder, K. (1993) *The New Politics of Class*, London: Sage.

Edgell, S. (1993) *Class*, London: Routledge.

Ellis, K. (1999) 'Welfare and Bodily Order: Theorising Transitions in Corporeal Discourse', in Ellis, K. and Dean, H. (eds) *Social Policy and The Body*, Basingstoke: Macmillan – now Palgrave.

Ellis, K. and Dean, H. (eds) (1999) *Social Policy and the Body*, Basingstoke: Macmillan – now Palgrave.

Elster, J. (ed.) (1986a) *Rational Choice*, New York: New York University Press.

Elster, J. (1986b) *Making Sense of Marx*, Cambridge: Cambridge University Press.

Engels, F. (1969) *The Condition of the Working-class in England*, St Albans: Panther.

Esping-Andersen, G. (1990) *The Three Worlds of Welfare Capitalism*, London: Sage.

Esping-Andersen, G. (ed.) (1996) *Welfare States in Transition*, London: Sage.

Esping-Andersen, G. (1999) *Social Foundations of Post-Industrial Economies*, Cambridge: Cambridge University Press.

Etzioni, A. (1994) *The Politics of Community*, London: Fontana.

Evason, E. (1999) 'British Pensions Policies: Evolution, Outcomes and Options', in Ditch, J. (ed.) *Introduction to Social Security*, London: Routledge.

Faludi, S. (1992) *Backlash*, London: Vintage.

Featherstone, M. (1991) *Consumer Culture and Postmodernism*, London: Sage.

Ferris, J. (1993) 'Ecological Versus Social Rationality: Can There Be Green Social Policies?', in Dobson, A. and Lucardie, P. (eds) *The Politics of Nature*, London: Routledge.

Field, F. (1995) *Making Welfare Work*, London: Institute of Community Studies.

Fitzpatrick, T. (1998) 'The Implications of Ecological Thought for Social Welfare', *Critical Social Policy*, **18**(1): 5–26.

Fitzpatrick, T. (1999a) *Freedom and Security*, Basingstoke: Macmillan – now Palgrave.

Fitzpatrick, T. (1999b) 'Social Policy for Cyborgs', *Body & Society*, **5**(1): 93–116.

Fitzpatrick, T. (2000) 'Critical Cyber Policy: Network Technologies, Massless Citizens, Virtual Rights', *Critical Social Policy*, **20**(3): 375–407.

Fitzpatrick, T. (2001) 'New Agendas for Social Policy and Criminology', *Social Policy & Administration*, 35(2): 212–29.

Fitzpatrick, T. and Cahill, M. (eds) (forthcoming) *Greening the Welfare State*, Basingstoke: Palgrave.

Foucault, M. (1967) *Madness and Civilisation*, New York: Pantheon.

Foucault, M. (1979) *The History of Sexuality:* Vol. 1, London: Allen Lane.

Foucault, M. (1984) *The Foucault Reader*, edited by Paul Rabinow, Harmondsworth: Penguin.

Fox Harding, L. (1996) *Family, State and Social Policy*, Basingstoke: Macmillan – now Palgrave.

Fraser, N. (1989) *Unruly Practices*, Cambridge: Polity.

Fraser, N. (1997) *Justice Interruptus*, London: Routledge.

Frazer, E. and Lacey, N. (1993) *The Politics of Community*, Hemel Hempstead: Harvester Wheatsheaf.

Freeden, M. (1990) *Rights*, Milton Keynes: Open University Press.

Friedan, B. (1983) *The Feminine Mystique*, Harmondsworth: Penguin.

Friedman, M. (1962) *Capitalism and Freedom*, Chicago: Chicago University Press.

Fukuyama, F. (1992) *The End of History and the Last Man*, New York: Free Press.

Fukuyama, F. (1999) *The Great Disruption*, London: Profile Books.

Gallie, D. (2000) 'The Labour Force', in A. H. Halsey with J. Webb (eds) *Twentieth-century British Social Trends*, Basingstoke: Macmillan – now Palgrave.

Gamble, A. (1988) *The Free Economy and the Strong State*, Basingstoke: Macmillan – now Palgrave.

George, V. and Page, R. (eds) (1995) *Modern Thinkers on Welfare*, Hemel Hempstead: Harvester Wheatsheaf.

George, V. and Wilding, P. (1994) *Welfare and Ideology*, Hemel Hempstead: Harvester Wheatsheaf.

George, V. and Wilding, P. (1999) *British Society and Social Welfare*, Basingstoke: Macmillan – now Palgrave.

Geras, N. (1989) *Discourses of Extremity*, London: Verso.

Geras, N. (1995) *Solidarity in the Conversation of Humankind*, London: Verso.

Geras, N. (1998) *The Contract of Mutual Indifference*, London: Verso.

Giddens, T. (1982) *Profiles and Critiques in Social Theory*, Berkeley, CA: University of California Press.

Giddens, T. (1984) *The Constitution of Society*, Cambridge: Polity.

Giddens, T. (1991) *Modernity and Self-identity*, Cambridge: Polity.

Giddens, T. (1994) *Beyond Left and Right*, Cambridge: Polity.

Giddens, T. (1998) *The Third Way*, Cambridge: Polity.

Giddens, T. (1999) *Runaway World*, London: Profile Books.

Gilmour, I. (1992) *Dancing with Dogma*, London: Simon & Schuster.

Gilroy, P. (1987) *There Ain't No Black in the Union Jack*, London: Hutchison.

Ginsburg, N. (1979) *Class, Capital and Social Policy*, London: Macmillan – now Palgrave.

Glennerster, H. and Hills, J. (eds) (1998) *The State of Welfare*, Oxford: Oxford University Press.

Goldthorpe. J., Llewellyn, C. and Payne, C. (1980) *Social Mobility and Class Structure in Modern Britain*, Oxford: Clarendon.

Goldthorpe, J., Lockwood, D., Bechhofer, F. and Platt, J. (1969) *The Affluent Worker in the Class Structure*, Cambridge: Cambridge University Press.

Goodin, R. (1988) *Reasons for Welfare*, Princeton, NJ: Princeton University Press.
Goodin, R. and Le Grand, J. (eds) (1987) *Not Only the Poor*, London: Allen & Unwin.
Goodin, R., Headey, B., Muffels, R. and Dervin, H.-J. (1999) *The Real Worlds of Welfare Capitalism*, Cambridge: Cambridge University Press.
Goodman, R., White, G. and Kwon, H.-J. (1998) *The East Asian Welfare Model*, London: Routledge.
Gordon, D., Adelman, L., Ashworth, K., Bradshaw, J., Lister, et al. (2000) *Poverty and Social Exclusion in Britain*, York: Joseph Rowntree Foundation.
Gorz, A. (1982) *Farewell to the Working-class*, London: Pluto.
Gorz, A. (1989) *Critique of Economic Reason*, London: Verso.
Gorz, A. (1999) *Reclaiming Work*, Cambridge: Polity.
Gough, I. (1979) *The Political Economy of the Welfare State*, London: Macmillan – now Palgrave.
Gough, I. (1996) 'Social Welfare and Competitiveness', *New Political Economy*, 1(2): 210–32.
Gough, I. (2000) *Global Capital, Human Needs and Social Policies*, Basingstoke: Palgrave.
Gowan, P. (1999) *The Global Gamble*, London: Verso.
Graham, C. (1994) *Safety Nets, Politics and the Poor*, Washington: Brookings Institute.
Gramsci, A. (1971) *Selections from Prison Notebooks*, London: Lawrence & Wishart.
Gray, J. (1993) *Beyond the New Right*, London: Routledge.
Green, D. (1996) *Community Without Politics*, London: Institute for Economic Affairs.
Green, T. H. (1986) *Lectures on the Principles of Political Obligation*, Cambridge: Cambridge University Press.
Greer, G. (2000) *The Whole Woman*, London: Anchor Books.
Habermas, J. (1975) *Legitimation Crisis*, London: Hutchison.
Habermas, J. (1984) *Reason and the Rationalisation of Society*, Boston: Beacon Press.
Habermas, J. (1987a) *The Theory of Communicative Action*, 2 vols, Cambridge: Polity.
Habermas, J. (1987b) *The Philosophical Discourse of Modernity*, Cambridge: Polity.
Habermas, J. (1994) 'Citizenship and National Identity', in Van Steenbergen, B. (ed.) *The Condition of Citizenship*, London: Sage.
Hajer, M. (1995) *The Politics of Environmental Discourse*, Oxford: Oxford University Press.
Hall, S. and Jacques, M. (eds) (1989) *New Times*, London: Lawrence & Wishart.
Hall, S., Critcher, C., Jefferson, T., Clarke, J. and Roberts, B. (1978) *Policing the Crisis*, London: Macmillan – now Palgrave.
Halsey, A. H., Lawder, H., Brown, P. and Wells, A. (eds) (1997) *Education*, Oxford: Oxford University Press.
Hardin, G. (1977) 'The Tragedy of the Commons', in Hardin, G. and Baden, J. (eds) *Managing the Commons*, San Francisco, CA: W. H. Freeman.
Harvey, D. (1989) *The Condition of Postmodernity*, Oxford: Blackwell.
Hayek, F. (1944) *The Road to Serfdom*, London: Routledge & Kegan Paul.
Hayek, F. (1960) *The Constitution of Liberty*, London: Routledge & Kegan Paul.
Hayek, F. (1976) *Law, Legislation and Liberty*. Vol. 2, London: Routledge.
Hayek, F. (1979) *Law, Legislation and Liberty*. Vol. 3, London: Routledge.
Heath, A. (1987) 'Class in the Classroom', *New Society*, (81): 13–152.
Heath, A. and Payne, C. (2000) 'Social Mobility', in A. H. Halsey with J. Webb (eds) *Twentieth-century British Social Trends*, Basingstoke: Macmillan – now Palgrave.
Hegel, G. (1967) *Philosophy of Right*, Oxford: Oxford University Press.

Hegel, G. (1977) *The Phenomenology of Spirit*, Oxford: Oxford University Press.

Held, D. (1995) *Democracy and the Global Order*, Cambridge: Polity.

Held, D., McGrew, A., Goldblatt, D. and Perraton, J. (1999) *Global Transformations*, Cambridge: Polity.

Herrnstein, R. and Murray, C. (1994) *The Bell Curve*, New York: Free Press.

Hewitt, M. (1992) *Welfare, Ideology and Need*, Hemel Hempstead: Harvester Wheatsheaf.

Hewitt, M. (2000) *Welfare and Human Nature*, Basingstoke: Macmillan – now Palgrave.

Hills, J. (1997) *The Future of Welfare*, 2nd edn, York: Joseph Rowntree Foundation.

Hindess, B. (1987) *Freedom, Equality and the Market*, London: Routledge.

Hindess, B. (1996) *Concepts of Power*, Oxford: Blackwell.

Hirsch, F. (1977) *The Social Limits to Growth*, London: Routledge.

Hirst, P. (1994) *Associative Democracy*, Cambridge: Polity.

Hirst, P. and Thompson, G. (1996) *Globalisation in Question*, Cambridge: Polity.

Hobbes, T. (1973) *Leviathan*, London: J. M. Dent & Sons.

Huby, M. (1998) *Social Policy and the Environment*, Milton Keynes: Open University Press.

Hume, D. (1969) *A Treatise on Human Nature*, Harmondsworth: Penguin.

Huntington, S. (1997) *The Clash of Civilisations and the Remaking of World Order*, London: Simon & Schuster.

Hutton, W. (1995) *The State We're In*, London: Vintage.

Hutton, W. and Giddens, T. (eds) (2000) *On the Edge*, London: Jonathan Cape.

Illich, I. (1990) *Tools for Conviviality*, London: Marion Boyars.

Inglehart, R. (1990) *Culture Shift in Advanced Society*, Princeton, NJ: Princeton University Press.

Jameson, F. (1991) *Postmodernism*, London: Verso.

Jessop, B. (1994) 'The Transition to Post-Fordism and Schumpeterian Workfare State', in R. Burrows and B. Loader (eds) *Towards a Post-Fordist Welfare State?*, London: Routledge.

Jessop, B. (1999) 'The Changing Governance of Welfare: Recent Trends in its Primary Functions, Scale and Modes of Coordination', *Social Policy & Administration*, 33(4): 348–59.

Jones, C. and Novak, T. (1999) *Poverty, Welfare and the Disciplinary State*, London: Routledge.

Jones, S. (1996) *In the Blood*, London: HarperCollins.

Jones-Finer, C. and Nellis, M. (eds) (1998) *Crime and Social Exclusion*, Oxford: Blackwell.

Jordan, B. (1985) *The State*, Oxford: Blackwell.

Jordan, B. (1996) *A Theory of Poverty and Social Exclusion*, Cambridge: Polity.

Jordan, B. (1998) *The New Politics of Welfare*, London: Sage.

Joseph Rowntree Foundation (1996) *Meeting the Needs of Continuing Care*, York: Joseph Rowntree Foundation.

Kant, I. (1999) *Critique of Pure Reason*, Cambridge: Cambridge University Press.

Keane, J. (1988) *Democracy and Civil Society*, London: Verso.

Kestenbaum, A. (1996) *Independent Living*, York: Joseph Rowntree Foundation.

Keynes, J. M. (1954) *The General Theory of Employment, Interest and Money*, London: Macmillan – now Palgrave.

Kierkegaard, S. (1992) *Either/Or*, Harmondsworth: Penguin.

King, D. (1987) *The New Right*, Basingstoke: Macmillan – now Palgrave.
King, D. (1995) *Actively Seeking Work?*, Chicago: Chicago University Press.
King, D. (1999) *In the Name of Liberalism*, Oxford: Oxford University Press.
Korpi, W. (1983) *The Democratic Class Struggle*, London: Routledge & Kegan Paul.
Kumar, K. (1978) *Prophecy and Progress*, Harmondsworth: Penguin.
Kumar, K. (1995) *From Post-industrial to Post-modern Society*, Oxford: Blackwell.
Kymlicka, W. (1990) *Contemporary Political Philosophy*, Oxford: Clarendon.
Kymlicka, W. (1995a) *The Rights of Minority Cultures*, Oxford: Clarendon.
Kymlicka, W. (1995b) *Multicultural Citizenship*, Oxford: Oxford University Press.
Laclau, E. (1990) *Reflections on the Revolution of Our Time*, London: Verso.
Laclau, E. and Mouffe, C. (1985) *Hegemony and Socialist Strategy*, London: Verso.
Lash, S. and Urry, J. (1987) *The End of Organised Capitalism*, Cambridge: Polity.
Laski, H. (1935) *The State in Theory and Practice*, London: George Allen & Unwin.
Lavalette, M. and Mooney, G. (eds) (2000) *Class Struggle and Social Welfare*, London: Routledge.
Lawson, G. (1998) *Netstate*, London: Demos.
Layard, R. (1998) *Tackling Unemployment*, Basingstoke: Macmillan – now Palgrave.
Le Grand, J. (1982) *The Strategy of Equality*, London: Allen & Unwin.
Lechner, F. and Boli, J. (eds) (2000) *The Globalisation Reader*, Oxford: Blackwell.
Leonard, P. (1997) *Postmodern Welfare*, London: Sage.
Levine, A. (1998) *Rethinking Liberal Equality*, Ithaca, NY: Cornell University Press.
Levitas, R. (ed.) (1986) *The Ideology of the New Right*, Cambridge: Polity.
Levitas, R. (1996) 'The Concept of Social Exclusion and the New Durkheimian Hegemony', *Critical Social Policy*, 16(1): 5–20.
Levitas, R. (1998) *An Exclusive Society?*, Basingstoke: Macmillan – now Palgrave.
Lewis, G. (2000) *'Race', Gender, Social Welfare*, Cambridge: Polity.
Lewis, G., Gewirtz, S. and Clarke, J. (eds) (2000) *Rethinking Social Policy*, London: Sage.
Lister, R. (1997) *Citizenship: Feminist Perspectives*, Basingstoke: Macmillan – now Palgrave.
Little, A. (1998) *Post-industrial Socialism*, London: Routledge.
Loader, B. (ed.) (1997) *The Governance of Cyberspace*, London: Routledge.
Loader, B. (ed.) (1998) *Cyberspace Divide*, London: Routledge.
Locke, J. (1960) *Second Treatise on Government*, Cambridge: Cambridge University Press.
Lukes, S. (1974) *Power: A Radical Agenda*, London: Macmillan – now Palgrave.
Lukes, S. (ed.) (1986) *Power: Readings in Social and Political Theory*, Oxford: Blackwell.
Lyotard, J.-F. (1984) *The Postmodern Condition*, Manchester: Manchester University Press.
McQuaig, L. (1998) *The Cult of Impotence*, Toronto: Viking Penguin.
Machiavelli, N. (1984) *The Prince*, Oxford: Oxford University Press.
Macintyre, A. (1981) *After Virtue*, London: Duckworth.
Macintyre, A. (1987) *Whose Justice? Which Rationality?*, London: Duckworth.
Macmillan, H. (1938) *The Middle Way*, London: Macmillan – now Palgrave.
Macpherson, C. B. (1973) *Democratic Theory*, Oxford: Oxford University Press.
Maheu, L. (ed.) (1995) *Social Movements and Social Classes*, London: Sage.
Mandeville, B. (1988) *The Fable of the Bees*, Indianapolis, IL: Liberty Press.
Mann, M. (1986) *The Sources of Social Power*. Vol. 1, Cambridge: Cambridge University Press.

Manning, N. and Shaw, I. (2000) *New Risks, New Welfare*, Oxford: Blackwell.

Marcuse, H. (1964) *One-dimensional Man*, London: Routledge & Kegan Paul.

Marcuse, H. (1969) *An Essay in Liberation*, Harmondsworth: Penguin.

Marquand, D. (1988) *The Unprincipled Society*, London: Fontana.

Marshall, G. (1997) *Repositioning Class*, London: Sage.

Marshall, P. (1993) *Demanding the Impossible*, London: Fontana.

Marshall, T. H. and Bottomore, T. (1992) *Citizenship and Social Class*, London: Pluto.

Marx, K. (1977) *Selected Writings*, edited by D. McLellan, Oxford: Oxford University Press.

Maslow, A. (1954) *Motivation and Personality*, 2nd edn, New York: Harper & Row.

Mead, L. (1986) *Beyond Entitlement*, New York: Free Press.

Mead, L. (1996) 'Citizenship and Social Policy: T. H. Marshall and Poverty', *Social Philosophy and Policy*, 14(2): 197–230.

Mead, L. (1997) *From Welfare to Work*, London: Institute for Economic Affairs.

Meadows, D., Randers, J. and Behrens, W. (1972) *The Limits to Growth*, New York: Universe Books.

Meiksins-Wood, E. (1985) *The Retreat from Class*, London: Verso.

Melucci, A. (1989) *Nomads of the Present*, London: Radius.

Merchant, C. (1992) *Radical Ecology*, London: Routledge.

Miliband, D. (ed.) (1994) *Reinventing the Left*, Cambridge: Polity.

Miliband, R. (1969) *The State in Capitalist Society*, London: Weidenfeld & Nicolson.

Mill, J. S. (1989) *On Liberty*, Cambridge: Cambridge University Press.

Millar, J. (1996) 'Women, Poverty and Social Security', in Hallett, C. (ed.) *Women and Social Policy*, Hemel Hempstead: Harvester Wheatsheaf.

Miller, D. (1990) *Market, State & Community*, Oxford: Clarendon.

Miller, D. and Walzer, M. (eds) (1995) *Pluralism, Justice and Equality*, Oxford: Oxford University Press.

Mills, C. W. (1956) *The Power Elite*, Oxford: Oxford University Press.

Mishra, R. (1999) *Globalisation and the Welfare State*, Aldershot: Edward Elgar.

Modood, T., Berthoud, R., Lakey, J., Nazroo, J. Smith, P., Virdee, S. and Beishon, P. (1997) *Ethnic Minorities in Britain*, London: Policy Studies Institute.

Montesquieu, C.-L. (1989) *The Spirit of the Laws*, Cambridge: Cambridge University Press.

More, T. (1989) *Utopia*, Cambridge: Cambridge University Press.

Morris, J. (1991) *Pride Against Prejudice*, London: The Women's Press.

Morris, L. (1994) *Dangerous Classes*, London: Routledge.

Murray, C. (1984) *Losing Ground*, New York: Basic Books.

Murray, C. (1990) *The Emerging British Underclass*, London: Institute for Economic Affairs.

Murray, C. (2000) 'Genetics of the Right', *Prospect*, April, pp. 28–31.

Newby, H. (1996) 'Citizenship in a Green World', in Bulmer, M. and Rees, A. (eds) *Citizenship Today*, London: UCL Press.

Nicholson, L. (ed.) (1990) *Feminism/Postmodernism*, New York: Routledge.

Nielson, K. (1985) *Equality and Liberty*, Totowa, NJ: Rowman & Allanheld.

Nietzsche, F. (1967) *On the Genealogy of Morals and Ecce Homo*, New York: Vintage Books.

Nietzsche, F. (1973) *Beyond Good and Evil*, Harmondsworth: Penguin.

Nisbet, R. (1986) *Conservatism*, Milton Keynes: Open University Press.

Nozick, R. (1974) *Anarchy, State and Utopia*, Oxford: Blackwell.

O'Connor, J. (1973) *The Fiscal Crisis of the State*, New York: St. Martin's Press – now Palgrave.

O'Connor, J. (1998) *Natural Causes*, New York: Guilford Press.

Oakeshott, M. (1962) *Rationalism in Politics and Other Essays*, London: Methuen.

OECD (1994) *New Orientations for Social Policy*, Paris: OECD.

Offe, C. (1984) *Contradictions of the Welfare State*, London: Hutchison.

Offe, C. (1985) *Disorganised Capitalism*, Cambridge: Polity.

Offe, C. (1987) 'Challenging the Boundaries of Institutional Politics: Social Movements since the 1960s', in Maier, C. S. (ed.) *Changing Boundaries of the Political*, Cambridge: Cambridge University Press.

Offe, C. (1996) *Modernity and the State*, Cambridge: Polity.

Ohmae, K. (1995) *The End of the Nation State*, London: HarperCollins.

Okin, S. M. (1979) *Women in Western Political Thought*, Princeton, NJ: Princeton University Press.

Oliver, M. (1996) *Understanding Disability*, Basingstoke: Macmillan – now Palgrave.

Oliver, D. and Heater, D. (1994) *The Foundations of Citizenship*, Hemel Hempstead: Harvester Wheatsheaf.

Olson, M. (1965) *The Logic of Collective Action*, Cambridge, MA: Harvard University Press.

Ophuls, W. (1977) *Ecology and the Politics of Scarcity*, San Francisco, CA: W. H. Freeman.

Oppenheim, C. (ed.) (1998) *An Inclusive Society?*, London: Child Poverty Action Group.

Oppenheim, C. and Harker, L. (1996) *Poverty; The Facts*, 3rd edn, London: Child Poverty Action Group.

Ostrom, E. (1990) *Governing the Commons*, Cambridge: Cambridge University Press.

Page, R. (1996) *Altruism and the British Welfare State*, Aldershot: Avebury.

Pakulski, J. and Waters, M. (1996) *The Death of Class*, London: Sage.

Paine, T. (1969) *The Rights of Man*, Harmondsworth: Penguin.

Parsons, T. (1961) 'The School Class as a Social System: Some of its Functions in American Society', in Halsey, A. H., Floud, J. and Anderson, C. A. (eds) *Education, Economy and Society*, New York: Free Press.

Pascall, G. (1997) *Social Policy: A New Feminist Analysis*, London: Routledge.

Pateman, C. (1988) *The Sexual Contract*, Stanford, CA: Stanford University Press.

Pateman, C. (1989) *The Disorder of Women*, Stanford, CA: Stanford University Press.

Pepper, D. (1993) *Ecosocialism*, London: Routledge.

Pepper, D. (1996) *Modern Environmentalism*, London: Routledge.

Petersen, A., Barns, I., Dudley, J. and Harris, P. (1999) *Poststructuralism, Citizenship and Social Policy*, London: Routledge.

Piachaud, D. (1997) 'The Growth of Means-testing', in Walker, A. and Walker, C. (eds) *Britain Divided*, London: Child Poverty Action Group.

Pierson, C. (1996) *The Modern State*, London: Routledge.

Pierson, C. (1998) *Beyond the Welfare State?*, 2nd edn, Cambridge: Polity.

Pierson, P. (1996) The New Politics of the Welfare State, *World Politics*, **48**(2): 143–7.

Pigou, A. C. (1965) *Essays in Applied Economics*, London: Frank Cass.

Piore, M. and Sabel, C. (1984) *The Second Industrial Divide*, New York: Basic Books.

Piven, F. (1995) 'Is it Global Economics or Neo-laissez Faire?', *New Left Review*, **213**: 107–14.

Plant, R. (1984) *Equality, Markets and the New Right*, Fabian Tract 494, London: Fabian Society.
Plato (1955) *Republic*, Harmondsworth: Penguin.
Polanyi, K. (1944) *The Great Transformation*, Boston, MA: Beacon Press.
Poulantzas, N. (1975) *Classes in Contemporary Capitalism*, London: New Left Books.
Przeworski, A. (1985) *Capitalism and Social Democracy*, Cambridge: Cambridge University Press.
Rand, A. (1961) *The Virtue of Selfishness*, Harmondsworth: Penguin.
Rawls, J. (1972) *A Theory of Justice*, Oxford: Oxford University Press.
Rawls, J. (1993) *Political Liberalism*, New York: Columbia University Press.
Reich, R. (1992) *The Work of Nations*, New York: Vintage.
Rex, J. (1970) *Race Relations in Sociological Theory*, London: Wiedenfeld & Nicolson.
Rex, J. (1986) *Race and Ethnicity*, Milton Keynes: Open University Press.
Rhodes, M. (1996) 'Globalization and West European Welfare States: A Critical Review of Recent Debates', *Journal of European Social Policy*, 6(4): 305–27.
Rich, A. (1983) 'Compulsory Heterosexuality and Lesbian Existence', in Abel, E. and Abel, E. K. (eds) *The Signs Reader*, Chicago: Chicago University Press.
Richardson, D. (2000) 'Constructing Sexual Citizenship: Theorising Sexual Rights', *Critical Social Policy*, 20(1): 105–35.
Rifkin, J. (1998) *The Biotech Century*, London, Orion Books.
Ritzer, G. (1993) *The McDonaldization of Society*, Thousand Oaks, CA: Pine Forge Press.
Robertson, J. (1983) *The Sane Alternative*, 2nd edn, Shropshire: James Robertson.
Robertson, R. (1992) *Globalisation*, London: Sage.
Roche, M. (1992) *Rethinking Citizenship*, Cambridge: Polity.
Rodgers, L.-F. (ed.) (1989) *The Black Woman*, London: Sage.
Roemer, J. (1993) 'A Pragmatic Theory of Responsibility for the Egalitarian Planner', *Philosophy & Public Affairs*, (22): 146–66.
Room, G. (ed.) (1995) *Beyond the Threshold*, Bristol: Policy Press.
Rorty, R. (1989) *Contingency, Irony and Solidarity*, Cambridge: Cambridge University Press.
Rose, N. (1999a) *Powers of Freedom*, Cambridge: Cambridge University Press.
Rose, N. (1999b) *Governing the Soul*, 2nd edn, London: Freedom Association Books.
Rothstein, B. (1998) *Just Institutions Matter*, Cambridge: Cambridge University Press.
Rousseau, J.-J. (1973) *The Social Contract and Discourses*, London: J. M. Dent & Sons.
Rowbotham, S. (1973) *Women's Consciousness, Man's World*, Harmondsworth: Penguin.
Sainsbury, D. (ed.) (1999) *Gender and Welfare State Regimes*, Oxford: Oxford University Press.
Sale, K. (1985) *Dwellers in the Land*, San Francisco, CA: Sierra Club Books.
Sandel, M. (1982) *Liberalism and the Limits of Justice*, Cambridge: Cambridge University Press.
Sandel, M. (1996) *Democracy's Discontent*, Cambridge, MA: Harvard University Press.
Sartre, J.-P. (1958) *Being and Nothingness*, London: Methuen.
Sassen, S. (1991) *The Global City*, Princeton, NJ: Princeton University Press.
Saunders, P. (1996) *Unequal But Fair?*, London: Institute for Economic Affairs.
Scase, R. (1992) *Class*, Milton Keynes: Open University Press.
Schmitt, C. (1976) *The Concept of the Political*, New Brunswick, NJ: Rutgers University Press.

Schorr, J. (1992) *The Overworked American*, New York: Basic Books.
Schumacher, E. F. (1973) *Small is Beautiful*, New York: Harper & Row.
Schumpeter, J. (1992) *Capitalism, Socialism and Democracy*, London: Routledge.
Sen, A. (1983) 'Poor, Relatively Speaking', *Oxford Economic Papers*, (35): 153–69.
Sen, A. (1984) *Resources, Values and Development*, Oxford: Blackwell.
Sen, A. (1985) *Commodities and Capabilities*, Amsterdam: North-Holland.
Sen, A. (1992) *Inequality Re-examined*, Oxford: Clarendon.
Sennett, R. (1998) *The Corrosion of Character*, London: W. W. Norton.
Shakespeare, T. (ed.) (1998) *The Disability Reader*, London: Cassell.
Shakespeare, T. and Kerr, A. (1999) *Genetic Politics*, Cheltenham: New Clarion Press.
Shiva, V. (1994) *Close to Home*, London: Earthscan.
Skellington, R. (1992) *'Race' in Britain Today*, London: Sage.
Smith, A. (1970) *The Wealth of Nations*, Harmondsworth: Penguin.
Smith, G. (2000) 'Schools', in A. H. Halsey with J. Webb (eds) *Twentieth-century British Social Trends*, Basingstoke: Macmillan – now Palgrave.
Solomos, J. and Back, L. (1995) *Race, Politics and Social Change*, London: Routledge.
Solomos, J. and Back, L. (1996) *Racism and Society*, Basingstoke: Macmillan – now Palgrave.
Soros, G. (1998) *The Crisis of Global Capitalism*, London: Little, Brown.
Spencer, H. (1969) *The Man Versus the State*, Harmondsworth: Penguin.
Steiner, H. (1994) *An Essay on Rights*, Oxford: Blackwell.
Steward, F. (1991) 'Citizens of Planet Earth', in Andrews, G. (ed.) *Citizenship*, London: Lawrence & Wishart.
Sumner, L. W. (1996) *Welfare, Happiness and Ethics*, Oxford: Oxford University Press.
Swain, J., Oliver, M., French, S. and Finkelstein, V. (eds) (1992) *Disabling Barriers: Enabling Environments*, London: Sage.
Talmon, J. L. (1952) *The Origins of Totalitarian Democracy*, London: Secker & Warburg.
Tawney, R. H. (1931) *Equality*, London: George Allen & Unwin.
Tarrow, S. (1994) *Power in Movement*, Cambridge: Cambridge University Press.
Taylor, C. (1989) *Sources of the Self*, Cambridge: Cambridge University Press.
Taylor, D. (1998) 'Social Identity and Social Policy: Engagements with Postmodern Theory', *Journal of Social Policy*, 27(3): 329–50.
Taylor, I. (1999) *Crime in Context*, Cambridge: Polity.
Taylor-Gooby, P. (1994) 'Postmodernism and Social Policy: A Great Leap Backwards?', *Journal of Social Policy*, 23(3): 387–403.
Taylor-Gooby, P. (1997) 'In Defence of Second-best Theory: State, Class and Capital in Social Policy', *Journal of Social Policy*, 26(2): 171–92.
Taylor-Gooby, P. (ed.) (2000) *Risk, Trust and Welfare*, Basingstoke: Macmillan – now Palgrave.
Temkin, L. S. (1993) *Inequality*, Oxford: Oxford University Press.
Thompson, S. and Hoggett, P. (1998) 'The Delivery of Welfare: The Associationist Vision', in Carter, J. (ed.) *Postmodernity and the Fragmentation of Welfare*, London: Routledge.
Titmuss, R. (1968) *Commitment to Welfare*, London: Allen & Unwin.
Titmuss, R. (1970) *The Gift Relationship*, London: Allen & Unwin.
Toffler, A. (1980) *The Third Wave*, London: Pan.
Tomlinson, J. (1991) *Cultural Imperialism*, London: Pinter.
Tonnies, F. (1955) *Community and Society*, London: Routledge.

Touraine, A. (1981) *The Voice and the Eye*, Cambridge: Cambridge University Press.
Townsend, P. (1979) *Poverty in the United Kingdom*, Harmondsworth: Penguin.
Townsend, P., Davidson, N. and Whitehead, P. (1988) *Inequalities in Health*, Harmondsworth: Penguin.
Turner, B. S. (1986) *Citizenship and Capitalism*, London: Allen & Unwin.
Turner, B. S. (1993) *Citizenship and Social Theory*, London: Sage.
Turner, B. S. (1996) *The Body and Society*, 2nd edn, London: Sage.
United Nations Development Programme (1997) *Human Development Report 1997*, Oxford: Oxford University Press.
Van Parijs, P. (ed.) (1992) *Arguing for Basic Income*, London: Verso.
Van Parijs, P. (1995) *Real Freedom for All*, Oxford: Oxford University Press.
Van Steenbergen, B. (ed.) (1994) *The Condition of Citizenship*, London: Sage.
Veit-Wilson, J. (1992) 'Muddle or Mendacity? The Beveridge Committee and the Poverty Line', *Journal of Social Policy*, 21(3): 269–301.
Vogel, U. (1991) 'Is Citizenship Gender Specific?', in Vogel, U. and Moran, M. (eds) *The Frontiers of Citizenship*, Basingstoke: Macmillan – now Palgrave.
Walby, S. (1997) *Gender Transformations*, London: Routledge.
Walker, A. and Naegele, G. (eds) (1998) *The Politics of Old Age in Europe*, Milton Keynes: Open University Press.
Walker, R. with Howard, M. (2000) *The Making of a Welfare Class?*, Bristol: Policy Press.
Walter, N. (1977) *About Anarchism*, 2nd edn, New York: Freedom Press.
Walzer, M. (1983) *Spheres of Justice*, Oxford: Blackwell.
Walzer, M. (1990) 'The Communitarian Critique of Liberalism', *Political Theory*, 18(1): 6–23.
Ware, A. and Goodin, R. (eds) (1990) *Needs and Welfare*, London: Sage.
Weber, M. (1978) *Economy and Society*. Vol. 1, Berkeley: University of California Press.
Weber, M. (1991) *From Max Weber*, edited by H. H. Gerth and C. W. Mills, London: Routledge.
Weeks, J. (1986) *Sexuality*, London: Tavistock.
Weiss, L. (1998) *The Myth of the Powerless State*, Cambridge: Polity.
White, S. (1997) 'What Do Egalitarians Want?' in Franklin, J. (ed.) *Equality*, London: Institute for Public Policy Research.
Wilkinson, R. (1996) *Unhealthy Societies*, London: Routledge.
Williams, F. (1989) *Social Policy: A Critical Introduction*, Cambridge: Cambridge University Press.
Williams, F. (1992) 'Somewhere Over the Rainbow: Universality and Diversity in Social Policy', in Manning, N. and Page, R. (eds) *Social Policy Review 4*, Nottingham: Social Policy Association.
Wilson, W. J. (1987) *The Truly Disadvantaged*, Chicago: Chicago University Press.
Wolf, N. (1991) *The Beauty Myth*, London: Vintage.
Wollstonecraft, M. (1975) *Vindication on the Rights of Women*, Harmondsworth: Penguin.
Woodcock, G. (1986) *Anarchism*, 2nd edn, Harmondsworth: Penguin.
Wright, E. O. (1985) *Classes*, London: Verso.
Young, I. M. (1990) *Justice and the Politics of Difference*, Princeton, NJ: Princeton University Press.
Young, J. (1999) *The Exclusive Society*, London: Sage.

CPSIA information can be obtained at www.ICGtesting.com
Printed in the USA
LVOW05s1635291014

411107LV00003B/50/P